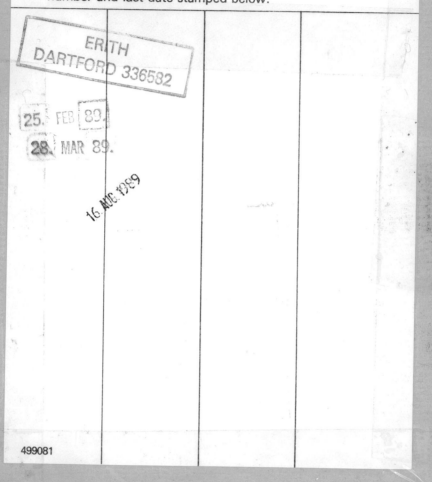

EDITED BY
GRAHAM WEBSTER

FORTRESS INTO CITY

The Consolidation of Roman Britain
first century AD

B.T. Batsford Ltd · London

Typeset by Servis Filmsetting Ltd, Manchester
and printed in Great Britain by
Anchor Brendon Ltd, Tiptree, Essex

for the Publishers B.T. Batsford Ltd
4 Fitzhardinge Street, London WIH OAH

ISBN 0 7134 5518 7

Contents

Foreword

This has been an extremely difficult book to assemble. It is not just that there are six different contributors, all with full commitments elsewhere, but in the very nature of the task. We have all tried to bring together new evidence from excavations which in three cases are still continuing. Thus, at Lincoln, Exeter and Colchester fresh information is still emerging, adding to, and, at times, even contradicting previous ideas. At Wroxeter, although the excavation finished in 1985, the post-excavation work, now in hand, is continually refining and changing previous assumptions. The problem has been 'at what point to stop' as the excavators naturally want the very latest to be presented. We had to bring down the curtain to get it published at all. So it remains, for the most part, a series of statements of work in hand. This may make it more exciting and immediate and the careful reader will find conflicting statements here and there. If an apology is needed the Editor willingly presents one.

Graham Webster

List of illustrations

Wroxeter

Lincoln

Glossary

Latin Words

aedes a shrine

ala(-e) literally a 'wing' – a unit of cavalry

armamentarium an equipment and weapon's store

ballista (-ae) a military catapult

basilica (-ae) an aisled building

basilica exercitoria a cavalry drill-hall

beneficiarius (-i) an old soldier seconded for civil duties

caldarium(-a) the very hot room in a bath-house

canabae ale-houses and brothels outside a fortress gate

castellum aquae a collecting point for a water supply

circus a race track

civitas (-ates) a tribal community and its lands

cognomen (-ina) the third name of a Roman citizen

colonia (-ae), a chartered settlement for retired veterans

conturbernium (-a) a tent-party or pair of rooms in a barracks shared by a group

curia(-ae) a meeting place for a *civitas* council

cohors(-tes) equitata(-ae) a part-mounted cavalry unit

cohors(-tes) peditata (-ae) a unit of infantry

damnatio memoriae the official expunging of all memory, an act against unpopular emperors

decurio (-ones) a member of a *civitas* council

denarius (-i) a silver coin

divide et impera divide and rule

Divus deified, a title given to emperors who had been deified after death

esc Celtic word for water

exedra a council chamber

fabri craftsmen

fabrica a work-shop

Fasti the Roman religious calendar

forum (-a), market-place

frigidarium the cold room in a bath-house

frumentarius (-ii) a collector of food supplies

groma (-ae) an instrument for setting out lines

hiberna (-ae) a winter camp

horreum (-a) a granary

imbrex (-ices) a curved roof tile

imperium the power to raise and maintain an army

incolae native residents

in deditionem acceperavit acceptance of a surrender

insula (-ae) a city block

labrum (-a) an ornamental water basin in a bath-house

legio (-ones) a legion

loc. cit. worked cited

lorica (-ae) segmentata (-ae) a cuirass formed of overlapping strips

ludus(-i) a place for festival rituals

lustrum a purification ceremony held every five years

macellum (-a) a small market

mercator (-es) a merchant

modius (-ii) a corn measure

municipium (-ae) a town with self-governing privileges

oppidum (-a) a native settlement

opus signinum a floor of pink cement

ovatio an ovation accorded to a successful general as distinct for the triumph, reserved for emperors

palaestra (-ae) the exercise area in a bath-house

peribolus (-oi) an enclosed portico

pes monetalis a Roman foot (=0.296mm)

pes Drusianus a Roman foot (=0.332mm)

piscina an open pool associated with a bath-house

pomerium the space within a town boundary

porta praetoria the gate leading into the *via praetoria*

praetorium the house of the commandant

prata the legionary grazing grounds

primus pilus 'first javelin' the senior legionary centurion
principales senior legionary officers
principia the head-quarters building in a fort or fortress
quaedam civitates certain tribes
quingenary a unit of 500
Res Gestae the title of the achievements of Augustus on the *Ara Pacis*
Res Publica Glevensium The Gloucester City Corporation
retentura the rear part of a fortress
rex king
rus in urbe the country in the town
sacellum the shrine of the standards in the *principia*
scamnum tribunorum the area of the tribunes' houses on the *via principalis*
sine ulla iactura 'without any loss', implying loss of face on the triumphal arch of Claudius
sub vallo outside the defences
taberna (-ae) a store room
tepidarium the warm room in a bath-house
terminus ante quem the date before which
terminus post quem the date after which (terms used when dating deposits by the artefacts found on them)

territorium (-a) the territory designated to a fortress or town
turma (-ae) a cavalry squadron
valetudinarium a hospital
via decumana the street in a fortress from the back of the *principia* to the rear gate
via praetoria the central street in a fortress at right angles to the *via principalis*
via principalis the main street crossing the front of the *principia*
via quintana the street crossing the rear of the *principia* at right angles to the *via decumana*
via sagularis the intervallum street behind the rampart
vicus a civil settlement without municipal status

Other Technical Terms

berm the space between the inner lip of a ditch and the front of a rampart
intervallum the space between the back of a rampart and interior buildings
revettment a structure supporting an earth mass
stylobate a low wall supporting a line of columns

Abbreviations

1 INTRODUCTION

Caesar's invasions of 55 and 54 BC and their effect on Britain

There had always been contacts and trade between Britain and the Continent since the early Palaeolithic period. This was due to the spasmodic migrations and to the barter trade in tools and weapons which had been on a small, but continuous scale throughout. This latter tended to grow under the influence of technical improvements in metallurgy in Central Europe and the growth in the numbers of sea-traders and venturers from the Mediterranean. Much of the early prehistoric trade was based on the considerable deposits of copper and tin in Britain and developed as soon as bronze became a metal of importance. The Cornish tin industry was developed by the Celts in the early fourth century BC, or earlier, but there were definite connections with the Greeks. One of the results of this kind of barter-exchange economy was the introduction of wine into Southern Britain. The British Celts, like their distant relations in Gaul, soon became addicted. There was a well-established trading connection between the Britons along the south coast and the people of north-west Gaul in the lands now known as Brittany (Macready and Thompson, 1984).

Caesar's motives in Gaul

Caesar has left us a very detailed account of his Gallic conquests, which has become a standard Latin text in schools, and has tended to inhibit discussion and analysis. Caesar felt obliged to publish his commentary to render an account of his activities to the Roman Senate and people, seemingly to justify his illegal act of crossing the Rubicon with his army. His real motives in Gaul are disguised and only careful reading of his text brings this to light. Before his appointment to Cis- and Trans-Alpine Gaul, he was a poor man, dependent for his political advance on his wealthy colleagues, Pompey and Crassus. Caesar was also extremely ambitious and he realized that he had gifts denied to ordinary men. He saw an opportunity in his provincial appointment to acquire a fortune which would enable him to pay off his debtors and able to take independent political action on his return to Rome. From the very start, when he prevented the Helvetii from crossing parts of Gaul and provoked them into battle, he skilfully devised openings for setting many of the Gallic tribes one by one against him, and was also able to exploit their ancient divisions and antipathies. His years as governor were spent entirely on campaigns from one end of Gaul to another. Any peoples who took up arms against Rome immediately forfeited any rights to their lands, possessions and persons. There was thus great booty to be had, and large numbers of the defeated tribes were taken as slaves and their chiefs and families held to ransom. A great retinue of traders followed Caesar's army, ready to step in and buy from Caesar the privilege of sacking *oppida*. This information slips out in the account of the reduction of the fortress of the Aduatuci (*BG* ii, 33). Caesar sold the booty of this *oppidum* as a single lot and the purchasers reported they had taken 35,000 persons, who were no doubt sorted out into categories of slaves and into those more suitable for ransom. The traders followed the army everywhere, even into hostile areas where heavy fighting and sudden attacks were to be expected. On several occasions they were caught in the mêlée. Once, when they ventured into the Rhineland, these followers were overrun by German horsemen dashing from the woods and not seen until they were near the camp. Caesar records that the traders (*mercatores*) encamped (*sub vallo*) presumably outside the defences had no chance of escape (*BG* vi, 37).

In his pursuit of conquests Caesar adopted the old Roman adage of 'divide and rule' (*divide et impera*). He needed friends and allies just as he needed enemies. In his expeditions to Britain he had the same basic purpose, and in his account of the second expedition, he includes one striking piece of information (v, 8). He tells us that when his ships made a landfall at Beachy Head, the Britons were not there to oppose him. He relates that he learnt later from prisoners that they had been alarmed at the size of his armada. This, he adds, consisted of 800 vessels, but he states elsewhere (v, 2) that there were 600 troop carriers and 28 men-of-war, from which it would appear that no less than some 70 ships were private vessels built or hired by the traders. Caesar's account of his activities in Britain in 54 BC was carefully structured to emphasize the glory of his victories and gains for Rome and to minimize the support from his British allies, a point brought out by Professor Christopher Hawkes in his British Academy lecture (Hawkes 1977, 125–92). Caesar produced Mandubracius, the young Prince of the Trinovantes, almost like the proverbial rabbit from the conjuror's hat. But it is stated elsewhere that the British Prince had sought his aid in Gaul and, in consequence, the plan of the campaign must have been a joint project since Caesar had agreed to restore him to his throne. Apart from the considerable aid and supplies brought to him by this tribe, Caesar lists five other allies, the Cenimagni, Segontiaci, Ancalites, Bibroci and Cassi, none of which are otherwise known except the 'Great Iceni', presumably a confederacy of East Anglian tribes, the chief of which was the Iceni.

. It has been generally assumed that Cassivellaunus, appointed by the hostile Britons to lead their army, was King of the Catuvellauni, but there is not a scrap of evidence to support this. It was an assumption made by Wheeler, on which he built his persuasive argument that the Wheathampstead earth-works near Verulamium were the *oppidum* taken by Caesar. But the evidence found by Wheeler is hardly adequate to date these earthworks, which in any case in recent years have been shown to be far more complicated than Wheeler had appreciated. The main difficulty, however, is that if the Catuvellauni had been the leaders of the anti-Roman faction against Caesar, it seems quite remarkable that by AD 43 they were the tribe most favoured by Rome. Furthermore, it has become increasingly evident that they took the greatest advantage of the trade with Rome which developed after Caesar. This is immediately apparent from the distribution maps of the wine *amphorae* and rich burials in the area of

the head-waters of the Lea Valley (Cunliffe 1984, figs. 7 and 8), where Clive Partridge has revealed evidence of a Roman trading post at Skeleton Green established by *c.* AD 10 and possibly earlier (Partridge 1981).

This is all of critical significance in the study of the reactions of the British tribes at the conquest and the process of Romanization which followed. The extent of the trade which Caesar had encouraged, and thereby enriched himself, has yet to be established. The distribution of pre-Caesarian artefacts is still very thin beyond the Thames Estuary, but there are already indications that it was far more extensive than had been thought possible. This could mean that most of the lowland tribes had become accustomed to the presence of Roman and Gallic traders and had established a rudimentary currency to make the trade effective. This was the first stage towards the adoption of a Roman-type economy and market system, based on urban centres. The bitter hostility met by the invasion army in the south-west was due to other factors, probably connected with the savage treatment of the Veneti and their commercial fleet by Caesar.

Caesar's opportunism and avid lust for power, and for the means to gain and support it, had a profound effect on the people of Southern Britain, which was to re-echo in the first century AD.

From Caesar to Claudius

When Augustus eventually came to power in 27 BC, his main aim was to bring peace to the Empire after a long and devastating civil war. He needed stability on the frontiers and attempted to establish it through friendly rulers and client relationships. The great improvements in communication, especially in the control of the Alpine passes, were necessary for rapid military deployment, but they were also an advantage for the growth of trade with the people on the fringes of Rome's influence. This was a necessary economic development, but there was also the extra financial gain to the state through the export duty of 25 per cent on goods travelling beyond the frontiers. It is not difficult to understand the policy of Augustus towards Britain, and the development of trade and friendly relations with the British kings. Strabo makes this abundantly clear in his famous passage listing the imports to and exports from Britain, but strangely omitting the most important of all – wine. No doubt quoting official sources, he stated that Britain was not worth occupying as Rome gained more economically by trade. It is doubtful if Augustus even seriously considered making Britain a province of Rome, but he attempted to maintain Rome's influence and trade based on the treaties made by Caesar, and extended this to the tribes south of the Thames. Tincommius of the Atrebates became a client king, and he received technical aid from Augustus which took the form of much-improved coins, the dies of which were cut by a Roman die-cutter copying Roman *denarii*, the types presumably chosen by Tincommius. But he was driven out by a younger scion of the royal house, Eppillus. The rightful king appears with another ousted British king, Dubnovellaunos, on the *Res Gestae* of Augustus as suppliants making offerings in the Capitol in Rome. Caesar's dramatic intervention in the affairs of Britain had the effect of polarizing the Britons into pro- and anti-Roman factions.

It was in the interests of the Druids to nurture and maintain hostility to Rome. Many of them had fled to Britain as a result of the rapid sweep of Caesar into central and north Gaul, fearful of their very lives. Caesar saw these powerful high priests and advisers to tribal rulers as representing a threat of a united Celtic nationalism. He had to break their political stranglehold in Gaul to achieve his rapid conquest. His anti-Druidic propaganda was to be very effective in Rome. It left Augustus in no doubt about the serious threat to his allies in Britain, of which Tincommius and Dubnovellaunos had been early victims. But it would be unwise to over-emphasize the role of the Druids since there were also tribal rivalries and dynastic struggles. These factors can be seen in the two main tribes north of the Thames. The evidence is too slight to do more than attempt a possible hypothesis of the causes of the changes in the fortunes of the Catuvellauni and the Trinovantes. The latter was certainly an important ally of Caesar, and without their aid it is doubtful if he would have achieved his success against Cassivellaunus. It was, however, the Catuvellauni who benefited most from Rome's trade, and the strong presumption is that they were also his allies. Under Tasciovanus, however, the power of the Catuvellauni waned: he amalgamated the two great tribes into a single kingdom, and transferred the power-centre from the Lea Valley to Camulodunon on the Colne. On the death of Tasciovanus, pro-Catuvellauni rulers (Dubno-

vellaunos and Andoco . . .) may have seized power, only to be driven out by Cunobelinos. This king extended his power and became the greatest ruler in south-west Britain. He achieved a delicate political balance between the anti- and pro-Roman elements he ruled, and only accepted Roman aid late in his reign, as indicated by a series of coins based on Roman types. On one coin he is actually styled *REX* (Mack 246). (Note, however, that Barry Cunliffe advises caution and sees no reason for equating coin distribution with political influence (Cunliffe 1981, 38).)

So, in spite of the Druids and the anti-dynastic struggles, Rome retained her influence and protected the trade routes to the depôts now established in Britain. It was the decline and death of Cunobelinos which created a change of allegiance. The first indication was the flight of Adminius (or Amminius), a son of Cunobelinos, to Gaius with a request for Roman intervention to reinstate him. But Gaius had more urgent problems on the Rhine, and could not afford troops for an invasion. Another British king, Verica of the Atrebates, soon followed, with a similar request to Claudius who succeeded Gaius in AD 41. It was now apparent that south-east Britain was wholly in the power of the anti-Roman forces under two sons of Cunobelinos, Togodubnus and Caratacus. The former had taken over his father's kingdom, while Caratacus had subdued the Atebates and probably the Regni. Claudius was faced with the choice of abandoning Britain altogether, or mounting an invasion. Galba had succeeded in stabilizing the Rhine frontier and there were no demands on the army elsewhere. Claudius badly needed a diversion of this kind as he had been thrust dramatically into power after the Senate had declared a new republic and annulled all the acts of the previous Emperors. Faced with a hostile Senate, he had to divert public attention from Rome by a glorious victory, and at the same time earn the loyalty of the frontier armies. The trade with Britain had given Rome some idea of its potential wealth, especially in iron, and, so it was thought, in silver. Claudius could also rely on the active assistance of his British allies; they would have included the Iceni, Catuvellauni, Atrebates, Regni and the northern Dobunni. The way was clear for Claudius to establish his power-base, win glory and extend the *imperium*, bringing to a satisfactory close what had been to the paternal head of the Julius-Claudian line no more than a large-scale raid to enrich his coffers and gild his military laurels.

The invasion force

The invasion army of AD 43 included four legions, II *Aug.*, IX *Hispana*, XIV *Gemina*, and XX, together with probably some 40 to 50 auxiliary units. For the initial phase extra troops were included, possibly legionary vexillations. These units would have returned to their establishments after the main resistance was overcome. The commander, who was to be the first governor of the new province, was Aulus Plautius, a 'safe' man with family connections with the Imperial House. The landing-place and main base of the operation was the land-locked harbour at Richborough, on the tip of East Kent, with the Wantsum Channel giving access to the Thames Estuary (Cunliffe 1968, 224–34). The landing was unopposed and the large army with all its stores and equipment was able to land and construct its base camp.

The army of resistance and
the Battle of the Medway

British resistance was led by the two brothers, Togodubnus and Caratacus, with their warriors, retainers and feudal-type levies, drawn from all the tribes over which the two kings exercised control. At the outset the northern Dobunni joined the Romans instead of the British, and one must assume from this that they had had previous diplomatic and/or trade contacts with Rome, and perhaps even an alliance.

The British leaders had decided to make their stand at the Medway crossing and assembled a large army there. Unfortunately, we have only a garbled account of this critical battle by Cassius Dio (lx.19–2) in the epitomized version which has survived. It is a great misfortune that the books of the *Annals* of Tacitus (books VII–X) which covered this period have not come down to us. It is evident that the Britons had little appreciation of the skill and professionalism of the Roman army, and in particular of their ability to cross wide rivers against opposition, usually by an outflanking manoeuvre. There were also the Batavian cohorts, who were specially trained to swim across rivers fully-armed. These created a diversion by attacking the British horse and chariots on one flank, while the legionaries quietly crossed at a narrow point on the other. Once the Romans had built up a large enough force on their bridgehead the main battle was engaged. Although it was a long engagement, there was no doubt about the outcome; superior discipline, armour and proven battle experience won the day. It was a devastating defeat for Caratacus and his brother since they must have realized that their troops could offer no further resistance in open warfare. Togodubnus died, probably from wounds, and Caratacus decided that the only hope for the freedom fighters was to retire to the hills in the west to gather strength to continue the struggle, but in a different form of warfare, the kind we have come to term guerilla tactics.

British opposition in the south-west

But the Roman army still had to face stiff opposition from the tribes of the south-west – the Durotriges, the southern Dobunni and possibly the Belgae. There was an old and serious grudge among these peoples against Rome from being cut off from north-west Gaul by Caesar's ruthless treatment of the Veneti and their trading fleet. A force led by *Legio* II *Aug* under Vespasian, aided by the complete control of the sea and the use of the invasion ships, swept rapidly westwards and took the Britons by surprise. Even so, Vespasian was forced to storm and capture some 20 hill-forts, including the greatest of them all, Maiden Castle, where Sir Mortimer Wheeler found graphic evidence of the assault in the war cemetery. This included a warrior who still had a Roman *ballista* bolt firmly wedged in his back-bone, giving vivid proof of this attack.

Claudius comes to Britain

There remained the final episode of the initial conquest, the visit of the Emperor himself to lead his victorious army into the British capital, Camulodunon. This was a carefully pre-arranged and stage-managed sequence. Its main object was to enable Claudius to display himself to his provincial army and thereby to secure their loyalty. The surviving pieces of the inscription from his Triumphal Arch in Rome (*ILS* 216) inform us that Claudius received the submission (*in deditionem acceperit*) of 11 British Kings, having made a conquest *sine ulla iactura*. This phase has caused some controversy as it has been taken to mean 'without bloodshed', which after the two-day Medway battle would be entirely false. It is more likely that Claudius with his sense of history, and piety towards his great forbear Julius Caesar, had actually used one of his phrases which at that time meant 'without loss of honour'. So, in a respectful literary gesture, Claudius was claiming that he had regained the territories Caesar had conquered and fulfilled Rome's obligations to the alliances he had created.

The occupying army

Having reduced all opposition, Plautius now disposed the army units which were to be the permanent garrison of the new province of Britannia. The land boundary of the province had no doubt been pre-determined, and was a wide strip from the Humber to the Bristol Channel, thence to the Exe Estuary. It included most of the lowland zone, much of the best agricultural land and what was more important to Rome, the most sophisticated peoples, many of whom had migrated to Britain in the first century BC, some in advance of Caesar's invasion of Gaul. It was probably thought by Rome that as these tribes were of recent Gallic origin, they would readily adapt to the Roman way of life and eventually provide a suitable body of citizens. The development of trade between Britons of the south-east and Gallic and Italian traders after Caesar's campaigns had been a great advantage to Rome in accustoming the Britons to Roman goods and also to a rudimentary currency.

The frontier problems

Rome had no need to occupy the highland zones which were inhabited by more barbarized peoples, since this would involve more fighting to gain control, and thereafter, more troops to occupy them. The main problem was the land boundary, but Rome had a time-honoured policy of organizing the security of her frontiers. This was done by means of friendly rulers in the territories adjacent to the bounds of the Empire. They were persuaded by smooth diplomacy to become clients of Rome, and duly rewarded by handsome gifts and honours. To secure the loyalty of these kings and queens, they were persuaded to allow their children to be educated in Rome, incidentally turning them into little 'Romans' used to a new way of life, but in reality they were hostages accountable for the good behaviour of their parents. It is more than likely that young Britons, scions of the client rulers, had been so treated in the post-Caesarian period. The building programme rapidly initiated by Cogidubnus seems evidence that he had become accustomed to life in Rome and the finds of the Lexden Tumulus at Colchester are suggestive of another example from the Trinovantian house (Foster 1986, 187–8).

Rome achieved one great diplomatic triumph by the creation of the large confederacy of the tribes of Brigantes and the placing of Cartimandua over them as a client queen. Her loyalty to Rome was to remain staunch, in spite of the pressures of the latter period. This effectively sealed the frontier of northern Britain, which as Rome was eventually to learn was to be the most difficult and vulnerable. No doubt attempts were made to induce rulers to the west to undertake similar responsibilities to provide buffer states against the tribes of the Welsh mountains. These attempts were no doubt frustrated by the presence and influence of Caratacus. This great British commander had rapidly established himself in Wales.

The experience gained at the Medway battle made it abundantly clear to Caratacus that no army of Britons could hope to face the Roman legions successfully in open battle. He therefore betook himself and his followers to the west to continue the struggle for freedom. His immediate acceptance by these remote people, who had no ethnic connection with the south-east tribes, remains a mystery. Perhaps he was a man of great charismatic power and they readily understood his passionate belief in their imminent loss of freedom and subjection to a foreign power. It would be much simpler to see the Druids as the agents for his success, since they had good reason to know that Rome had not tolerated their strong influence over the tribal kings and chiefs of Gaul, and were not likely to do so in Britain, especially if many of the priesthood had fled here after the collapse of the revolt of Vercingetorix. Their main sanctuary was presumably near the British capital Camulodunon, but this would have been abandoned with the Roman victory on the Medway. They may have joined Caratacus in his westward trek, to establish themselves in the island of Anglesey, a place rich in good agricultural and mineral wealth where they may already have had a major shrine, as may be indicated by the Llyn Cerrig Bach hoard (Fox 1946). Although this is supposition, it would help to explain the background to the flight of Caratacus, and the presence of the Druids on Anglesey, as recorded by Tacitus in AD 60.

All Rome could do in these circumstances was to protect this section of her new frontier defences with her own troops. Rome had at this time no concept of the secure barriers which were to become necessary some 75 years later. Large rivers

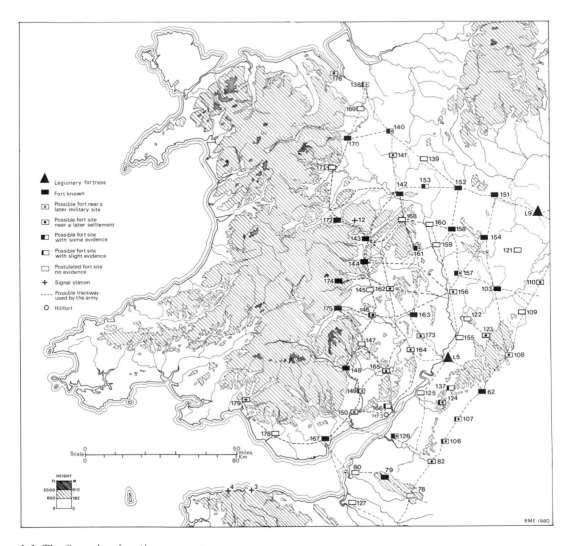

1.1 The Scapulan frontier, *c*. AD 50.

like the Rhine and Danube gave a great advantage in controlling tribal movement and trade, but the British rivers were very small in comparison, only the Humber Estuary and Bristol Channel offering any serious protection; the rivers Trent and Warwickshire Avon hardly constituted a defence line. The answer, as already established over the desert edges of Africa and the East, was to establish a wide control zone some 20–30 miles wide with auxiliary units stationed in it. These were mainly cavalry which was better-suited to long-distance patrol. A lateral line of communication in this zone became known later as the Fosse Way, stretching from the south bank of the Humber down to the head of the Exe Estuary. This had forts spaced along it at intervals, a number of which are known (fig. 1.1). The key sites on this route would probably have been Lincoln, Leicester, Cirencester and Exeter, but of these there is evidence of a fort only at Cirencester which has also produced two fine tombstones of troops of two different *alae*, the crack cavalry regiments. The legions were normally kept well in reserve and not subjected to the rough-and-tumble of frontier forays. Of the four invasion legions, the XXth was established by the British capital at Camulodunon; II *Aug.* on the south-west at Chichester near the large naval base at Fishbourne; IX *Hispana* on the River Nene at Longthorpe; and XIV *Gemina* must have been somewhere in the Midlands, possibly at Towcester,

16

a nodel point in the communication system. The auxiliary units were spread in a network controlling the routes. The army would not at this early stage have constructed roads, but relied on passable tracks suitable for horses and pack-mules. Some of the old British trackways would have been useful, but they needed to be straightened. The army was capable of laying down timber causeways over marsh and bog and making fordable crossing points over rivers. But the dispositions were also determined by the presence of large British settlements. Some of the British tribes may have appeared to be friendly, but their real feelings were as yet unknown. The army had, therefore, to keep a wary eye on all the Britons. Even the friendliest of allies had troops in their territory – pieces of equipment have, for example, been found at Silchester – but here the troops may, of course, have been to protect Cogidubnus.

Very little excavation has so far been carried out on these early military sites, but the few examples have produced peculiar results. At both Dorset sites of Hod Hill and Waddon Hill there may be evidence of legionaries and auxiliary together in the same fort,* and it is now also clear that the legionary fortress at Colchester is not the full size. This suggests that legionary cohorts were on outpost duties with auxiliaries represented also, by part of their unit. This partition of units indicated that the commander-in-chief was forced to split his normal units to spread them over the province. Counting the number of possible forts on the communication network, the total is far more than the auxiliary units one would expect to be in Britain at this time. The army thus appears to be spread thinly over the ground, but it must be emphasized that the available sample is far too small for any firm general conclusion and can only be regarded as an indication (Webster 1980, pp. 111–67).

Caratacus strikes

Whatever one may conclude from the distribution of possible forts and units, it was a system which lasted a very short time. Aulus Plautius retired from his governorship to his well-deserved *ovatio* in the winter of AD 48, having completed a five-year stint. This means that most of the forts could not have been in existence for more than three to four years. By striking in mid-winter when the governors were changing over, Caratacus hoped to cause the greatest confusion. He had had the same short time to win over the mountain tribes and train them in what was to them a new type of warfare. His objective was to link up with the anti-Roman forces in the south-west, still smarting under the ruthless onslaught of Vespasian. So he crossed the lower Severn somewhere near Gloucester, avoiding, one would presume, the part-mounted cohort of Thracians stationed there. When the new governor Ostorius Scapula arrived, he found the province in a state of great confusion and a strong enemy raiding party supported by a general uprising in the south-west. Fortunately we now have the terse but careful accounts of Tacitus to follow (*Annals* xii,41–40). Scapula had to call his troops out of their winter quarters, put down the rising and clear the province of the invaders.

Scapula takes stock

He then had to consider his next move. It would have been very unwise to allow Caratacus the freedom to attack the frontier zone at any point; besides, Rome had suffered an injury not only to its people and property, but to its pride. Such a powerful enemy could not be allowed to escape capture or punishment. This required a large-scale expedition into Wales as a search and destroy operation, and Scapula could use only the troops actually in Britain, spread thinly over the province. He must have been very uncertain about the reaction of some of the British tribes if he took most of the soldiers from their territories. The raid by Caratacus must have left the province in a very restless state. It is even possible that some of the tribes had taken advantage of the confusion to raid and loot Roman property, especially with traders by now well established.

The governor's solution to this problem was drastic but typically military: he ordered the disarming of all the tribes within the province. Although the sentence in which Tacitus describes this action is unfortunately a corrupt text, and the emendation may not be correct, it would, however, seem to fit the circumstances. (*Annals* 12, 31, *detrahere arma suspectis cunctaque cis Trisantonam et Sabrinam fluvios cohibere parat*, i.e. 'prepared to disarm those suspect on this (i.e. the Roman) side of the Trent and Severn'). The effect of this decision was for the army to go into the settlements and farms searching for arms and if any were found, or resistance offered, instant reprisals

---

* Some doubt may be expressed over this, as the evidence on which it was based was exclusive use of the *lorica segmentata* by legionaries, but it now seems certain that this type of body armour was also worn by auxiliaries in the *cohorts peditata*.

would be taken. It would appear to be a tactic of sheer brutality and terror, intended to crush the Britons into stunned submission to enable units to be withdrawn for the campaign. It was a piece of military expediency which was to have grave political consequences. Nor were loyal allies exempt, since a section of one of the oldest British allies, the Iceni, reacted strongly and fortified themselves in a stockade, which was stormed by the army.

Scapula decided to take the troops he needed from the safest areas in the south-east, but somehow law and order had to be maintained. He used the old Roman device of coercing reliable rulers to take responsibility with the creation of the two client kingdoms of Cogidubnus and Prasutagus. The time of this action has been thought to have been part of the arrangements of Claudius on his visit to Britain in 43, but it makes no geographical or political sense to create two such kingdoms within the area of the new province, unless it was decided to concentrate the army in the northern and western parts of the province from the outset. This appears to be disproved by the presence of troops in the areas of these kingdoms under Claudius, but more evidence is needed before one can be certain of this. An important fragment comes from *Agricola* 4, where Tacitus summarized the early conquest period and states that Cogidubnus received *quaedam civitates*, i.e. certain tribes. This clearly indicates that the king had more than one tribe to govern, possibly even three, the Belgae as well as the Atrebates and Regini. Also in this passage, this comes after Scapula and is linked with another action, that of the founding of a *colonia*. It was often the practice of commanders before regular retirement was introduced, to thin out their legions before any campaign, so that older men were pensioned off. A method of achieving this was the establishment of a chartered town, built as an urban model with a plot of land for each colonist. The site for this was the British capital Camulodunon, and the archaeological evidence for this is described below by Philip Crummy. It is presumed that the royal lands of the Trinovantian house were taken for the allotments, but so far no trace of their regular pattern has been discovered in the vicinity.

The main purpose of Scapula was to plant a strong military reserve in this area to keep a firm eye on the Britons. *Legio* XX was now needed to plug the gap on the lower Severn and a fortress was built at the crossing of the river at Kingsholm. Unfortunately, sand-pits, factory and housing development have removed almost all trace of this site. Although an alignment of military defences is now known (Atkins 1986, 3–11), this and other excavations since have cast doubt on Kingsholm as a fortress. There was a general move of units to the west. In the south, Hod Hill was given up and Waddon Hill built. *Legio* II *Aug* moved from Chichester, probably to Lake Farm, near Wimborne, still maintaining a naval presence but now at Hamworthy in Poole Harbour. *Legio* XIV now appears at Mancetter near Atherstone along the main north route, but the IXth stayed at Longthorpe, now acting as the legionary reserve but watchful of the Corieltauvi of Leicestershire and Lincolnshire, and of the peoples to the south whose name has not survived (fig. 1.1).

Scapula's campaign

Scapula was now prepared for his campaign, which can be considered here only in brief outline (for more detail, see Webster 1981 – but since outdated by recent discoveries). The first action was a strong task force to do a reconnaissance along the edge of the Welsh foothills, subduing hostile tribes, mapping the country and also sealing off contact between Caratacus and any potential Brigantian support. It is hardly likely that Cartimandua, crafty and powerful as she was, could control all her varied peoples. Scapula may have first attempted to encircle the enemy in his stronghold in the Black Mountains by an advance up the Wye, but Caratacus frustrated him by moving to central Wales. So the Roman campaign was concentrated on the Severn and the great tactical advantage of the site at Wroxeter was immediately appreciated. Tacitus gives us a very telescoped account of the Roman assault and the subsequent events – suffice it to say here that Scapula had not been able to prevent either the escape of Caratacus or of the Britons who melted away in the woods and swamps, more determined than ever to continue the struggle.

Scapula's frontier

The governor was now in a dilemma. He was unable to advance westwards and complete the conquest of Wales, since it was beyond his intentions merely to search for and destroy his enemy. Further advance would have needed imperial authority and it is doubtful if this would have been forthcoming. Having taken the army beyond the Severn, he could hardly withdraw to the boundary of the province as this would appear to be a retreat. So he was obliged to construct a new frontier along the foothills with forts in each valley to stop the hostile tribesmen from gaining access to the Severn and crossing it (fig. 1.1). Tacitus' account is very brief but it disguises heavy Roman losses incurred while the troops were building the new forts. The Britons, used to their own terrain, would appear suddenly, strike hard and vanish. At one point there was a more serious engagement in which a legion was defeated in the field under Manlius Valens, whose career suffered in consequence (*Annals* 12,40; Birley 1981, 230). The position was indeed serious, and Scapula died worn out by effort and frustration. He was immediately succeeded by a more elderly but highly experienced senator, Didius Gallus. For reasons unknown to us, Tacitus disliked this man and dismissed him in disparaging terms (*senectute gravis et multa copia honorum* i.e. 'weighed down by years and honours' *Ann.* xii, 40). However, Gallus consolidated the Welsh frontier and dealt successfully with new troubles from the north, caused by Cartimandua's divorce.

Britain after the reign of Claudius

The future of Britain in the balance

It may have been during this period, in the early years of Nero's reign, that those in power in Rome were debating the future of Britain. Suetonius informs us that Nero contemplated giving up the province altogether (*Nero* 18). Seneca, who was one of the Emperor's advisors, was active in recalling loans made to the British chiefs, according to Dio, who may have been guilty of exaggeration (lxii, 1,1). A bold decision was certainly needed over Britain's future, but the young Nero resolved the problem by deciding not to give up a province gained by his distinguished forbear, referring no doubt to Caesar and not Claudius. So a very able governor, Q. Veranius, was sent to advance into Wales. In his first and only season he destroyed the power of the Silures; on his untimely death he was immediately succeeded by another military man, Suetonius Paullinus, who completed the conquest in the north-west and also destroyed the Druidic sanctuary on Anglesey. It was probably the threat to the Druids that precipitated the great revolt of Boudica in AD 60 or 61 (Carroll 1979), which brought any further conquest to a halt. The army

returned into the lowland zone to crush the rebels. The legionary dispositions had remained the same, except that Veranius had moved the XIVth to Wroxeter, and *Legio* XX built a legionary store base at Usk for his campaign. At the same time he also probably moved *Legio* II *Aug* to Exeter.

Post Boudica

A period of consolidation and reconciliation was necessary after the holocaust of the revolt, but Britain was peaceful enough by AD 66 for Nero to withdraw the XIVth for an eastern project which never materialized. This involved a redistribution of the legions. *Legio* XX moved to Wroxeter to replace the XIVth, and its place at Gloucester was taken by *Legio* II *Aug.* on a new site, while Exeter was retained as a military base for legionaries and auxiliaries or remained under care and maintenance. It was now also that the IXth moved north to Lincoln to build its fortress on the dominant hilltop. So matters remained until the civil war of AD 69, when the British garrison was depleted to provide troops for Vitellius. This was the moment for Venutius to strike in the north by forcing his divorced Queen Cartimandua off her throne, and taking over the kingdom; the northern frontier was now in a state of hostility. But Rome could not deal with the problem of Britain until 71, when Petillius Cerealis was sent with a large body of reinforcements including *Legio* II *Adiutrix* to deal with the hostile British king, who was defeated, presumably at the great Iron Age fort at Stanwick. The northern advance continued under Agricola and the shape of the province changed dramatically.

Agricola, although with a reduced army, having been obliged to release troops to Domitian for a serious crisis on the Danube, defeated Calgacus, the war-leader of the Caledonian tribes, at the famous battle of Mons Graupius. The permanent garrison for the north now included *Legio* XX which was constructing its new fortress at Inchtuthil in AD 85–6. The demands of the Danube were still pressing and Domitian decided he needed more troops, including a British legion. The withdrawal of *Legio* II *Ad.* from Chester upset the whole military balance in Britain, and Caledonia could no longer be held. A slow, steady retreat was organized and *Legio* XX was ordered to stop building when its fortress was almost complete, but still lacking a full-size *principia*, a *praetorium*, barrack blocks and probably granaries (Pitts and St Joseph, 1955). The comments of the troops would

1.2 Legionary dispositions in the first century.

have been worth recording. The obvious site for the legion was now the vacated fortress at Chester on the Dee Estuary, where control could be exercised on the tribes of both North Wales and those on the north-west side of the Pennines.

The effects of the army relinquishing its fortresses
By *c.* AD 90 there were in Britain four vacant fortresses under care and maintenance, which had long ceased to have any military importance, since the army had moved so far to the north and west, and the province of Britannia was now at peace. These four fortresses were at Lincoln, Gloucester, Exeter and Viroconium, *Legio* IX having moved forward to York and *Legio* II *Aug.* to Caerleon. Exeter had ceased to be a legionary fortress by AD 66, but could have been replaced by an auxiliary unit, and if so, was now transferring to another place, while *Legio* XX had now occupied the Chester fortress made vacant by the withdrawal of *Legio* II *Adiutrix*. The long retention of fortresses and forts in areas now at peace had had a serious effect on inhibiting the development of urbanism, an important aspect of Roman provincial policy. The spreading of the old urban ideal may be now have been considered as an outdated concept by realists in Rome, but it had the enormous advantage in establishing properly organized and governed communities with ample market facilities for the expansion of trade, a hidden and often overlooked aspect of imperialism. The cities of the south had developed along these lines soon after the conquest; as a result, Verulamium, Silchester, Canterbury, Chichester and Winchester had been subject to large-scale building programmes on the Roman urban model by the middle of the first century. To spread this into the areas of the west and north required a new imperial initiative and this was supplied by the much-maligned Domitian.

It was decided that one solution was the founding of *coloniae* for the settlement of retired army veterans, but this required large areas for the land allotments, and after the period of conquest the emperor could no longer claim ownership without breaking established treaties with the tribes. So only two fortresses – Lincoln and Gloucester – were selected for this special treatment, and the other two were handed over to the civil authorities in the form of the *civitates* of the two tribes, the Cornovii at Viroconium and Dumnonii at Exeter, as also was the site of the auxiliary fort at Cirencester (to the Dobunni), and presumably at Leicester (to the Corieltauvi).

The great advantage of founding model cities at Exeter and Viroconium was the presence there of considerable numbers of citizens, due to the discharges from the legions, which probably became regular under Vespasian. The legionaries were obliged to retire after 20 years' service and discharges from each legion took place every other year (Watson 1969, 217f.519). This would have amounted to about 200 men per legion per year, but some would have continued in service as centurions and *beneficarii*. Not all would have wished to stay near the fortress, but moved away into trades and crafts, or bought land and settled on it. It is, however, a reasonable assumption that the majority would have stayed near their old comrades-in-arms. There was another important factor – the customary practice for soldiers to form alliances with local women and raise families on the expectancy of these unions becoming legal on discharge. There was little inducement for the men to return to their original families, since they had been recruited at an early age of 15/18 in frontier areas of distant provinces. In the absence of a general postal system, and as they were virtually illiterate, it is hardly likely that contact would have been maintained. After about 35 years at Wroxeter there may have been as many as 3000–4000 men settled near the fortress, and to this should be added their wives and families, servants and slaves, as well as traders and craftsmen and others drawn towards the civil settlement. This has not yet been located at Viroconium, but it could not have been too far from the fortress. It had to be outside the areas under military control, and a reasonable site would be the later village of Wroxeter along the road leading to the bridge over the river. There is, however, little evidence of this apart from odd pottery sherds found in cottage gardens.

A serious problem for the imperial authority may have been to devise means by which the inhabitants of the civil settlement could have been induced to abandon their houses to move into the new city. No-one would willingly leave the home to which they had grown accustomed over many years and where they had brought up a family. Old soldiers might have responded to a call of duty: they had endured a life under constant discipline for 20 years, and in a Roman household the husband was always technically the master. This in itself seems hardly enough and it can reasonably be assumed that there may have been considerable inducements, probably financial. The state could at least give the veterans the building plots, but they would also have needed help towards building their new houses. At least technical aid was readily available from the legion, and it may be possible that the military craftsmen actually built the houses and public buildings, and installed the services. There is a suggestion of this from the recent excavations at Viroconium (see p. 137 below). Whatever method was employed, it was evidently successful since the new city prospered to such an extent that Hadrian chose it as part of his policy of bringing urban prosperity into the frontier zones.

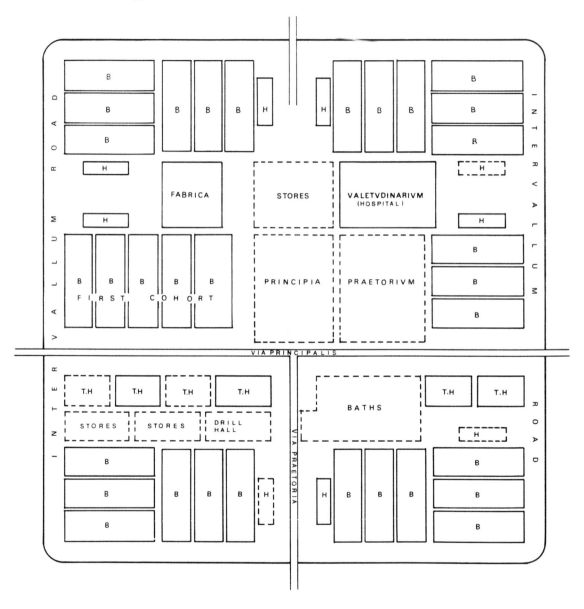

1.3 Plan of a legionary fortress based on Inchtuthil, showing the general layout and arrangement of buildings. It must be borne in mind, however, that no two fortresses are identical.

B. BARRACK BLOCKS
IN TWO CENTURY UNITS

H. HORREA

T.H. TRIBUNES HOUSES

Bibliography

Atkins, Malcolm, 1986 'Excavations at Gloucester 1985 – an Interim Report' in *Glevensis*, no. 20, 3–11

Birley, A.R. 1981   *The 'Fasti' of Roman Britain*

Caesar   *De Bello Gallico*

Cunliffe, B., 1968   *Fifth report of the excavations at Richborough, Kent*, Soc. Antiqs. Res. Rep. No. 23

Cunliffe, B. 1981   'Money and society in pre-Roman Britain' in *Coinage and Society in Britain and Gaul*

Cunliffe, B. 1984   'Relations between Britain and Gaul in the first century BC and early first century AD' in Macready, S. and Thompson, F.H., 1984 3–23

Foster, Jennifer, 1986 *The Lexden Tumulus*, BAR 156

Fox, Sir Cyril, 1946   *A find of the Early Irish Age from Llyn Cerrig, Bach Anglesey*, Nat. Museum of Wales

Hawkes, C.F.C. 1977   'Britain and Julius Caesar', *Proc. Brit. Acad.* 63, 175–92

Macready, S. and Thompson, F.H. 1984   *Cross-Channel trade between Gaul and Britain in the Pre-Roman Iron Age*, Soc. Antiqs. Occ. Pap. No. 4

Partridge, C. 1981   *Skeleton Green: a late Iron Age and Romano-British Site, Brit.* Monograph Ser, No. 2

Pitts, Lynn F. and St. Joseph, J.K. 1985   *Inchtuthil, Brit.* Monograph ser. No. 6

Watson, G.R. 1969   *The Roman Soldier*

Webster, Graham, 1981   *Rome against Caratacus*

2 COLCHESTER
(Camulodunum / Colonia Victriciensis)

Introduction*

Colchester occupies a place of special importance in the study of the Roman colonization of Britain (Crummy 1982a; *CAR* **3**, 9–10). The destruction of the early town by fire during the native revolt in AD 60 or 61 left in the ground a remarkable three-dimensional freeze-frame of the civilian settlement when it was little more than a decade old. Archaeological excavations of the remains of the Boudican holocaust have led not only to the discovery of the legionary fortress predating the town but also to the realization of the fact that, despite the withdrawal of the legion over ten years earlier, many of the streets and buildings of the military base were still in use at the time of the catastrophe. Some stumps of walls survive in the debris to a height of half a metre or more, so that the layer is all the more important for the information it provides about the surprising variety of structural techniques used in the construction of the military and early civilian buildings.

The discovery of the fortress at Colchester is a comparatively recent event although the presence of a base in the locality was suspected for many years. The site was finally located in 1972 when, principally as a result of discoveries made during large-scale excavations at Lion Walk, it was realized that the remains of the fortress underlay the central and western part of the walled area of the Roman town (fig. 2.1; Crummy 1977; *CAR* **3**, 3–5).

Subsequent work at two other large sites (Balkerne Lane and Culver Street) threw more light on the plan and buildings of the base (fig. 2.2; *CAR* **3**, 3–5) whilst exploration at the Gilberd School in 1984–5 provided significant new information about the internal layout of the barracks (Frere 1985, 295–6). (1).

* This chapter was written after the excavations at Culver Street had finished but before all the results could be assessed and fully taken into account.

Camulodunum: the Iron Age settlement

At the time of the Claudian invasion of Britain, *Camulodunum* (the Celtic name was '*Camulodunon*') was probably politically and economically the most powerful centre in southern Britain. Claudius underlined its pre-eminence by contriving to make his brief visit to Britain coincide with the point in the military campaign which would allow him to lead his troops in triumph into the conquered settlement.

Most of *Camulodunum* lay on a tongue of land bounded on the north by the River Colne and on the south by the Roman River (fig. 2.3). The settlement was protected by a series of earthen dykes totalling an impressive 24km (15 miles) in length. The agricultural base of the estate was at Gosbecks and the fertile lands along the northern edge of the Roman River valley, whereas its industrial and commercial centre was the riverside site of Sheepen. Via the mouth of the River Colne *Camulodunum* imported and exported much agricultural and industrial produce and no doubt in its heyday served a great hinterland north of the Thames, encompassing the Trinovantian and Catuvellaunian territories and perhaps beyond (Collis 1984, 155–62).

Sheepen has been the subject of two major excavations (Hawkes & Hull 1947; Niblett 1985) which have yielded substantial evidence of pottery and metalworking of various kinds, including 'moulds' believed to have been used in the manufacture of coins in pre-Roman times. Surprisingly, finds from the site have proved to be extraordinarily plentiful and of high quality particularly when compared with the material recovered so far from the earliest levels in the town centre. Yet there can be little doubt that Sheepen provided a labour-intensive manufacturing and trading base for at first the Iron Age settlement, then the Roman fortress, and finally the pre-Boudican town.

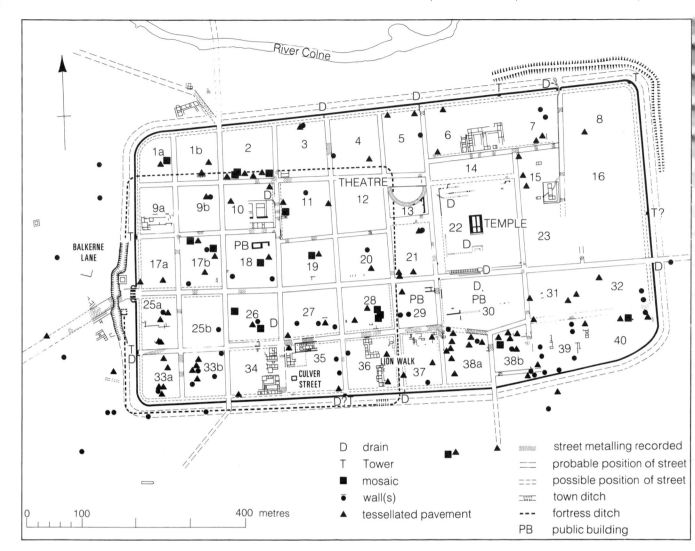

2.1 Roman Colchester *c.* AD 300 showing the position of the filled-in fortress defences.

By contrast, little excavation has been carried out at Gosbecks but, being today largely under the plough, much is known about the site from crop marks (fig. 2.4). Two distinct periods of occupation or activity can be detected: the area was at first given over mainly to intensive native farming (Hull 1958, 260), but later, presumably sometime after the revolt of AD 60–1, the site survived primarily as an important tribal sanctuary later dignified by a temple and a theatre. The heart and earliest part of the complex was a large native farmstead, the main buildings of which were enclosed within a large trapezoidal enclosure.

Possibly representing a century or more of development, there were complicated multi-period systems of trackways, ditched fields and defensive dykes, all leading to the main enclosure. The latter was remodelled several times, later phases being represented by straight-sided enclosures. The temple stood inside a square ditched enclosure which was probably laid out in the late Iron Age period as a site of considerable religious importance. Against the inside of the innermost dyke was a small Roman fort, sited to police the native settlement in the conquest phase whilst causing minimal disturbance to its layout.

Camulodunum and its immediate environment must have been densely inhabited; the presence after the conquest of the fortress and the Gosbecks

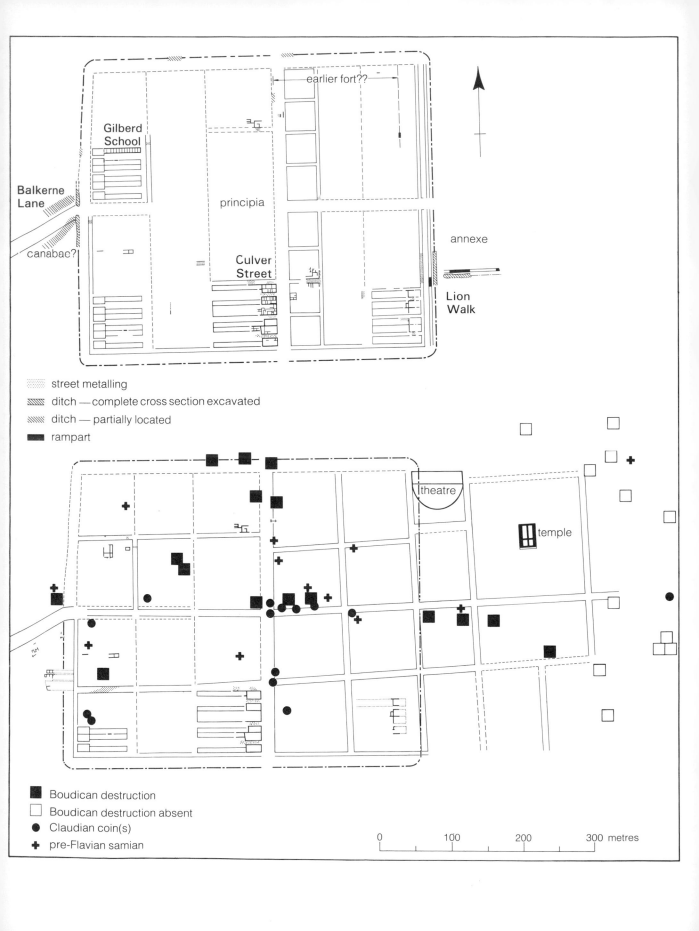

earlier fort??

Gilberd
School

Balkerne
Lane

principia

canabac?

Culver
Street

annexe

Lion
Walk

street metalling

ditch — complete cross section excavated

ditch — partially located

rampart

theatre

temple

Boudican destruction

Boudican destruction absent

Claudian coin(s)

pre-Flavian samian

0   100   200   300 metres

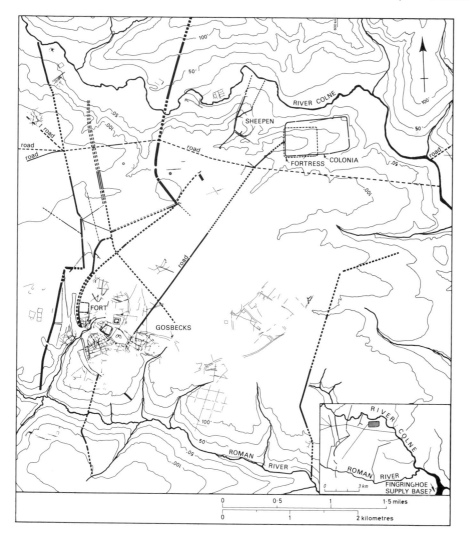

2.3 *Camulodunum* in the Roman military period.

fort implies a large indigenous population in the vicinity and so too does the scale of the native defences and the large investment of manhours which their construction must represent. Yet the focus of the settlement was the comparatively small trapezoidal-shaped enclosure at Gosbecks to which the trackway systems led. It is this convergence which suggests that within the enclosure were the houses of the successive native kings and that *Camulodunum* was in essence a huge royal estate, which through its extraordinary success

2.2 *Above left*: the fortress at Colchester; *below left* the pre-Boudican colony.

provided its owners with far-reaching political and economic power (Crummy 1980a and 1980b).

The site of the fortress

The fortress was carefully sited in relation to the local topography. First and foremost the chosen site had to be inside the defences of the native *oppidum*. Also the base had to be built on unoccupied land so as to disrupt the native settlement as little as possible; it had to be near the river to take advantage of waterborne transport and yet be sufficiently high to command a good view of the surrounding area; it had to guard the main river crossings into the *oppidum*; and it had to be close to a good supply of water.

27

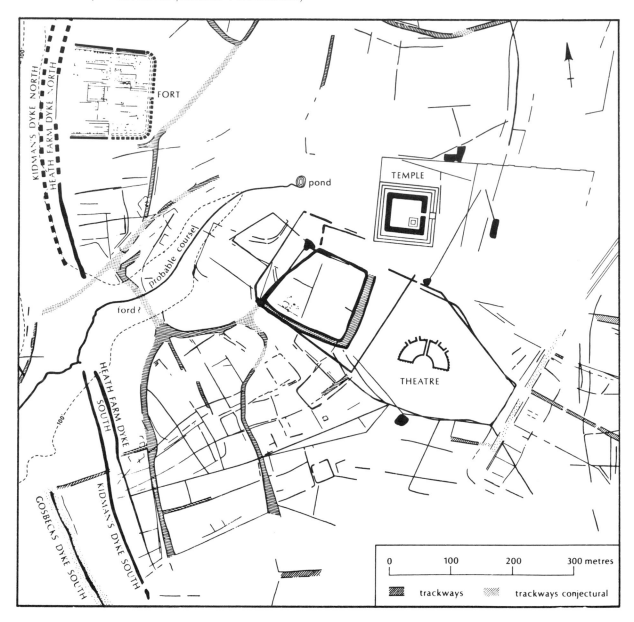

2.4 Gosbecks, showing the temple, the theatre, trackways, fields, and dykes.

The site which met all these requirements was a spur of land immediately downstream from the Sheepen site where in *c.* AD 44 work on building the base began. The longitudinal axis of the fortress was placed on the crest of land formed by the steep slope down to the River Colne on the north and the more gentle slope forming the northern side of the valley of a little stream immediately to the south.

(The latter may have silted to such a degree that the stream had become an underground water-course – as in fact it is today.) Thus the fortress was sited neatly along a low east-west ridge. The northern half lay on a 1-in-11 slope formed by the Colne valley and overlooked a considerable expanse of land to the north of the Colne; the *principia* and the line of buildings to the east and west would have been visible on the horizon from one to two kilometres to the north. The buildings on the north side of this line would have had to be terraced into the natural slope. The water-table coincides very approximately with the 15m (50ft) contour which is the level at which the glacially-deposited sand and gravel under most of Colchester meets the underlying London clay. Ground-water passes down through the sand and gravel to form water-courses along the top of the clay which then emerge near the foot of the valley sides as a series of springs. The north side of the fortress lay just above the 15m (50ft) contour so that there was plenty of spring water just outside the northern defences of the base.

The fortress may well have been aligned deliberately on the true north: it was in fact orientated to within half a degree of this point. The base faced east so that the principal gate (*porta praetoria*) would face seawards rather than westwards towards the land route to the west and south as might have been expected.

On the east side of the fortress was a large annexe, the precise size and position of which are yet to be established. To judge by military annexes elsewhere, it probably extended north of the street passing through the *porta praetoria*. If we assume that the built-up area of the pre-Boudican colony (fig. 2.2) coincided with the area occupied by the fortress and its annexe, then the latter may have been about a third the size of the original fortress enslosure. (The existence at this time of the streets south of Insulae 29 and 30 is not certain so that early occupation need not have extended south of the position of the southern boundary of the annexe.)

The fortress may have been preceded by a Roman fort which was abandoned unfinished. The evidence for this is insubstantial and rather inconclusive and takes the form of a deep pre-Boudican north–south ditch found in 1963 and an early east-west rampart discovered in 1964 about 175 metres (190 yards) to the east of the ditch. Neither can be satisfactorily rationalized in terms of the plans of the fortress or pre-Boudican town and thus they have been tentatively linked together as being part of a fort predating the fortress (*CAR* **3**, 5).

Planning of the fortress

The layout of the fortress is sufficiently well known to enable a reconstruction of the strategy of the military planner who devised its layout. The plan was formulated in terms of round figures and the planning of the buildings was secondary to the street system. In other words, the buildings were made to fit the street plan rather than *vice versa*.

Taking measurements east-west (fig. 2.5), the ground area of the fortress can be divided up into six north–south strips 300 and 200 Roman feet (*pedes Monetales*) across. The area east of the *via principalis* can be divided into two squares 650 feet across. In one of the 200-foot-wide strips lay the tribunes' houses and the *via principalis*. Thus the strategy of the planner can be summarized as follows (fig. 2.6). First he marked out on his plan, at an appropriate size, strips 300 and 200 feet wide. Then he set out the *via praetoria* and the *via decumana*, so that these were 60 feet across. He allocated a 60-foot wide strip for the *via principalis* and marked off the northern and southern limits of the street system at a distance of 650 feet from the north and south frontages of the *via praetoria* and the *via decumana*. Thus the street plan of the fortress covered a theoretical area of 1360 by 1600 feet.

The next stage involved delineating the minor streets. These have been assumed to be 20 feet wide, but apart from the *via sagularis* (the *intervallum* road) they could have been as much as 30 feet. The *via sagularis* has been excavated in two places and its width has been established as having been approximately 20 feet.

Finally the building plots were marked out. Those for the tribunes' houses seem to have measured 140 feet east to west. There were at least two sizes of barrack. Those of the First Cohort (excavated at Culver Street) were the biggest and are likely to have occupied practically the full width of a 300-foot strip. The others were at the most the width of a 300-foot strip minus the widths of two north-south streets.

The defences of the fortress

The defences of the fortress and its annexe were of identical construction. The ditch was V-shaped in profile. Being cut through soft sand and gravel, the sides were always susceptible to collapse so that the dimensions of the backfilled ditch do not necessarily reflect its original size. The ditch has been sectioned at Lion Walk and Balkerne Lane where it was about 2.5m (8ft) deep and 5.0m (16ft 6in) wide. The rampart was made of sand revetted with vertical faces made of coursed blocks of sun-dried sandy clay. The blocks were irregular in size except for their thickness (100–120mm; 4–5in) which was

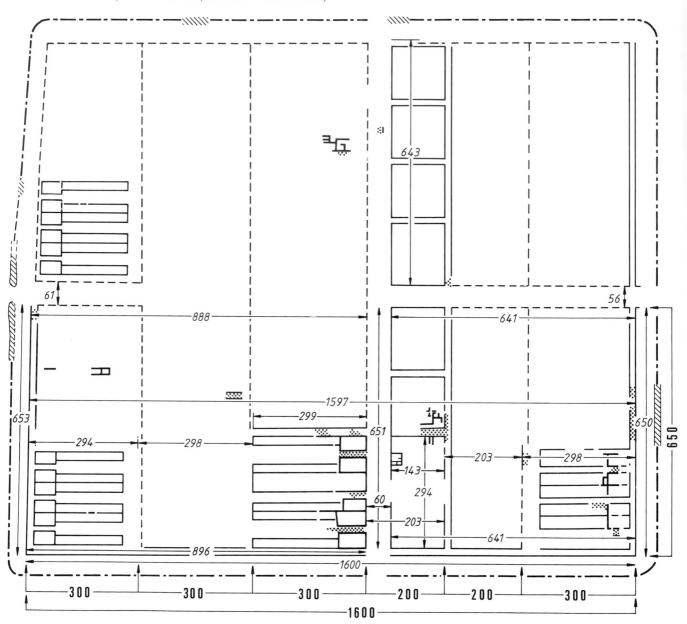

2.5 The dimensions of the fortress at Colchester in *pedes Monetales*. The actual measurements are shown in italics and the theoretical dimensions are shown in bold around the edges of the plan.

more or less uniform so that the faces of the rampart could be coursed. The annexe rampart seems to have been slightly wider than that round the fortress proper (3.8m; 12ft 6in as opposed to 4.1m; 13ft 6in). In each case, the topsoil had been removed and the rampart built over a layer of timbers laid across its full width. The best preserved part of rampart excavated so far belonged to the section of annexe defences excavated at Lion Walk where it stood to a height of 0.7m (2ft 4in). If the rampart had been timber-laced, then the lacing must have occurred vertically at intervals greater than 0.7m (2ft 4in) because no trace of any has yet been found. There was a berm between the rampart and the ditch which was at least 1.8m (5ft 11in) wide. (Erosion into the ditch makes it impossible to establish the original width.) At Lion Walk, a layer

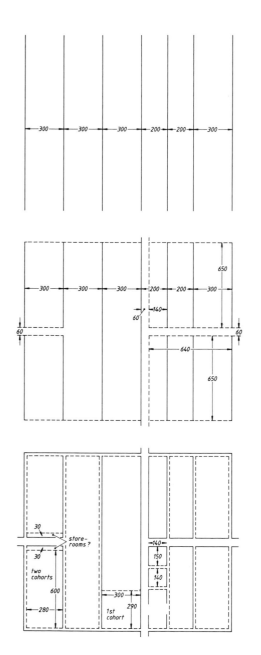

2.6 Three stages of the formulation of the plan of the fortress at Colchester.

the faces of the rampart. The *via sagularis* was set back 9.0m (29ft 6in) from the inner face of the rampart. (No *via sagularis* has been recognized in the annexe.) The space between the rampart and the street has only been excavated at one small area (Lion Walk, Site B), where it appeared to have been used for digging pits and for dumping unwanted debris. Unfortunately nothing is known of the gates of the fortress other than their positions.

The building techniques used in the fortress

The buildings in the fortress were well constructed and clearly intended to last. In the light of their quality and the efforts expended in their construction, it is not surprising that the decision was made not to demolish the fortress when it was no longer needed by the army but to keep it and convert the base into a town. The barracks were very soundly built. The main load-bearing walls were of an elaborate design consisting of three main structural components (figs. 2.7.2, 2.8). The base of each of these walls was a mortar-and-stone plinth made by pouring a mixture of mortar and stones (almost exclusively water-worn pebbles) into two lines of vertical shuttering 0.6m (2ft) apart. The shuttering was made of wooden planks set on edge end to end. When at its required level, the mortar was tamped flat to obtain a neat horizontal surface. After the mortar had set, the planks were removed to leave the finished free-standing plinth. Generally less than the lowest 100mm (4in) of each plinth was below ground level. Care was taken to make the tops of the plinths as level as possible, which meant that on sloping ground as at Culver Street, shallow construction trenches sometimes had to be dug to take the bottom edges of the planks.

The northern and southern plinths forming the western *contubernia* at the Gilberd School barrack were markedly different in height but, because of the steep natural slope between the two, were carefully constructed so that the tops of both plinths were at the same level. Two substantial squared oak timbers were laid along the top of each plinth. On top of these was then built a wall of sun-dried blocks set in courses 90mm (3.5in) thick. The blocks were similar to those used to make the faces of the military ramparts except that they were all the same size (i.e. 430 × 290 × 90mm; 17 × 11.5 × 3.5in) and they seem to have been

of sandy clay extended from the base of the rampart to well down the side of the ditch. It lay directly on the natural sand and may have been a deliberate lining to prevent erosion of the soft sandy sides of the ditch. Alternatively, the layer could have resulted from the demolition of the rampart since it was made of the same material as

31

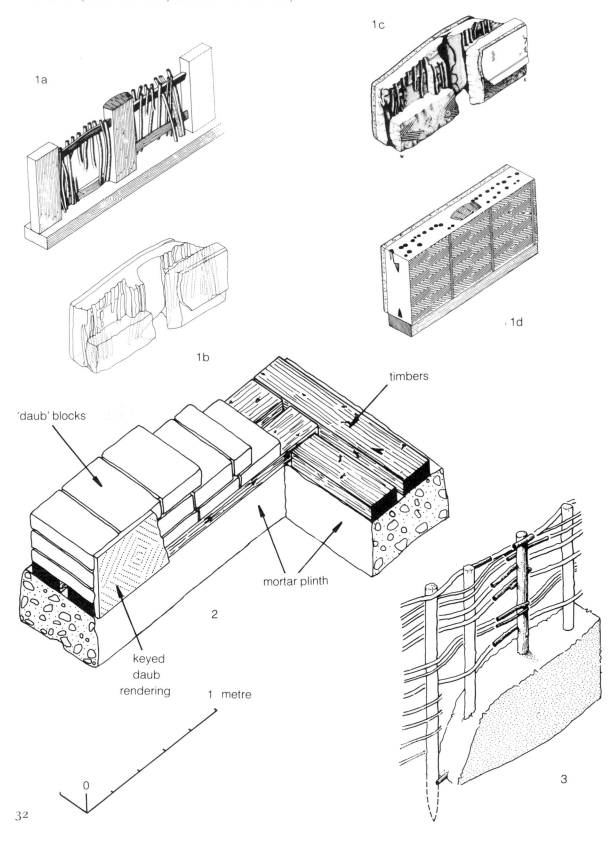

1a

1c

1b

1d

'daub' blocks

timbers

mortar plinth

keyed
daub
rendering

2

1 metre

0

3

2.8 Part of a well-preserved stump of an external wall of the northern barrack of the First Cohort (Culver Street). Burnt during the Boudican Revolt.

tempered with vegetable matter. At Culver Street, an external corner of the superstructure of one of the barracks survived to a height of 0.65m (2ft 2in) and was made only of sun-dried blocks. The absence of vertical timber studs at the corner is most significant since it must imply their almost certain absence elsewhere in walls of this type. The purpose of the horizontal timbers on the plinths is not readily apparent since they were not part of a

2.7 Some of the types of wall which occurred in pre-Boudican Colchester: 1 Stud-and-wattle (Lion Walk, Site J, Building 8, F312). 2 Daub block (Culver Street, BF487). 3 Stake-and-wattle (Balkerne Lane, Site J, north wall of Building 44).

timber-frame. Presumably their function was to spread the load of the roof and superstructure along the plinths and prevent localized subsidence into the backfill of any earlier features over which the plinths passed.

The inner surface of each wall was made smooth with a layer of sandy clay applied in much the same way as walls are plastered today. Then the internal surface of the wall was scored, marked, or moulded in a variety of ways to provide a crude, decorative finish. The treatment of the walls always involved diagonal lines either cut individually or made with a stamp (probably) which was in the form of a chevron pattern. Exceptional was a pre-Boudican civilian wall at Lion Walk where neat horizontal lines were formed by running a finger along taut strings held against the face of the damp wall (*CAR* **3**, 23–4). The use of diagonal lines rather than

33

figurative or abstract designs supports the view that the primary purpose was to make a key for plaster. Although many of these 'keyed' walls were indeed plastered, there is as yet no unequivocal proof to indicate that wall plaster was used in the fortress since the pre-Boudican plaster found so far could all be civilian in origin. Where plastered walls exist which were of military origin, it is usually impossible to tell if the plaster was primary or if it had been applied in the civilian period.

Internal walls were built in a variety of ways. Normally these all involved an oak ground-plate laid directly on the natural sand. Being indoors there was little fear of damp rotting the timbers so that plinths were not necessary. One type of internal wall (which may in fact have been introduced into the military buildings in the civilian period) was very similar in construction to medieval timber-framed buildings in that each wall was framed top and bottom with horizontal plates into which were tenoned a series of vertical studs at roughly 0.55m (1ft 10in) centres (fig. 2.7.1). The spaces between the upright timbers were filled with wattles and the whole frame then encased with daub, which was keyed either in readiness for plastering or, less likely, as a form of decoration. Like medieval and later timber-frames, the structure would have probably been wind-braced with diagonal timbers to stop the building folding over in the wind. The braces would probably have been tenoned into the horizontal plates and the principal studs. They would have either been nailed to the studs or cut through them so that each of the affected studs would have been in two parts and fixed to the brace in some way. The manner in which the gaps between the studs were filled with wattles is shown clearly by the stump of wall which survived to a height of 0.5m (1ft 8in) at Lion Walk (fig. 2.9). (This particular example was part of a pre-Boudican civilian building rather than a military one.) Using a chisel, vertical notches were cut downwards into the sides of each stud. These were made as matching pairs down the sides of each panel. Each notch increased in depth downwards to end as a little horizontal ledge cut in the face of the stud. Small, stiff 'rails' slightly wider than the panels were dropped into each pair of facing notches so as to rest on the ledges in the faces of the studs. Flexible wattles were then woven around the rails to fill the panels and provide the daub with something on which to bind as it dried and hardened.

A variation on this type of construction took the

2.9 Stud-and-wattle wall (Lion Walk, Site J, Building 8, F312). Reconstruction shown on figure 2.7.1.

form of timber-framed walls with panels filled with small, sun-dried blocks used in the same way as 'brick nogging', found in some post-medieval timber-framed houses. The blocks were of the same type as those used to build the superstructure of the main load-bearing walls of the barracks except that they were smaller in size. Yet another variation is represented by a few examples of wall which appear to have been built entirely of small sun-dried bricks set on a single oak ground-plate. These were a cross between the fully-framed internal wall and the external type incorporating a mortared plinth.

In complete contrast, the building technique of palisade-trench construction usually associated with the Roman army was used in the fortress. Two large buildings lining the *via principalis* at Culver Street were built by first digging trenches up to 1m (3ft 3in) deep along the lines of the proposed walls. Substantial posts of roughly-square section were then dropped into the trenches as they were backfilled. The gaps between the posts were filled with daub blocks and the finished walls left unplastered. In this way the frames of the walls could be erected quickly. However, being set in the ground, the bases of the posts were very susceptible to wet rot which is possibly why, unlike the barracks, these buildings were not retained for use in the new town (see below). No other examples of this type of construction have as yet been recognized in the Colchester fortress although the buildings in the small fort at Gosbecks seem to have been built in this way (see below).

A much simpler form of construction was discovered at the Balkerne Lane site and is thus associated with buildings erected outside the base. Here the walls were formed by applying sandy clay as a daub to a frame made by hammering a row of stakes into the ground and then weaving wattles round them (fig. 2.7.3). Almost all the walls of these buildings seem to have been of this type although they were clearly incapable of supporting the same degree of loading as the types of walls described above.

Although roof tile seems to have existed in the military period, few if any of the military buildings excavated so far have produced conclusive evidence of tiled roofs. Their absence in any quantity in the Boudican destruction debris of the reused barracks is probably significant in this respect (particularly at Culver Street where there was so much of it). The materials used seem to have left no trace so that shingles or thatch must be tentatively presumed.

The buildings of the fortress

Although the layout of the fortress is broadly known, very few of its buildings have been examined and, of these, none have been more than half uncovered. In all the picture is very inadequate. At Lion Walk, the areas of the excavated military buildings consisted only of parts of the centurions' quarters of six barracks, a few being represented only by little more than a fragment of a plinth. At Culver Street, parts of the centurions' quarters of the six barracks of the First Cohort were examined as well as areas of two large buildings fronting the eastern side of the *via principalis* (for brevity referred to below as the '?tribunes' houses'). In contrast to Lion Walk and Culver Street, the Gilberd School site provided an opportunity to examine the *contubernia* of a barrack, parts or all of nine being available for study. And at North Hill in 1965, Miss B.R.K. Dunnett uncovered part of an early building which she interpreted as a possible military store building. In the light of the discoveries since made at Lion Walk and elsewhere, the character of the North Hill building points to it certainly having belonged to the fortress (because it had the mortar plinths characteristic of the military base) and its position, if not its plan, indicates that it may have been the southern barrack of a group of six. To judge by more completely excavated fortresses elsewhere, there would have been many other types of buildings in the base. For example, there would have been store buildings, workshops, latrines, a hospital, a headquarters building (*principia*) in the centre of the fortress, and the legionary commander's house (*praetorium*). There would have been at least 60 barracks – more if an auxiliary unit had been garrisoned with the legion – and stables for the horses of the cavalry unit which the legion would have incorporated.

Each barrack was at least 69m (227ft) long and provided the accommodation for a 'century' of soldiers. About one third of each barrack was taken up by the centurion and took the form of a semi-detached block at the end of the barrack adjacent to either the *via principalis*, the main north-south street of the fortress, or the *via sagularis*, the street around the inside of the military defences. Some of the rooms were heated with hearths which were placed against a wall presumably with some kind of hood above to conduct the smoke through a chimney or louvre in the roof. The bases of these frequently survived and take the form of one or two tiles or bricks set flat in the ground. The floors, being nearly always of sand or sandy clay, were rudimentary but at Culver Street, in the centurion's quarters of the most northerly barrack, at least two floors had been made of planks (fig. 2.10).

2.10 Traces of a timber floor in the northern barrack of the First Cohort at Culver Street, Colchester.

The internal arrangements of the centurion's quarters varied from barrack to barrack as if each occupant had a hand in how his quarters were laid out.

To judge by fortresses elsewhere, the rest of a typical legionary barrack block was divided into a row of pairs of rooms (*contubernia*) usually sharing a common verandah along the side of the adjacent street. The front room (next to the verandah) was the smaller of the two, and is generally believed to have been used primarily for the storage of the soldiers' kit. The back room was usually roughly square and provided the sleeping and living area. The Gilberd School barrack provided the first opportunity to examine the men's quarters in Colchester. Its layout fits the normal pattern except that in common with other early barracks there does not appear to have been the customary internal partition dividing the *contubernia* into two compartments. There was exactly the space for 14 *contubernia* but only 13 seem to have been built, the two western rooms being enlarged accordingly. There is also the possibility that the barracks contained no verandahs.

With the excavation of the Gilberd School, Lion Walk, and Culver Street sites, the intended layout and dimensions of the barracks are becoming clearer (figs. 2.11, 2.12, 2.13). The key distance was 12.5 Roman feet (*pedes Monetales*). The internal partitions were half a Roman foot wide so that each *contubernium* measured 12 × 20 Roman feet internally (fig. 2.11). The centurions' quarters were more or less equivalent to the area occupied by five *contubernia* plus the adjacent section of (?)verandah thus making them measure 60 × 30

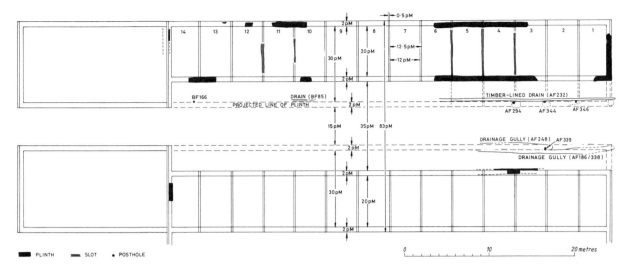

2.11 Reconstruction of the ground plans of the two barracks at the Gilberd School site.

Roman feet (a ratio of 2:1) (fig. 2.13). The streets between each pair of facing barracks were 15 feet wide (figs. 2.11, 2.12, 2.13).

Probably in the 70s, in the reign of Vespasian, the First Cohort was restructured so that instead of the customary six centuries there were five of double size. With the increased responsibility, the size of the centurions' accommodation was enlarged appropriately. The reorganization may not have been a sudden event but may have been a process which was embryonic in the Claudian period because at Culver Street all but one of the barracks of the First Cohort, whilst still six in number, were bigger than those elsewhere (fig. 2.13). Four appear to have been enlarged so that they were equivalent in area to six *contubernia* (i.e. 75 × 37.5 Roman feet). (This still maintains the 2:1 ratio.) Another was larger still and was 45 Roman feet wide, the additional 7.5 Roman feet being obtained at the expense of the facing barrack which was of normal size (i.e. 60 × 30 Roman feet).

Apart from barracks, the only other buildings examined in the fortress are two large buildings which fronted the east side of the *via principalis* at Culver Street. These were two of the eight large buildings normally found taking up the entire length of one side of this street in fortresses elsewhere. Six of these buildings are usually thought to have been occupied by tribunes so that the chances of at least one, if not both, of the Culver Street buildings having been so used are high. The southern building had a series of hearths and shallow burnt pits in its northern range of rooms. Crucible fragments and other metal-working debris from this area have been analysed by Justine Bayley of the Ancient Monuments Laboratory who has found that brass-making took place in these rooms. The presence of this material and the associated hearths indicate that the building may have been a workshop rather than a tribune's house (or even that part of the tribune's house was used for metal-working). A third (?)tribune's house ought to have been found at Culver Street but, although access was gained to the appropriate parts of the site, there was unfortunately not enough time even to establish its existence.

The annexe of the fortress would have been used as an area for stores and, more importantly, may conceivably have contained the large set of baths which the fortress would have needed for the comfort of its soldiers. Any legionary baths would almost certainly have been kept for civilian use in the new colony, but so far the site of this building has remained elusive. In 1983 during a small excavation at 61–2 High Street (the former 'Spendrite' site), what appeared to be a cavity formed by a massive hypocaust was seen just off the limits of the site under Moel's shop to the east. Although the site itself did not appear to contain part of a public building, a loose fragment of a very thick slab of mortar found in the area looked, from its construction, as though it may have been part of a suspended floor of a substantial hypocaust. Tentative though it is, could the baths have occupied the eastern half of Insula 30 (fig. 2.1)? If

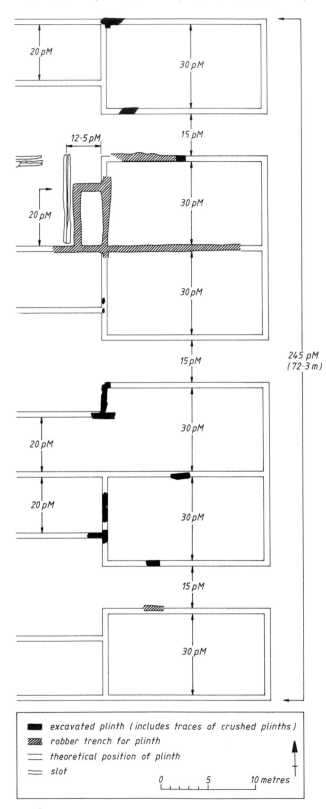

excavated plinth (includes traces of crushed plinths)
robber trench for plinth
theoretical position of plinth
slot

0   5   10 metres

so, this could place them in the legionary period in the south-eastern corner of the annexe.

The streets of the fortress, like those of the later Roman town, were made of packed gravel. By the end of the Roman period, frequent resurfacings of the streets in the colony resulted in accumulation of gravel up to a 1.0m (3ft 3in) deep. However, metalling the streets was not a priority in the fortress; at the Gilberd School barrack only part of the narrow street to the south was ever metalled, and impressed in a thin patch of sandy soil underlying the street between the fifth and sixth barracks at Culver Street were wheel ruts and a remarkable hoof print probably of an ox, cow, or bull indicating use of the street when it could have been no more than a muddy track.

The garrison of the fortress

The famous tombstones of two soldiers come from Colchester. One was erected in honour of Longinus Sdapeze, officer of the First Squadron of the Thracian cavalry (Toynbee 1964, 189–90) and the other, for Marcus Favonius Facilis (fig. 2.15; Toynbee 1964, 185), a centurion of *Legio* XX. These two stones have for many years been taken to point to the presence of a fortress in the Colchester area and, in the case of Facilis, to indicate which of the invading legions had been in occupation.

Military installations outside the fortress

The fort at Gosbecks mentioned above is known only from crop marks. It measures about 1.6ha (4 acres) inside its ramparts thus implying a probable garrison of cohort size (fig. 2.3; Crummy 1980b, 78). The buildings were predominantly east-west and the road system consisted of the *via principalis*, the *via praetoria* but, in common with contemporary forts such as Hod Hill and Valkenburg, apparently no *via decumana*. The positions of the buildings and the revetments of the rampart are indicated on aerial photographs by long straight trenches dug to take the lower ends of

2.12 *left* Reconstruction of the ground plans of the barracks at the Lion Walk site.

2.13 *right* Reconstruction of the ground plans of the barracks at the Culver Street site.

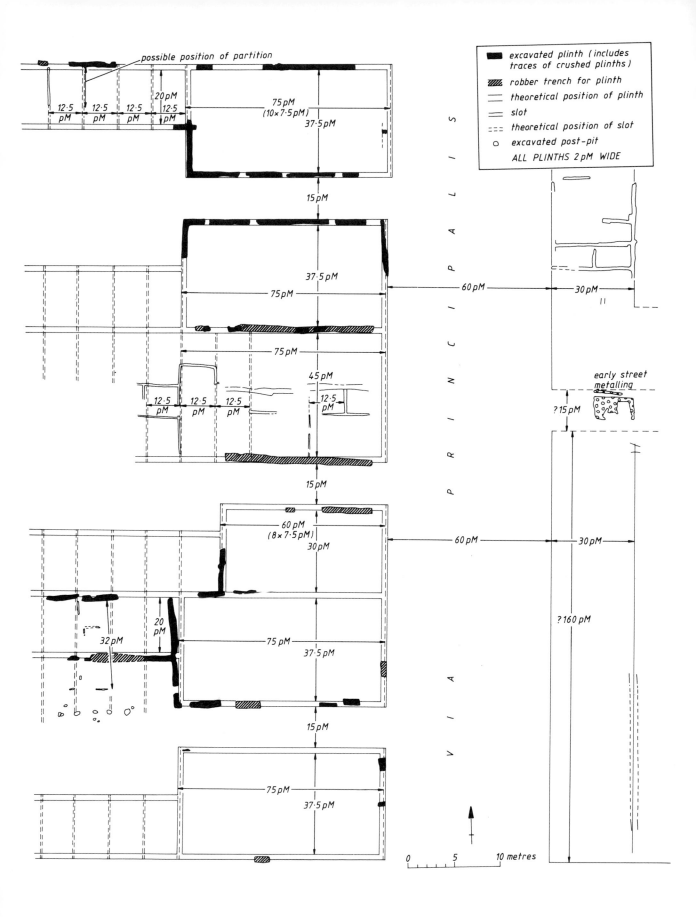

possible position of partition

12·5 pM 12·5 pM 12·5 pM 12·5 pM 20 pM

75 pM
(10×7·5 pM)
37·5 pM

15 pM

37·5 pM

75 pM

60 pM

30 pM

75 pM

45 pM

12·5 pM 12·5 pM 12·5 pM 12·5 pM

15 pM

60 pM
(8×7·5 pM)
30 pM

60 pM

30 pM

?15 pM

early street metalling

?160 pM

20 pM

32 pM

75 pM
37·5 pM

15 pM

75 pM
37·5 pM

P R I N C I P A L I S

V I A

excavated plinth (includes traces of crushed plinths)
robber trench for plinth
theoretical position of plinth
slot
theoretical position of slot
excavated post-pit
ALL PLINTHS 2 pM WIDE

0   5   10 metres

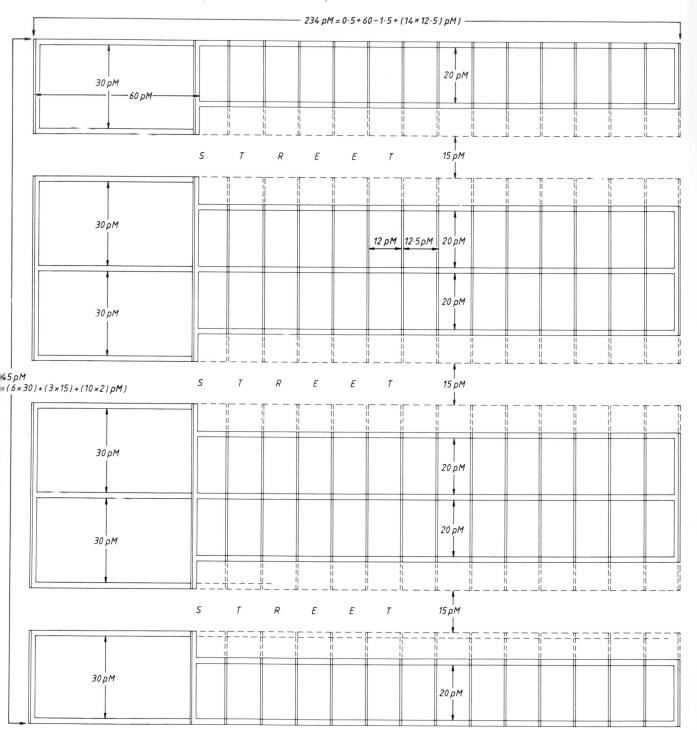

2.14 Conjectural reconstruction of the ground plan of
the barracks for a typical cohort (not the First
Cohort) at Colchester. Based on the Lion Walk and
Gilberd School sites.

2.15 The tombstone of Marcus Favonius Facilis, a centurion of the Twentieth Legion.

upright posts. Also visible are lines of rubbish pits at the rear of the rampart and alongside many of the roads.

In addition to Sheepen, another landing area may have existed further downstream at Fingringhoe where gravel and sand quarrying in about 1930 produced Roman military equipment and substantial quantities of pottery and coins, of Claudian date (Hull 1963, 130–2). Although destroyed with only the slightest of records, the evidence suggests the presence in the area of a military stores base contemporary with the legionary fortress. The River Colne is much deeper at this point so that Fingringhoe would have been accessible to much larger ships than could have reached Sheepen. The sketchy records mention rows of pits filled with dark soil, bones and shells, within a ditched enclosure at least 3.2 ha (2 acres) in area. This description is reminiscent of the lines of pits at the little fort at Gosbecks although, unlike the latter, most of the buildings at Fingringhoe would have been granaries as at Richborough (Cunliffe 1968) rather than barracks.

On the Colne between Sheepen and Fingringhoe lies the Hythe, the landing area established probably in the Norman period as a replacement for Old Heath, '*Ealdehethe*', further downstream (*CAR* **1**, 47). No significant Roman structures or finds have been recorded from this area but in 1974 Mr. R.H. Farrands discovered a Roman road leading from Manningtree (on the Orwell) to the west bank of the River Colne at the Hythe (Farrands 1975). The road was traced as a series of crop marks over a distance of 10km (6 miles) to within a mile of the Colne. This could point to the position of a bridge or ford across the river or it may imply the presence of a more convenient 'deep-water' port for the fortress and subsequently the Roman town. The known pattern of approach roads to Colchester supports the view that the Hythe was the site of a landing area in the Roman period (fig. 23). Many of the known Roman roads converge on a spot in the grounds of the Colchester Royal Grammar School. Although the precise alignment is obscure, if projected eastwards from this point, the main road leading from the west would have bypassed the fortress and later Roman town, as if it had originated before the fortress, and headed for a landing area established at the Hythe shortly after the conquest.

The building of the new colony

The new town, known as '*Colonia Victricensis*', was made by adapting the redundant fortress. The conversion process was extensive and involved considerable building work. The legionary defences were filled in and a new street grid laid out at a slightly different angle so that it covered the area of the legionary annexe and the eastern half of the fortress. The *via principalis* and the north-south streets to the west of it were retained for the colony. The *via sagularis* was also kept, except on the east side of the fortress where it was replaced by a new street built over the levelled legionary defences. The area of the annexe seems to have been given over partly, if not entirely, to public buildings including the Temple of Claudius and probably the theatre. About two-thirds of the 18 or so military buildings so far excavated in Colchester were destroyed in the fire of AD 60/1. This fact, combined with the number of re-used streets, suggests that a substantial proportion of the military buildings must have survived the transition from fortress to town.

The centurions' quarters of barrack blocks were ideally suited as houses because they fronted on to a principal street and were divided up internally into small rooms. The men's quarters were not so readily converted being in effect a series of small independent compartments and were perhaps less desirable because they fronted on to minor streets. For these reasons, only parts of the barracks were re-used in the new colony. All of the northern barrack at Lion Walk was converted into houses as well as the centurions' quarters of the two adjacent blocks. The rest were knocked down and their sites used for cultivation. The fate of the barrack at the Gilberd School is more difficult to establish because of the circumstances of the surviving remains. A new east-west street was laid out to the north of the barrack in the early colonial period. This shared the alignment of the eastern street grid and was set back about 7.0m (23ft) from the barrack. Small houses were built along the southern frontage of the new street, one being terraced into the natural slope (rising to the south) so that it cut into the central area of the former barrack, thereby partially destroying it. Parts of the military building seem to have been re-used but perhaps only because it was marginally easier to do this than knock the barrack down. Part of the north wall at the western end appears to have been incorporated in the south wall of the civilian house

to the north. There were indications that the eastern end of the building may have seen some re-use but this may also have been as a secondary process associated with new houses to the north. In contrast, all of the barracks of the First Cohort at Culver Street seem to have been made into houses, including (as far as could be judged) all the men's quarters. These were probably more desirable as residences because of their more central position, being just off the principal north-south street of the former fortress.

Probably there would have been insufficient space within the former fortress for all the large civic buildings which the colonists required. Accordingly the military defences were levelled so that the area of the annexe could be given over primarily to buildings of this type. This explains the otherwise puzzling statement by Tacitus, 'It seemed easy to destroy the settlement; for it had no walls. That was a matter which the Roman commanders thinking of amenities rather than needs, had neglected' (*Annales*, xiv, 32). The 'amenities' must be the group of public buildings which, as already explained, would only have been laid out after the defences had been levelled. Excavations at Balkerne Lane have confirmed Tacitus's statement that the colony was unprotected in AD 60, because it was found that houses burnt in the revolt had been constructed over the levelled military defences and that these defences were not replaced until after the fire (Crummy 1977, 96).

At least four buildings existed on the site of the military annexe: the Temple of Claudius (figs. 2.1, 2.16), the theatre (fig. 2.1), and at least two others, one in Insula 29 and one or more in Insula 30. The building(s) in Insula 30 probably contained columns 0.9m (3ft) wide, covered with fluted stucco (Hull 1960, 310, 316). The theatre is not necessarily the one referred to by Tacitus when he described the omens seen in Colchester foretelling the impending Boudican disaster (*Annales*, xiv, 32). But the remains of a pre-Boudican theatre may lie underneath, although no trace of this was noted during the small exploratory excavations of 1981 (Crummy 1982b). The major building was the Temple of Claudius. Certainly no expense seems to have been spared because, as a study in 1955 of the marble and porphyry fragments from around the temple indicated (Morris 1955, 48–9; *CAR* **3**, 29), the building had been decorated with types of stone imported from various parts of the Mediterranean world. The stones and sources cited are: Rosso Antico marble, Cipollino marble, and green

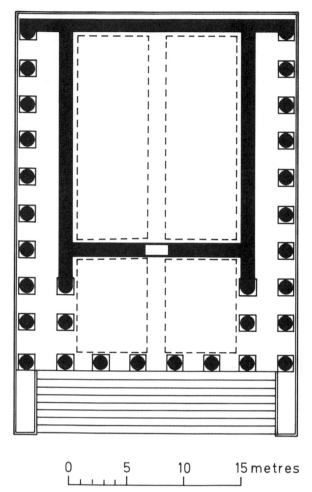

2.16 Conjectural reconstruction of the ground plan of the Temple of Claudius, Colchester. The 'vaults' are shown by dotted lines.

porphyry from Greece; Giallo Antico marble from Tunisia and Algeria; Carrara marble from Italy; Pavonazzetto marble from Asia Minor, and Africano marble probably from the same source. (Identification of the sources of marbles and porphyry can be difficult even with modern techniques so that this list should be regarded as tentative.)

Converting the fortress into a town may have taken several years. The evidence for this comes from three places: (i) the Temple of Claudius; (ii) the backfilling of the legionary ditch; (iii) the theatre. It has been argued that the Temple of Claudius could not have been started until after the death of Claudius in AD 54 (Fishwick 1972). Since the *insula* containing the temple is apparently the dominant feature of the eastern grid and is an integral part of its layout, then either the grid was set out no earlier than AD 54 or, before this date, the focal point of the *insula* was an altar as, for example, at Lyons and Cologne. Tacitus of course tells us that during the revolt a last stand was made by the veterans in the Temple (*Annales*, xiv, 32).

The legionary defences at Balkerne Lane had been much neglected before being levelled. Debris had been tipped into the butt ends of the ditch, pits dug on its western side, and at least one building, probably a workshop, had been built up against the southern butt end so that it encroached on to the main street. Since no military commander would have tolerated such treatment of his defences, the bank and ditch must have been intact for some time after the evacuation of the garrison (Crummy 1977, 76).

The western side of the theatre appears to have overlain the levelled defences of the fortress (fig. 2.1). Moreover, it was not on the alignment of the eastern grid as might be expected, but shared the same alignment as the fortress. These two factors seem to indicate that, between the destruction of the defences and the laying out of the eastern grid, there was a hiatus long enough for the construction of the theatre to begin.

Taken together the various strands of evidence indicate that the eastern grid may not have been laid out until the mid 50s. The process could have been quite complex, with various stretches of the defences being levelled independently over a period of years.

The inhabitants of the new town

Most sites excavated in Colchester reveal evidence of the Boudican attack showing that by AD 60 the town must have had a substantial population. The numbers of inhabitants at this time can only be guessed, but crude comparisons with the medieval town point to a population of up to five or ten thousand (Crummy 1975, 8). Being a colony and thus technically a self-governing extension of Rome itself, only Roman citizens could hold property in the settlement. Retired veteran soldiers and their families would presumably have made up the most important component of the population.

Quite how the veterans acquired redundant military buildings is obscure. The army at this time

2.17 Lamps and moulds for the manufacture of lamps. From a workshop in Insula 10, Colchester. The lamps are approximately 90mm long.

usually gave veteran soldiers either allotments of land or a lump sum as a kind of annuity for their retirement. The normal practice was for the land to be divided up on a grid system (centuriation) and the blocks apportioned accordingly. Such a scheme has not as yet been positively recognized in Colchester probably because its traces are now difficult to detect. Tacitus indicated that sometimes at least the process of land acquisition in Colchester was not as orderly and structured as it ought to have been. 'The settlers drove the Trinobantes (the natives) from their homes and land, and called them prisoners and slaves. The troops encouraged the settlers' outrages, since their own way of behaving was the same – and they looked forward to similar licence for themselves' (*Annales*, xiv, 32). This apparent unrestrained free-for-all could be taken to imply the absence of centuriation. More likely, Tacitus may have been referring to large-scale unofficial excesses which occurred after the initial allocation of centuriated land – excesses which were to prove one of the contributory factors behind the native revolt in AD 60/1. As mentioned at the start of this chapter, the topographical relationships of the fortress and the

Gosbecks fort to the occupied areas of the native settlement hint that the Roman army made some attempts to live with the local population in as unabrasive a manner as the circumstances would allow. Rather than court conflict in the way described by Tacitus, the Romans may have initially acted diplomatically by not centuriating the most contentious land. After all, tolerance of native rights and traditions resulted in the survival of the Gosbecks site throughout the Roman period (it was clearly never confiscated for centuriation) and extended to permitting the subsequent development of the native sanctuary (Crummy 1980a, 258–64; 1980b).

In addition to the veterans, the new settlement and the fortress before it would have attracted tradesmen, merchants, and other business men of various sorts who would have attended the local markets or resided permanently in the area. Figuring prominently among this group would have been immigrants, especially those from Gaul. They would have come to Colchester in the hope of making a good living, attracted by the enormous purchasing power of the army and subsequently of the new frontier town. Those fortunate enough to hold Roman citizenship would probably have lived and worked in the town, whilst some of the others may have set up shop along one of the approach streets. Of those in the colony, notable is the discovery made in 1964 of a workshop for the manufacture of clay lamps (fig. 2.17). Apart from being a unique discovery in Roman Britain, the find provides exceptionally vivid proof of artisan activities within the limits of the colony proper. For those without Roman citizenship, the Balkerne Lane site was perhaps the predominant area, where small buildings huddled along both frontages of the road leading from Colchester to London and the west. In this area too were likely to be at least some of the native members (*incolae*) whom Tacitus tells us were present in the town at the time of the Boudican revolt (*Annales*, xiv, 32).

Although devastating in its consequences for the inhabitants, the Boudican revolt was a great boon for archaeologists. Apart from the wealth of structural detail in the form of stumps of walls already described above, the layer of Boudican destruction lying under most of the walled part of Colchester contains a variety of important finds, particularly organic remains which, but for being carbonized, would not have survived today. Included in the latter category are wheat, oats, barley, flax, dates, and figs (fig. 2.18, *CAR* **3**, 40, 105, 108, & 110).

2.18 Organic remains from Colchester, burnt in the Boudican Revolt dates from Lion Walk.

Remarkable was a charred bed in the corner of a room in a house at Lion Walk (*CAR* **3**, 432–7). Measuring 1.9m (6ft 4in) by 1.0m (3ft 2in), the bed consisted of two mattresses each made of a casing woven in two-over-two twill and stuffed probably with wool.

In 1927, workmen working on a building site in the High Street discovered part of the burnt and smashed stock of a pottery-and-glass shop (Hull 1958, 152–8). The fragments were so loose in the ground that when touched, they fell out in a 'tinkling shower'. The pieces collected were thought to have been only a hundredth part of what survived. The vessels had been stored in stacks, the pottery being below the glass in piles on the floor or on a shelf. The intense heat of the fire left much of the glass as shapeless fused lumps and the pottery below covered in drips of melted glass. The bulk of the pottery is red-glazed *terra sigillata* and much of the glass is thin-walled and delicately coloured. The entire stock probably ran to thousands of vessels, most (if not all) of which was imported. A second shop, similarly destroyed in AD 60–1, was discovered in 1947 on the south side of the High Street. In this case, the vessels were restricted to *terra sigillata*; whether the stock included other types of vessels is uncertain (Hull 1958, 198–202).

In summary, the early colony would have been markedly agricultural in character and, as in immediate pre-conquest days, would have served as the main market place in the region for agricultural produce of all types. Opportunities would have abounded in what must have been a fast-developing commercial and industrial boom town. The expanding civilian population (containing many men newly retired from the army with substantial cash sums), the port, the large native population in the area, and the prospect of lucrative military contracts to help supply a large campaigning army would have combined to act like a magnet for the skilled craftsman and the determined entrepreneur alike, regardless of whether or not he was a veteran soldier. The extent of the early town and the density of occupation demonstrate the success of the venture: the ubiquity of the famous 'Boudican layer' testifies to the abruptness with which it all but ended.

Problems for the present and future

The discovery of the site of the fortress at Colchester and of the manner in which it was subsequently adapted to make the new town represents a major breakthrough in the study of Colchester's past. However, the work is far from over, because in reality our knowledge of the fortress and early town is still very incomplete. For example, few of the barracks have as yet been excavated, and none completely so. All the other buildings in the fortress are obscure. None of the gates have been examined, even in part. And what was inside the annexe? Where and how extensive was the military cemetery? Was there more than one area? Presumably the tombstones of Facilis and Longinus point to the main burial area – or is this only an early civilian one? Where did the troops live whilst the fortress was being built? Indeed, was it ever finished? Where were the landing facilities for waterborne transportation of goods via the River Colne? How extensive were the legionary *prata* and to what extent did they represent confiscation of native land? Presumably the *prata* were assigned to veterans on their retiral, but was there centuriation around Colchester and how extensive was the colony's *territorium*? What was the latter's relationship to the former legionary *prata*, the surrounding native farms, and the remnants of *Camulodnum*? To judge from the limited evidence available at present, there were probably many villas surrounding the early town. Yet despite the obvious economic and social importance of the group to the town, they remain enigmatic and largely unstudied. What was their relationship to the colony and its inhabitants? Many parts of the *territorium* of the colony would have almost certainly extended too far out to allow those areas to be worked by colonists living in the town. What proportion of veterans lived in villas rather than the town? Would most of the common soldiers not have preferred to make a living on the land rather than try to provide a specialist service in the town? What proportion of villa owners within the *territorium* were veterans (presumably the vast majority)? And how did the early villas compare in plan and construction techniques with the first houses in the town?

Recent advances in our knowledge about the origins of Colchester have been made possible because of several large-scale redevelopment projects in the town centre. Although the pace of change is slowing down, key sites will continue to arise over the next few decades at least. Also the land surrounding Colchester is almost entirely arable; all around the plough bites deeply into the remains of many of the villas which could reveal so much about the early days of Roman Colchester. In the years to come, the opportunities will be there; let us hope that archaeologists will be too.

Bibliography

Abbreviations

CAR **1** P. Crummy, *Aspects of Anglo-Saxon and Norman Colchester*, CBA Research Report, 39 (1981)
CAR **3** P. Crummy, *Excavations at Lion Walk, Balkerne Lane, Middleborough, Colchester, Essex* (1984)

References

Collis, J. 1984	*Oppida, Earliest Towns North of the Alps*
Crummy, P. 1975	*Not Only a Matter of Time*
—— 1977	'Colchester: the Roman fortress and the development of the *colonia*', *Britannia*, 8, 65–105
—— 1980a	'The temples of Roman Colchester', *Temples, churches and religion, recent research in Roman Britain* (ed. W. Rodwell), BAR, 77
—— 1980b	'Crop marks at Gosbecks, Colchester', *Aerial Archaeology* 4, 75–81

—— 1980a | 'The origins of some major Romano–British towns', *Britannia*, 13, 125–34

—— 1982b | 'The Roman theatre at Colchester', *Britannia*, 13, 299–302

Cunliffe, B. 1968 | *Fifth Report on the Excavations at the Roman Fort at Richborough, Kent*

Farrands, R.H. 1975 | 'Evidence for a Roman road linking Mistley with Colchester', Colchester Archaeological Group Bulletin, 18, 5–7

Fishwick, D. 1972 | '*Templum divo Claudio constitutem, Britannia*', *Britannia* 3, 164–81

Frere, S.S. 1985 | 'Roman Britain in 1984', *Britannia* 16, 252–316

Hawkes, C.F.C. and Hull, M.R. 1947 | *Camulodunum*

Hodder, P.A. 1982 | *The Roman Army in Britain*

Hull, M.R. 1955 | 'The south wing of the 'forum' at Colchester', *Trans Essex Archaeol. Soc.*, 2nd Ser, 25 (1955–60), 24–61

—— 1958 | *Roman Colchester*

—— 1963 | *A History of Essex*, 3, The Victoria History of the Counties of England (ed. R.B. Pugh)

Morris, M.O. 1955 | 'Notes on the decorative and building stones from the temple sites', in Hull 1955, 47–50

Niblett, B.R.K. 1985 | *Sheepen: an early Roman industrial site at Camulodunum*, Council for British Archaeology Research Report, 57

Toynbee, J.M.C. 1964 | *Art in Britain under the Romans*

3 GLOUCESTER
(Glevum)

Gloucester was arguably the most military city of Roman Britain in its shape and, as we shall suggest, its fabric; and the exploitation of resources in the surrounding countryside was initiated and organized by the army to a great extent. It was also a *colonia*, like Colchester and Lincoln, which meant that it was probably settled on its foundation with veteran soldiers to take the part of leading citizens. Yet what emerged fairly rapidly was an average-sized Romano-British town, with strengths and weaknesses which can be matched elsewhere. These are the main themes of the present study, which is based on a general reappraisal and reinterpretation of the evidence for the military occupation and start of the city. An earlier view by the writer of the ground covered in the present study was published as Hurst 1976. The present chapter represents the position at the end of 1987.

A general point must first be made about method. In Roman archaeology we usually work with a mixture of written source material (in the ancient authors and in inscriptions) and straight archaeological evidence. It has to be said that this is often done badly, normally because an interpretation of the written evidence is set up as a framework for studying the archaeology. At best the framework is liable to be inappropriate; at worst it leads to aspects of the archaeological evidence being ignored or misinterpreted. This has been the case with the military occupation at Gloucester. Here, therefore, the archaeological evidence is deliberately presented within its own terms first, and novel interpretations follow from this; the written evidence is also discussed, as it needs to be, in a separate section (given as an Appendix).

Part I: the physical heritage of the military occupation

The setting of the site (figs. 3.1–3)
Gloucester overlooks the lowest point where the Severn could be bridged until the Industrial Revolution. The building of the first Roman bridge made this the main route from England into South Wales, and thus of key strategic importance. As the river itself was a natural communications line, the site also occupies an important crossroads. The major land route was the east-west road, Ermin Street, but in the first years of the Roman occupation a north-south road was also built along the east bank of the Severn.

In Roman and early medieval times there was a more easterly major branch of the Severn at Gloucester, which appears to have been captured by the present eastern channel (Rowbotham 1978). This flowed close to the Roman sites at the city centre and Kingsholm 1km to the north. It seems to have determined the alignment of the buildings on both these two sites and possibly in the area between them, in the modern Hare Lane area, where there appears to be yet another distinctive building alignment (Hurst 1985, 2–3; Hurst 1986, 1–4).

Roman settlement was therefore strung around a curve in the Severn. Kingsholm has been shown to be the earliest site and it is the point on the river bank which Ermin Street aims for. However, there is some evidence that the river crossing at Gloucester was used even at the time of the Kingsholm occupation. This involved a branch road, which ran southwest from Ermin Street to the river at Gloucester. The branch road has sometimes been seen as a secondary feature, dating from the time the city-centre fortress was established, but in the excavation of the North Gate, at 45–9 Northgate Street, fragmentary remains of the earliest Roman features were aligned with the

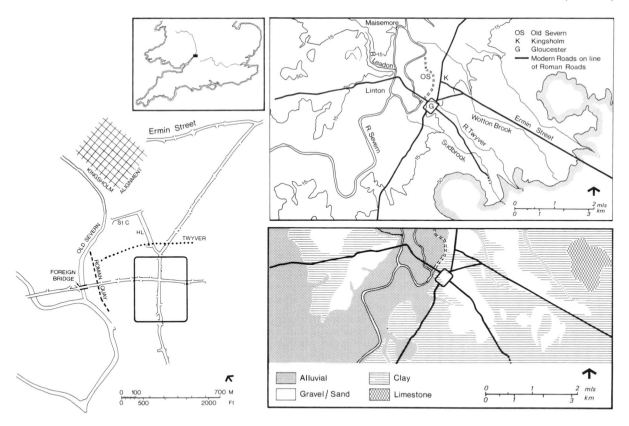

3.1 Location map, showing Kingsholm and city-centre sites (latter marked by outline of defences) and earlier course of river (old Severn). Drawn by P.A. Moss.

branch road, at an angle to the fortress remains (Heighway 1983, 20, fig. 11), thereby suggesting that the road existed before the fortress. Also this road has a similar alignment to the Kingsholm fortress, which would be explained if the two were laid out together, or if Kingsholm were laid out with respect to the road. (This is a revision of my earlier view of the river crossing: Hurst 1985, 119 and fig. 40).

The military sequence

It is suggested here that the military occupation at Kingsholm and the city centre was represented by four major periods or sets of structural evidence, which extended for half a century from the invasion of AD 43; there were extramural structures associated with the occupation of both sites. The first three periods require only brief mention, but the last is discussed in more detail, both because it is now included within the military sequence for

the first time, and also because it is closest to the succeeding civilian occupation, and therefore exercised most influence on it.

(1) *Kingsholm, first period:* site of unknown size, pre-60s AD. Timber buildings of post-in-trench construction, gravelled roads, ditches and other features typical of an early military site, have been found on the same alignment over an area of up to *c.* 8ha (20 acres), from existing discoveries (Hurst 1985, chapter 4). Contemporary defences have been proved on one side only (to the north (Atkin 1986)). Military equipment, including an unfinished cheekpiece from a cavalry helmet and three cavalry pendants, were possibly associated with one of these buildings. No useful dating evidence was found (but predating period 2).

(2) *Kingsholm, second period:* timber-sill buildings on same site and alignment as period 1, covering an area of up to 22ha (*c.* 56 acres; same line for northern defences as above, but possibly extending further south). The occupation of one of these buildings was ended by a series of pits containing abundant finds dating to the 60s AD, including a coin of 64–8. Here and on a nearby site there were no later coins among 40

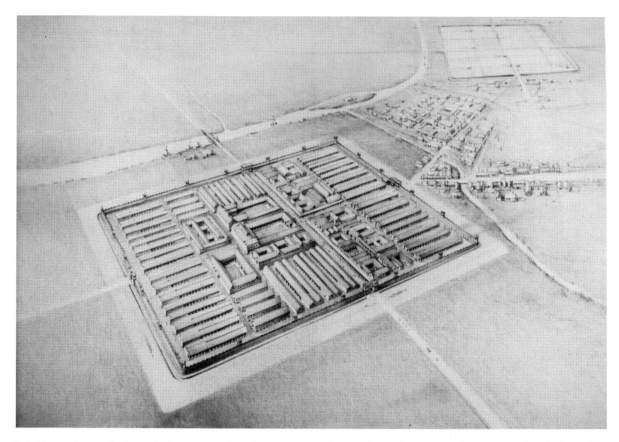

3.2 Reconstructed view of city-centre first fortress, looking north-west, with extramural areas and Kingsholm in background. Drawn by P.A. Moss, reproduced by kind permission of Gloucester City Museums.

first-century examples found in excavations (*op. cit.*, chapters 2, 3).

Kingsholm extramural, north: To the north of the main Kingsholm site, there was a further area of early Roman occupation, with ditches and one possible building. These produced finds, including military objects, again dating no later than the 60s. The general alignment of features in this area was that of nearby Ermin Street and it was clearly extramural to the main military site. (See Garrod 1984, 1985.)

Presumed ditto, south: At the city centre site, 1km south of Kingsholm, a series of small ditches and pits on no overall alignment, found over an area of about 0.7ha (1.7 acres) in the central part of the later fortress, were in use before the buildings of the fortress were constructed. These had been filled with rubbish, probably when the site was cleared for building; the rubbish contained Claudian-copy

coins and samian ware characteristic of the mid-60s, with both military and non-military objects and a large collection of locally-made pottery including the earliest examples of Severn Valley wares. This pottery assemblage differs markedly from that in the abandonment pits at Kingsholm, which must be exactly contemporary; and this fact, combined with the irregular layout of structural features, argues for civilian use of the site within the general context of the military occupation centred on Kingsholm (Hurst 1972, 53, and forthcoming (1); Darling 1977).

(3) *City centre, first-period fortress* (figs. 3.2, 3.4, 3.6): a legionary fortress of *c.* 17 ha (43 acres), whose defences have been established on all four sides. The rampart was turf-faced with timber gates and interval towers and a single ditch. Internal buildings were of post-in-trench construction, except for the back and end walls of the *contubernia* (barracks), where there appear to have been stone-and-clay ground sills, probably for timber and clay walls – clay was the main walling material elsewhere between the timber posts. A small fragment of a building identified as the

3.3 Vertical aerial view of centre of Gloucester, showing outline of fortress defences clearly reflected in street plan towards east (r.) (Copyright: Cambridge University).

principia had a gravelled courtyard, defined by foundations of stones and clay. Parts of the barrack buildings for three cohorts, including the first, have been excavated, together with small fragments of other internal buildings. Two coins of AD 64 and another of AD 66 have been found sealed into the construction levels of these buildings and a road between two barrack buildings. The latest coin so far found in an occupation level within the buildings dates to AD 77–8, though the buildings may only have been demolished on the occasion of the general rebuilding (Hassall and Rhodes 1974; Hurst 1972, 1974, 1986; Heighway 1983).

(4) *City centre, second-period fortress* (figs 3.5, 3.7): a general rebuilding of the fortress, previously interpreted as the buildings of the *colonia*. Barrack

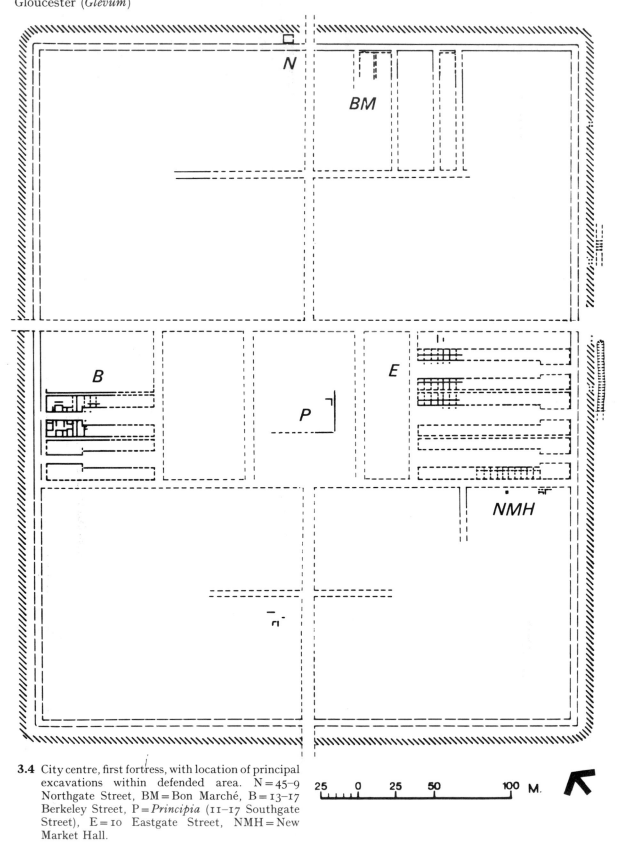

3.4 City centre, first fortress, with location of principal excavations within defended area. N = 45–9 Northgate Street, BM = Bon Marché, B = 13–17 Berkeley Street, P = *Principia* (11–17 Southgate Street), E = 10 Eastgate Street, NMH = New Market Hall.

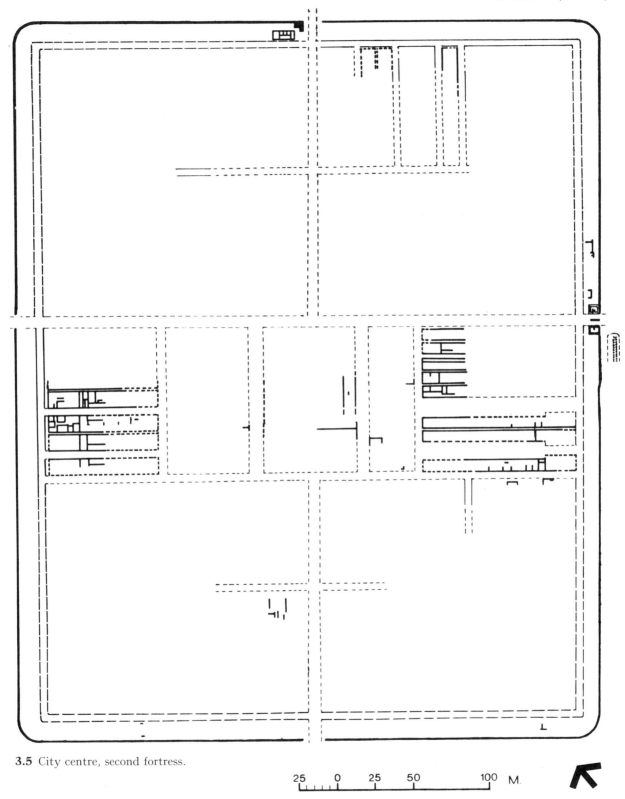

3.5 City centre, second fortress.

25 0 25 50 100 M.

buildings and centurions' houses were rebuilt with external walls of mortared masonry and internal walls based on timber sills or masonry footings carrying timber ground sills. Evidence for the internal plan of the buildings has so far been unravelled in detail for part of two centurions' houses and barrack blocks on the west side of the fortress (at 13–17 Berkeley Street: Hurst 1972, 1974), but it matched wall for wall the plan of the same buildings in the earlier fortress.*

In the area of the first cohort only the outline of buildings has been established, but here also there were barrack-like buildings with mortared masonry outer walls (Hurst 1972; Hassall and Rhodes 1974). One of the roads between a pair of barrack blocks in the earlier fortress had been replaced by an additional building as if an extra century of soldiers had to be accommodated. These buildings were dated not earlier than AD 87–8 by three coins, one in the area of the first cohort and two from the more extensively excavated buildings on the west of the fortress. Here there was also stratigraphic evidence, which showed that in the case of one building there had been a lapse of time between the demolition of the barrack block of the first fortress and the building of the second one. At least one pottery kiln had been established on the site of the earlier building and was earlier than the construction levels of the second building. (This is a revision of the sequence given in Hurst 1972, 40.) Elsewhere no time gap is apparent, since clay from the demolished first buildings was used directly as the floor make-up for the second period. Evidence for the occupation and date of destruction of these second fortress buildings is discussed below.

On the site of the *principia* and later forum, a second building period, represented by part of a gravelled courtyard and masonry structures, was excavated beneath the paved court, basilica and east range of the civilian forum. These structures

also probably represent part of an eastern range and basilica to the south and thus could belong to either a military *principia* or a forum, both of which generally have a similar plan in Roman Britain. Nevertheless the eastern range in this period (as in the first period) seems to be represented by continuous foundations for external walls with a possible internal colonnade, a plan which is more characteristic of an armoury (*armamentarium*) in a military *principia* than the shops or offices which are found in the side ranges in civil *fora* (Hurst forthcoming (1); Johnson 1983, 108–9). Direct dating evidence on this site was minimal, but at least does not contradict a late first-century date for these structures.

Work on the defences has shown that the first-period rampart was faced by a drystone wall of large cut blocks of stone (with rubble packing behind); at the north and east gates the timber first-period gates were also replaced with stone gates of similar construction (Heighway 1983; Hurst 1986). The north gate, or *porta praetoria* (the main gate of the fortress) was probably an impressive structure in the form of a triumphal arch flanked by towers. Part of the west side of the gate was excavated by Heighway (1983), who reconstructed its plan as inturned L-shaped structures flanking a single carriageway (Heighway 1983, 29–30, fig. 4). This plan was partly based on the assumption that the city wall had an irregular line (similar to its post-Roman line) at this point; with a regular line, the gate would have substantial flanking towers (cf. Hurst 1986, 107). The single carriageway arises from a projection of the line of the main north-south street (*via praetoria*), which is also probably erroneous. Thus the excavated fragment, at first thought to be of a modest gate of unusual type, is now seen to belong to something grander and more common. A new ditch was possibly also dug at this time; and outside the wall generally there was a cleared strip of ground with a metalled surface extending for as much as 50m (160ft) from the wall. Most of the direct dating evidence for this new period of defences would allow a late first-century *terminus post quem*, although a single sherd of Trajanic-Antonine samian was embedded in the rubble core behind the wall facing (Heighway 1983, 47; discussed in Hurst 1986, 118–19).

As has been noted, this whole set of constructions had until now been set into the context of the Roman *colonia* traditionally founded in AD 96–8: why should it now be regarded as another military

---

* This is true of the area excavated under controlled archaeological conditions, but it modifies an earlier statement of mine, Hurst 1976, 69–71. There I made much of two or three masonry walls which run across the width of the barrack block, stressing that this conflicted with the barracks plan and suggesting they were major divisions of a block into colonial properties. These walls were recorded in salvage conditions, where it was possible only to establish that they were earlier than substantial second-century or later masonry buildings. They may, therefore, have been secondary additions to the barrack buildings or even an intervening structural period between the barracks and substantial masonry buildings. (See further below on the sequence at 13–17 Berkeley Street.)

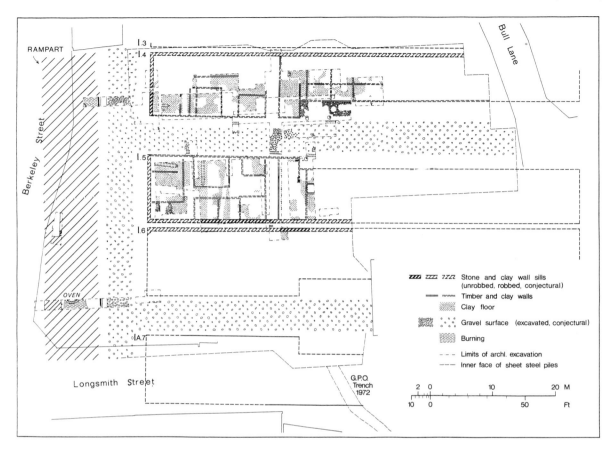

3.6 13–17 Berkeley Street, first fortress buildings.

period? The question should rather be put the other way round: unless we were excessively on the lookout for evidence for the *colonia*, would it ever have occurred to us that these structures were anything but military? In my earlier interpretation assigning them to a primary *colonia* context I pointed to differences in their plan from military buildings and to features associated with them such as an iron-smithing hearth in one room of a centurion's quarters and ovens in two rooms at the ends of *contubernia* (Hurst 1976, 69–71). The differences of plan can be disposed of (as note, above), the smithing hearth is discussed further below, and the ovens are in the area of the *principales'* quarters (end of *contubernia* nearest to centurion's quarters), where perhaps some domestic activity was allowed, as in the centurions' house. None of the objections to these being military buildings are therefore insuperable, while the positive arguments of their plan and character, plus a rather similar assemblage of finds from their

floors to those of the earlier known military period, together with the evidence for a rebuilding of the *principia* and renewal of the defences (even if there are questions over its dating), constitute a powerful case for a rebuild of the fortress.

The implications of this reinterpretation are so far-reaching, both for Gloucester and more widely, that we should briefly take stock. In Gloucester the main impact is to remove the evidence for a deliberately-built *colonia* and the arguments for its initial high population (Hurst 1976, 73). More widely we would have here the earliest stone barrack buildings known in Roman Britain (assuming they were constructed shortly after their *terminus post quem* of AD 87–8), perhaps a decade or more earlier than the conversion of the legionary fortresses at Caerleon, Chester and York into stone. However, these are strictly part-stone buildings, with internal partitions of timber, and thus they mark a transitional stage towards the fully stone second-century buildings; already in the first-period fortress some walls were based on stone ground sills. The notion of a new period of military

55

buildings at Gloucester not earlier than AD 87–8 – as opposed to the idea of the earlier fortress being kept on – also makes us look at the military occupation of Britain generally in a new light. Not only is this a decade and a half after the initial construction of Caerleon, which until recently was thought to have replaced Gloucester, but it is also after the campaigns of Agricola in the north which used to be regarded as ending the military occupation in southern England. By a process of elimination, the most plausible legion to have been rebuilding the Gloucester fortress at that date would be the XXth on its return from Scotland; it is also the case that there is documentary evidence for this legion at Gloucester (see Appendix) and there is an interesting parallel between the architecture of the stone defensive walls at Gloucester and at the XXth legion's later fortress at Chester (Strickland 1982, 1983; discussed in Hurst 1986, 119). Other considerations would follow from this, but unfortunately they cannot be pursued here. The point which does need emphasis is that made at the start: up to now we have misread this key archaeological evidence by thinking in terms too rigidly defined by an interpretation of the documentary evidence.

The earliest civilian activity within the city centre fortress

It is more difficult than one might expect to define the start of civilian activity on a former military site. Positive structural evidence – new buildings – should be decisive where building plans are characteristic of either military or civilian functions, but this is not always clear (as here, for example, with the *principia* and city wall assigned to the second fortress). The piecemeal demolition and replacement, or especially non-replacement, of buildings should be a pointer towards the civilian use of an area, although again there are many exceptions. Even when structural changes can be defined convincingly as civilian they only provide a *terminus ante quem* for the start of civilian occupation. The question now has to be posed at Gloucester, as at Colchester, of the secondary use of military buildings for civilian purposes: how much did that happen and how long did it go on for? It might be thought that this could be answered by the small objects found in occupation levels, but here too there are difficulties. Many common finds, such as brooches, gaming counters, glass beads etc., occur in both military and civilian occupation levels. Conversely, individual finds of small pieces of military equipment are not necessarily a sign that the army is still in occupation since retired ex-soldiers might have held onto bits of their equipment (perhaps too there were army surplus stores!) and there is always the danger of objects turning up residually.

The evidence from 13–17 Berkeley Street (figs. 3.7, 3.9)

Thus there are no easy answers, but these questions can be resolved by excavations which are both large-scale and detailed at the same time: the most extensive excavations so far carried out within the defended area at Gloucester has been on its western side at 13–17 Berkeley Street (Hurst 1972, 1974, forthcoming (2)). Here the finds associated with the second fortress buildings (4, above) followed the pattern just described. As an assemblage they were similar to those found in the first fortress levels, but they were mainly objects at home in either military or civilian contexts. Ambiguity remains even with objects which might seem to be distinctive. For example, a bronze steelyard with lead weights and bronze measuring horn, found together in a pit which seemed to be earlier than the demolition of a centurion's house in the second fortress period (Building I 11, fig. 3.7), would normally be associated with a shop or small commercial premises, but such items are also found in military contexts. (Dr G. Webster kindly informs me that two scalebeams are known from the fort at Rheingönheim, for example.)

A more convincing argument for civilian activity is provided by a large circular iron-smithing hearth in the neighbouring centurion's quarters (Building I 12, fig. 3.7). This was stratigraphically later than a certain amount of use and resurfacing of the floor, so that it could fit a sequence of military followed by civilian use. In this case a coin of AD 103–111, as well as samian pottery of a similar date, may be earlier than the destruction of the building, so that it very probably did remain standing into the civilian period (see Appendix, no. 8, on starting date of the *colonia*). An indication that military buildings were retained for civilian use is also provided by another nearby centurion's house, where an external wall, originally constructed in the second fortress period, was retained in successive rebuilds and was still standing in the fifth century (Buildings Ia 14, Ia 23: cf. figs. 3.7, 3.9).

The Berkeley Street excavations also produced evidence for the demolition and non-replacement

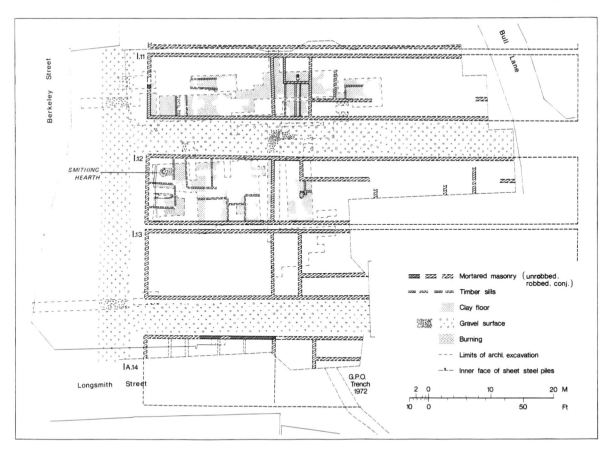

3.7 13–17 Berkeley Street, second fortress buildings.

of buildings ascribed to the second fortress. The top floor levels of the centurion's house (I 12) were beneath a deposit, generally *c.* 0.5m (1ft 8in) thick, of clayey loam with fragments of building materials, charcoal, pottery and other finds scattered through it. This deposit directly overlay, and sometimes penetrated through, the floors as if it resulted from a disturbance of the building levels; where subsidence had taken place in the lower levels, the building's destruction layer of clay, stone and plaster from the walls and tile fragments survived beneath the disturbed deposit. Was this therefore open ground, where cultivation was producing a loamy deposit from the (mainly) clayey matrix of the building's destruction? Of the four barrack blocks/centurion's houses where some evidence was retrieved, this type of deposit was present in two cases (I 11, I 12), the evidence was uncertain in a third (I 13) and might not have been present (excavations over a very small area) in the fourth case (IA 14), this being the building whose

external wall was retained throughout the Roman period.

This disturbed loam deposit nevertheless itself fits into a fairly tight building sequence since it was partially sealed by buildings with an early to mid-second century *terminus post quem* (the loam postdates the coin of 103–111 and the Flavian-Trajanic samain referred to above). The buildings which covered the loam (fig. 9) – which were unquestionably civilian – consisted of a small structure (I 17) one room's depth, with an added corridor on the site of the centurion's house (I 11), perhaps leaving an area of open ground behind it, and a large courtyard house (I 18) completely occupying the site of the next two centurions' houses and part of the *contubernia*. This had grown out of a more modest building on the site of the centurion's house (I 12) with rooms on two sides of a gravelled yard. In one of the rooms there was a hearth with a brick in position carrying the stamp *RPG* (generally interpreted as standing for *Res Publica Glevensium*, 'Gloucester Corporation' in a free translation) thus providing direct evidence for

57

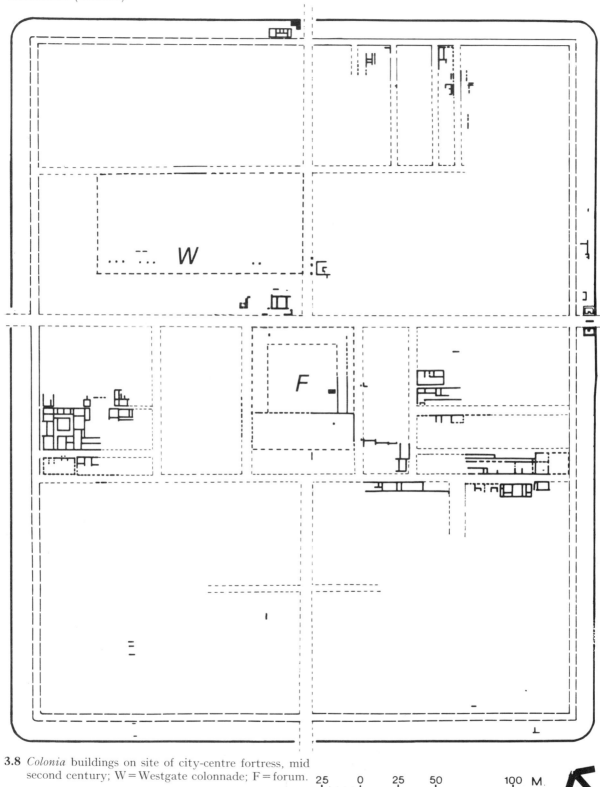

3.8 *Colonia* buildings on site of city-centre fortress, mid second century; W = Westgate colonnade; F = forum.

civilian use. Next to the large courtyard house was the centurion's quarters whose wall was retained. This was rebuilt in the second century as a small courtyard house (IA 23) having a paved court with dwarf colonnades and an external porch carried on a pair of columns.

This complex picture from Berkeley Street may therefore be summed up as follows. At least some buildings of the second fortress may have been used secondarily for civilian purposes. They appear to have been demolished piecemeal. The replacement of demolished buildings sometimes did not occur immediately, allowing time for the ground to show signs of having been turned over, perhaps for cultivation. The replacement buildings varied in size and character and they too left areas of open ground. By the mid-second century – a date by which all the buildings in fig. 3.9 seem likely to have been standing – this small sample area of Roman Gloucester looked like any other Romano-British town, say Silchester, as far as the density of buildings went. Architecturally, however, there were still reminders of the army, and this deserves further brief comment.

The large courtyard house (I 18) is of a recognizable type found in towns throughout the Roman empire, but it is also paralleled by tribunes' or commanders' houses on military sites, and one of the closest parallels is the commander's house in the fort of Housesteads on Hadrian's Wall (Johnson 1983, 132 ff.). The present house was evidently built in a civilian context, but was its owner making a show of his Romanness, evoking the buildings of Mediterranean cities, or of his status in the army? Perhaps the latter, since the only British parallels so far for this type of a house in an urban setting are from Colchester and Caerwent, both cities with strong military associations (Caerwent being situated close to the fortress of the IInd legion at Caerleon). However, most of the British town houses whose plans we know date from the third or fourth centuries, so this impression could be transformed by a small number of new discoveries.

Military associations are also evoked by the building in which the external wall of the second fortress period was retained (IA 23). Only a small part of it was excavated, but as its limits can be defined in the unexcavated areas by the lines of streets, it would seem to occupy precisely the same area as the underlying centurion's quarters. The constraints of space were such, that despite the difference of the courtyard, its internal layout must have resembled that of the centurion's quarter, with ranges of rooms on each of its long sides.

Berkeley Street as a sample of the fortress area (figs. 3.4, 3.5, 3.8)
The evidence described above was obtained from controlled excavation over an area of about one per cent of the defended enclosure (a more or less equal area was recorded on the same site under salvage conditions). Deliberate excavations, as opposed to salvage recording, of the earliest levels elsewhere in the fortress probably account for only another one to two per cent of the defended area and are split into a number of different sites. The main ones are: the *principia* (11–17 Southgate St.: Hurst 1972, 52–8, and forthcoming (1)); first cohort, north-west and south-east parts (respectively 10 Eastgate St. and New Market Hall, Bell Walk: Hurst 1972, 50–2; Hassall and Rhodes 1974); north-east quarter of fortress (Bon Marché: Hunter 1963, although the author did not believe that there was a fortress at the city centre); intervallum area west of the north gate (45–9 Northgate St.: Heighway 1983, 20–8). Salvage recording, which on the whole only readily picks up unrobbed masonry structures, accounts for the extensive look of the plans of the walled area (figs. 3.4, 3.5, 3.8). The record of the early levels is thus too fragmented and/or lacking in detail for any of these sites to provide a full comparison for the evidence provided by Berkeley Street. Nevertheless all these sites have provided complementary information and it is fair to say that all evidence known to the writer for early structures within the walled area is explainable in terms of the broad pictures just set out. Of course there are likely to be differences of detail, but there is nothing to suggest that Berkeley Street is not representative.

Built-up areas outside the fortress defences (figs. 3.10, 3.11)
Here the evidence is more fragmentary than in the defended area, and it is worth highlighting this fact at once as it is liable to distort our overall picture of Roman Gloucester. The main inhabited areas beyond the defences were on the north and north-east and, to a lesser extent, the west of the fortress. A masonry courtyard building has also recently been excavated south of the south gate (unpublished), but both on this side, further to the south-west, and around the south-east and east sides of the fortress there is evidence of Roman cemeteries.

In the main urban area north of the fortress, the

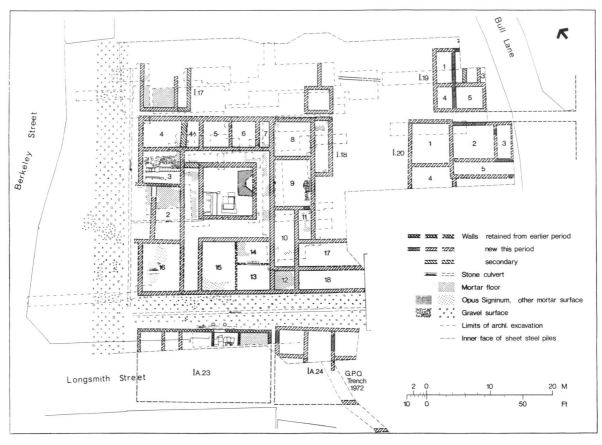

3.9 13–17 Berkeley Street, mid-second century.

military legacy would have been: stone or part-timber structures in the Hare Lane–St Catherine Street area (if these were military), which could still have been standing; Kingsholm, where the military structures had certainly been demolished; and Northgate Street–London Road, the branch road between the fortress and Ermin Street, which was flanked by buildings of timber and then stone, whose function was probably civilian since they included shops or commercial premises fronted by colonnades at 96 Northgate Street (J. Rhodes in Hurst 1974, 31–3). Buildings also spread over to the north-east corner of the fortress in a less rigidly planned way than in other areas, so that this area seems likely to have been where the main nucleus of the *canabae*, or extramural civilian settlement, was situated. London Road–Northgate Street was the main approach to the fortress, and close to it the Roman street was flanked by at least one monumental building at 63–71 Northgate Street (Hurst 1972, 63–5), possibly another at 82–4 Northgate

Street (Hurst 1974, 30–1) and, as already mentioned, the shop fronts at 96 Northgate Street were treated monumentally. A recent interpretation of a robbed foundation in the road nearby as the remains of a triumphal arch (Garrod and Heighway 1984, 1, 36) is not impossible, although a more mundane alternative is that it was the abutment for a bridge taking the road over one of the streams of the river Twyver which cross in this area.

Roman features within the Hare Lane–St Catherine Street area further west include an east-west road or metalled area and other features just north of St Catherine Street, a masonry building at the north end of Park Street (the western 'carriageway' of Hare Lane on fig. 10) and a timber building, later replaced by a stone one, east of Hare Lane at 35 Worcester Street (excavation at Worcester St. by Garrod; Hurst 1974, 39–41). At St Catherine Street the earliest road surface was associated with first-century pottery, and at 35 Worcester Street occupation of the timber building was associated with coins of AD 71/2 and 77 and its

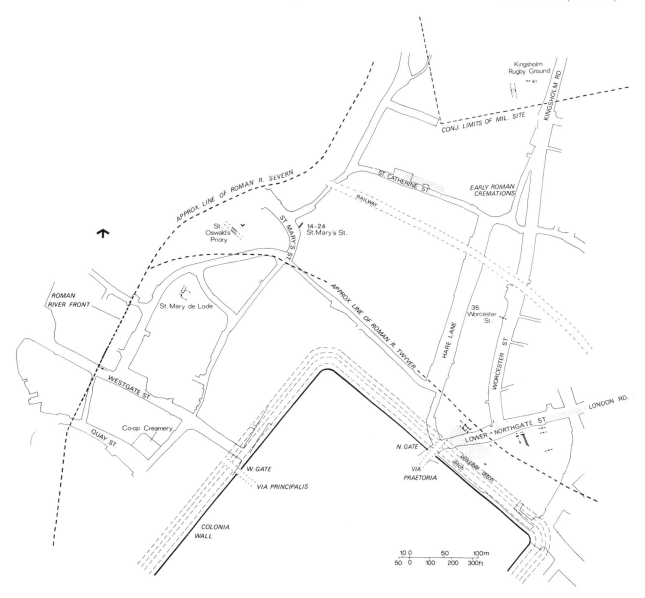

3.10 Extramural areas to north and west of city-centre fortress and *colonia*. Stipple represents Roman metalled surface. Drawn by K.P. Forrester.

destruction with a coin of AD 87/8. This seems to suggest a sequence tying in with the main occupation periods in the city centre fortress, and there may have been a distinctive alignment of structures, represented by the remains at 35 Worcester Street and by the lines of Hare Lane and St Catherine Street (which may have been influenced by Roman structures), which is different from those of both the Kingsholm and city centre sites,

perhaps indicating an actively defined area. The area is sufficiently close to the fortress defences to have served as an annexe for one of the many types of activity which took place in the immediately extramural areas. At all events, there seems to be a contrast here with the ribbon development of commercial and other buildings fronting the main road (Lower Northgate Street and London Road) leading from the north gate of the fortress.

The limits of the built-up area of the city can broadly be defined in an arc extending from north-east round to north-west. Some 700m along London Road from the north gate of the fortress there was an extensive lime-burning area on the side of the road, suggesting that this was outside the main nucleus. West of this, there are hints of one or two structures in the southern part of the Kingsholm site, but there are positive signs of ground under cultivation further to the north, again from *c.* 500m outside the fortress defences. However, the road or large metalled area and other features just north of St Catherine Street (referred to above) suggest a low density of building in this area, which is much closer to the fortress; also some early cremations have been found in this area (see below). Further west, the site of St Oswald's Priory, where abundant finds of stamped tiles suggest the municipal tilery was located – and therefore that the area was not densely built up – was only some 200–300m from the fortress defences. Evidence of timber buildings, together with finds of unstamped tiles in first-century contexts, led the excavators to suggest that tile-making on this site may have originated in the military occupation. This seems highly probable given all the other evidence for the survival of the military framework, and this is an obviously appropriate riverside site (Heighway and Parker 1982).

The riverside area west of the fortress was also built up, and there is evidence for buildings with mosaic floors at St Mary de Lode Church (Bryant 1980) and the site of the Co-op. Creamery in Upper Quay Street (Knowles 1938). Recently there has also been speculation that the Roman defences may have been extended in this area, but this partly results from misinterpretation. So far there is clear evidence for the reclamation of some ground on the river frontage, probably in the second to third century; a proposed possible city wall need only be a retaining wall on the river frontage and is quite unlike the city wall elsewhere in Gloucester (Hurst 1986, 115–6). Where found in Lower Westgate Street, this wall overlay the remains of a substantial masonry platform situated at a low level and partly covered by river alluvium. The latter structure was perhaps part of an earlier quayside, or it might have been part of a bridge pier, since the discovery was close to the line of the *via principalis* (main east-west street) of the fortress. There are also masonry structures at a very low level further south at Quay Street and The Quay, suggesting a line parallel to the present river frontage (Garrod 1986, 28).

Cemeteries (fig. 3.11)

The location of cemeteries on Roman urban sites is of key topographical importance, since they always lie outside the area formally set apart for urban purposes and usually begin just beyond its limits. The Gloucester cemeteries containing cremation burials, and therefore dating to the first and second centuries AD, lie just north of the former Kingsholm military site at Coppice Corner (or Gambier Parry Lodge), at Wotton Pitch (and St. Margaret's Hospital) *c.* 1km (0.6 mile) along London Road from the fortress, and isolated cremation burials are known from the area of the Docks to the southwest of the fortress. There is also a major cemetery with cremation burials at Barnwood on the main Ermin Street, about 2km ($1\frac{1}{4}$ miles) from the city centre. A single late Roman cremation is also known from 3 Barton Street, just outside the east gate, and inhumations have also been found outside the east defences, but so far there is no evidence of early Roman cemeteries in this area. (A gazetteer of burials is given in Heighway 1980, 62–3.)

Recently up to three cremation urns were discovered in contractors' excavations to the north of St Catherine Street (Frere 1987, 341), one vessel which was retrieved was of an early, but not closely datable, Severn Valley ware. We may nevertheless guess that these burials may have been associated with the Kingsholm site, since there is evidence for later habitation (perhaps initiated by the move to the city centre site) in the vicinity. Excluding this small group, the cremation burials define the urban area on the north-east to north-west and south-west, suggesting that it extended for at least 150ha (400 acres). Within this area were all the former military installations, including Kingsholm, even though its buildings had been demolished perhaps 30 years before Gloucester became a city. The fact that the Coppice Corner cemetery begins just to the north of the bounds of the Kingsholm site indeed gives a positive indication that these limits still mattered.

The dating of the cemeteries raises a different point of interest. Where recent work has been done

3.11 The *colonia* and its cemeteries: **a** Cremations, first–second centuries, **b** Inhumations (mainly), fourth century or later; stipple represents area presumed to have been under urban use. Key to cemeteries, CC = Coppice Corner (Gambier Parry Lodge), WP = Wotton Pitch, B = Barnwood, D = Docks, K = Kingsholm, O = St Oswald's Priory, BR = Brunswick Road.

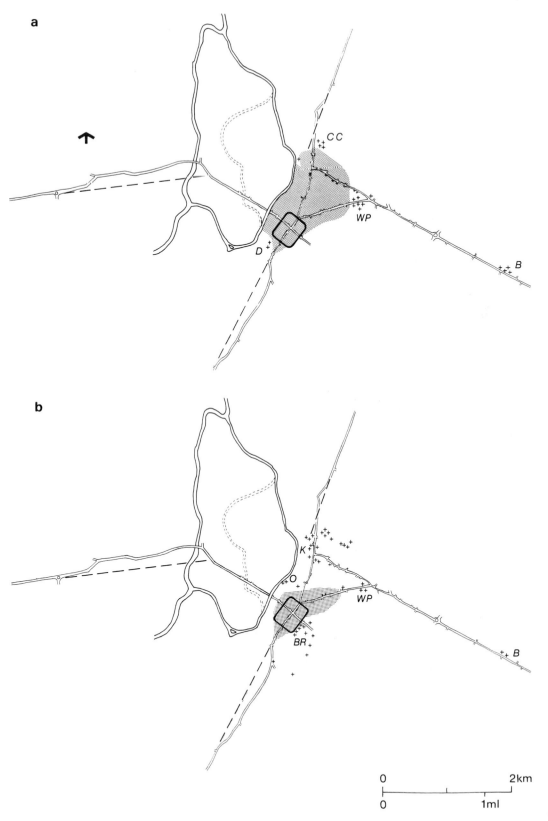

at Coppice Corner (Garrod 1984, 1985); and St Margaret's Hospital by Wotton Pitch (by Garrod: cf. Heighway 1980, 63–6), the earliest burials found so far have been late first/early second century. Since Wotton Pitch produced the Rufus Sita auxiliary cavalryman's tombstone (*RIB* 121) and a tombstone of a serving soldier of the XXth legion (*RIB* 122), it would seem that it was a military cemetery, but at which point in the military sequence as now revised?

With the late- or sub-Roman cemeteries, in particular those containing unaccompanied inhumation burials, perhaps of late fourth or fifth century date, a very different picture is presented. Many inhumations have been found on the former military site at Kingsholm, extending certainly as far south as modern Sebert Street at the limits of the built-up urban area described above. There were also late Roman inhumations on the site of the former tilery at St Oswald's (Heighway 1980b, fig. 1) and two, of uncertain but probably late Roman date, were found in 1984 at the north end of Park Street (information supplied by M.J. Watkins). This gives a hint of an inner band of cemetery, occurring at a distance of only 200–300m north-west and north of the *colonia* walls on sites which had been built up previously. Unaccompanied inhumations of uncertain date were also found between the walled area and the river, above the building containing the mosaics of St Mary de Lode Church, where they postdated occupation of the second to fourth centuries (Bryant 1980, 7–8). To the east there were inhumation cemeteries immediately outside the walls, in Brunswick Road and at the College of Art site. North-east of the walled area, fourth-century occupation levels are recorded in buildings fronting Lower Northgate Street and London Road as far as the Bristol Omnibus Depot, some 500m from the walls, but inhumations also edged their way along the London Road towards the city centre, the nearest known examples being at 50–52 London Road, some 700m from the walls (Garrod *et al.* 1982, 32; 1983, 28). The inhumations therefore enclose a much smaller area than the cremation cemeteries, and towards the north, north-west and probably west of the walled area there are indications that they encroached on former built-up areas. None of the extramural areas appears so far to have produced evidence of occupation continuing as late as within the walled area.

The overall picture from the cemeteries, then, is that to begin with a vast area, related to the military occupation, was formally set aside for urban uses. The actual town never filled this space, although at its maximum it was a respectable size, with the built-up area occupying about 50ha (120 acres) a third or about of the space, and fields and scattered dwellings outside this nucleus. In due course, perhaps only very late in the Roman period, the earlier formal urban limits were relaxed, and inhumation burials came to define a town which was withdrawing inside its walls.

Part II: a successful city?

Theoretical outline

The view has been expressed that Gloucester was a failure by comparison with nearby Cirencester because of its rather military, conservative character, lacking a population of risk-taking entrepreneurs (Wacher 1974, 155). Delightful as the picture is, with its implied contrast between a Roman Cheltenham, full of red-faced ex-centurions, and a Roman Dallas, it is misleading. No doubt Roman Gloucester had its share of backward-looking ex-soldiers, but having a population of risk-taking entrepreneurs had nothing to do with why Cirencester seems to compare favourably with Gloucester. Cirencester was the centre for the *civitas* of the Dobunni, one of the most powerful and socially developed tribes or groupings in Britain at the time of the Roman conquest. There were some twenty or so other examples of this type of city in Britain, generally the centres of major pre-Roman political groupings which had been re-established within the Roman system, wearing the Roman dress of rectangular buildings, gridded streets etc., instead of the pre-Roman one of a defended *oppidum*. What made Roman Cirencester set out in a particularly ambitious way was no doubt the wealth and importance of the territory of the Dobunni. In the conventional view most of this would have been under the control of a small number of individuals. These would be the key figures in the success of Cirencester as a Roman city: what mattered was that their political aspirations and sense of status should be expressed through public building projects and the provision of communal services. These activities made the cities cultural centres, and they generated as a consequence a class of shopkeepers, craftsmen and service-suppliers.

While the army was stationed in a particular area, it was a substitute for a local élite in terms of its economic impact, since it promoted the physical development of the area and also had surplus wealth to spend on services and goods. A colony of veteran soldiers settled on a former military site was a very different affair, for while all the settlers had some wealth, there was no natural 'upper class' or powerful landholding element among them. Thus an economic vacuum must, to some extent, have been created on the removal of the legion and foundation of the colony. A further disadvantage of such a city may simply have been the size of its territory. The most likely pattern of events is that the legion controlled a tract of land around the fortress and this was either transferred directly or sold off in lots to the new veteran settlers in the *colonia* (sold if they received cash donatives rather than land on retirement from the army). A calculation is made below of the possible size of this territory, based on the needs of the legion, but however big it was it seems inconceivable that it could have matched the territory of even a fairly modest British *civitas*. Thus a city such as Gloucester started with some marked disadvantages at a theoretical level; true, its citizens did not have the tax burdens of the rest of the province, but again these would have presented no problems to the élite in less privileged cities.

This is all theory, but it has set up a number of possibilities, which we can look at in the archaeological record. Firstly, the activities of the élite: how do Gloucester's public buildings and rich houses compare with those of other cities? Secondly, the economic vacuum: is this what the archaeological record shows?

Public buildings (fig. 3.8)

The little we know suggests Gloucester compares favourably with other Romano-British cities. Its forum, as rebuilt in the second century, was just smaller than that at Silchester but more architecturally elaborate than the usual reconstructions of Silchester, having a basilica with internal colonnades defining a nave and two aisles and a colonnaded facade, as well as flanking colonnades in the forum (Hurst 1972, 52–8, and forthcoming (1); Fulford 1985, esp. 49–53). The variety of colour in the architectural treatment – whitish-yellow oolitic limestone for the colonnades, red Old Red sandstone for the ground-level gutters and green-grey Forest of Dean (Old Red) sandstone for the courtyard paving slabs – was also a typically Roman effect, although the use of local stones instead of the coloured marble characteristic of the larger Mediterranean cities gave it a modest,

'provincial' feel. The excavation carried out in 1968–9 also revealed the remains of a monumental cast bronze statue, almost certainly an equestrian figure, situated in the southeast corner of the courtyard. This had first been set up in association with the second-century forum, and was then re-erected on a crudely-built base of reused stones, perhaps some time in the fourth century.

The most intriguing Roman public building is represented by remains of huge columns (*c.* 1m shaft diameter, the same dimensions as those of the basilica nave) found along the north side of modern Westgate Street at various times in the nineteenth century, in 1971 and in 1977–8 (Hurst 1972, 62, and forthcoming (1); Heighway and Garrod 1980, 79–82). Reference used to be made to the 'Westgate colonnade' in a manner reminiscent of the Bailgate colonnade at Lincoln, though in fact these columns are substantially larger (Richmond 1946, 72–3). When two columns were found at 4 Westgate Street in 1971, up to 100m east of the westernmost of the columns previously known, it seemed probable that they were from a separate building; the possibility was raised of a baths basilica. The later discovery of another column towards the west, at 30 Westgate Street, however, argues strongly for a single colonnade, since not only is it exactly in line with the two at No. 4, its plinth is at the same absolute level (and this despite a probable natural slope down to the west). If a single colonnade is represented, with columns of 1m shaft diameter and extending for over 100m, what could it be? It cannot be any sort of streetside colonnade because the columns are too large and, in any case, the nearest major street, on the line of the *via principalis* of the fortress, is some 30m (100ft) to the south. It can hardly be a basilica, since it would then be virtually the largest such building in Roman Britain, having roughly the same dimensions as the London civil basilica, and would dwarf the known forum basilica of Gloucester, which cannot be more than *c.* 65m long overall (its internal colonnades would, of course, be shorter). An attractive solution is that it might be the internal colonnade of a *peribolos* (surrounding range) of a temple enclosure, like the well-known examples at Colchester (Temple of Claudius) or Bath (*Sulis Minerva*); in both these cases, however, only the limits of the *periboloi* are known, not their internal treatment. As a colonial foundation, Gloucester must have had at least one major classical temple. This suggested *peribolos* could then be the southern side of a precinct, which extended for *c*. 62m (70yds) to the west of this; the temple within such an enclosure could be aligned east-west, with its front to the east (fig. 3.8).

As noted, at least one monumental building is known from outside the fortress defences, while water pipes and traces of a possible fountain within the defences show that the city was supplied with an aqueduct. This would probably have brought water from Robinswood Hill, slightly over 3km (2 miles) southeast of the centre, like its medieval and post-medieval successors. The evidence described above for land-reclamation and monumental structures in the waterfront area may be added to the list, although the latter may date back to the last stage of the military occupation.

The city walls and gates can also be considered in this same context, as reflecting the community's sense of status. On present understanding of the evidence, the army's legacy was particularly rich – an ornate city wall and probably both the east and north gates which have been partially excavated. Neither of these gates seems to have been replaced later in the Roman period. The original city wall seems to have stood until the late third century, when it was rebuilt on the same line, making Gloucester unlike both Colchester and Lincoln in not extending the walled area beyond that of the fortress. The inference made from this, that it was a community with only modest aspirations, has gained wide acceptance. However, now that we understand much more about the background to the building of town walls in general we can no longer reach the simple conclusion that the city did not grow – its extent beyond the walls has been described. The most telling comparison should be with Lincoln, since Colchester was plainly marked out to be special from the start, with the Temple of Claudius attached to it. With Lincoln and Gloucester the question arises of what the walls were intended to enclose: were their whole communities, those dwelling in the former *canabae* as well as the veteran settlers in the former fortress, given full colonial status with the rights of Roman citizenship? Or was there a double-status community, as is implied for Colchester by an inscription of a census official (*CIL* XIV 3955)? Hence at Lincoln the double-fortified enclosure, one for each community, while at Gloucester only the *colonia* was enclosed within its former military fortifications? Gloucester nevertheless has a similar chronology to Lincoln's for its defences, with the addition of late-second century earthworks and

stone towers (this was when the 'Lower Colonia' at Lincoln was first enclosed), followed by the building of massive walls and external towers at the end of the third century.

Rich dwellings

Luxurious residences are known both within and outside the city, but there is not enough information yet to suggest any overall pattern. A building with a paved courtyard and ranges of rooms floored with mosaics covering not less than 1500 sq m (1800 sq yds) was recorded as 12–36 Eastgate Street (regrettably in salvage conditions, so that its plan is not understood in any detail: Hurst 1974, 27) and there are other rich town houses. Great Witcombe, 8km (5 miles) to the south-east, is the richest villa from the vicinity of Gloucester. Richmond (1946, 72–3) and others have drawn attention to the lack of figured mosaics and the poverty of art generally in the city, but here a misleading impression may have been created. Figured mosaics from the city are known (Neal 1981, pls. 52, 56), but third- and fourth-century levels, in which they would normally be found, survive more rarely than those of the first and second centuries, in which mosaics are less common and less frequently have figured designs. A work of art which has in the past been made to play far too large a part in value judgements on the 'Romanness' of Roman Gloucester is the Bon Marché head, a more-or-less lifesize male head in oolitic limestone. For a long time it was seen as a hybrid of Romano–Celtic sculpture: a Roman city producing monumental sculpture with such 'native' traits had to be rather backward, and so forth. Greene has effectively argued the case for this piece being Romanesque architectural ornament, and it was indeed found on the site of the medieval church of St Aldate (Greene 1975).

Economic activity

From archaeological evidence it is possible to present a picture of virtual economic collapse after the departure of the army, since a range of products ceased to be made in the city. However, in describing them, we must bear in mind the fundamental difference between a modern and an ancient city – that there were no urban industries (of any importance) in the Roman world: all types of production from pottery to ironworking were equally at home in the city and the countryside, and in civilian Roman Britain the tendency was on the whole towards rural production.

Taking pottery first: under the army there was extensive local production of pottery, first at Kingsholm, and then in the city centre. Kilns have been excavated at the College of Art site (Rawes 1972, 1978), and at Berkeley Street (Hurst 1972, 41). This included 'continental forms' such as flagons, mortaria and imitations of some imported table ware, destined obviously for use by the army. But there was also local production of native Iron Age forms in typically Roman wheel-thrown well-fired fabrics. This class of pottery as found at Gloucester (together with other locally-produced wares) was called 'Glevum ware' by Green (Green 1943), but it belongs within a larger class of typologically similar pottery known as Severn Valley ware, produced all along the Severn valley up to Wroxeter (Webster 1976; Rawes 1982). The earliest of these wares occurs in military contexts at Kingsholm and Gloucester, and wasters of one of the wares have been found at Kingsholm, so the initial impetus for their presence at Gloucester was certainly military. After the departure of the army around AD 100 local pottery production at Gloucester goes into a decline: production of the continental forms stops; Glevum ware or the local variant of Severn Valley ware still forms a significant part of second-century pottery groups, but its position is progressively taken over by other Severn Valley wares and Dorset Black Burnished (both essentially rural industries) so that by c. AD 200 there may have been no directly local pottery production in Gloucester. This continues to be the case in the third and fourth centuries.

Tile production seems to behave in the same way as the pottery industry. The municipal tilery at St Oswald's Priory was producing early in the second century (Heighway and Parker, 1982). Fired clay tiles on Gloucester sites are the standard roofing material in the second fortress buildings at the city centre and through the first quarter of the second century. From around the middle of the second century, however, sandstone from the Forest of Dean begins to be used as a roofing material and thereafter it appears to be dominant. Fired clay tiles continue to be found in later destruction levels, but it is difficult to say how much, if any, was newly produced after AD 200. This is perhaps a less significant change than it might appear, since by AD 150 the main sequence of building was completed, leaving Gloucester a city largely of stone buildings with a long potential life ahead of them. The drop in the scale of demand for new building materials may have occasioned the change of roofing material.

Similar comments could be applied to the use of stone. Again it was the army which developed the exploitation of the two common building stones – the Lower Lias limestone, a mudstone available in the Severn Valley (in medieval times it is documented as having been brought for the castle from Denny Hill on the riverbank c. 12km (7½ miles) downstream from Gloucester), and the higher-quality oolitic limestone from the Cotswold edge. Both of these stones were used in the first city centre fortress from the mid-60s (and undressed oolitic limestone is present at Kingsholm in a still earlier context), but dressed oolitic limestone is first found on a large scale in the masonry of the first city wall and buildings of the second city centre fortress. The large-scale quarrying of oolite is evident from the series of buildings constructed up to c. AD 150, but again it is difficult to demonstrate the use of newly quarried material for buildings constructed after the second century, even if this seems probable. What survives of the late city wall is substantially reused material, although the small oolite courses in the upper part of the third build may have been newly quarried. Perhaps before the end of the fourth century, certainly in the early fifth century (if that is the date of the relevant buildings), Gloucester like Wroxeter had reverted to timber as the standard building material.

The only local 'industry' which is more strongly attested in the third and fourth centuries than in the first and second seems to be ironworking, as evidenced by the use of slag in the metalling of streets and other surfaces and its general occurrence in levels throughout the city. The Forest of Dean was one of the main iron-producing areas in Roman Britain and again, to judge by the evidence of the major ironworking site of *Ariconium* (Weston-under-Penyard, near Ross-on-Wye), this resource was first exploited and developed by the army in the pre-Flavian period. The abundance of iron slag in the late Roman levels at Gloucester is interesting in view of the predominance of this industry in the early medieval city: Domesday Book records that part of the city's taxes were paid in iron rods (Fullbrook-Leggatt 1952, 42).

What emerges from this short survey, therefore, is that the city was on the whole unable to take over the role of the fortress as a centre for production and the exploitation of resources. Its economy came to look like that of other Romano–British towns, with rural production dominating, and eventually its ability to manipulate resources became very limited.

The territorium

An unbalanced picture would be given if the city was not considered in relation to its dependent territory. Where and how big was Gloucester's *territorium*? This is likely to remain one of those unanswerable questions in terms of precise boundaries or measurements, and here it would be profitable to move the argument in a new direction from that followed up to now. Some familiar points must, however, first be discussed. We can now exclude once and for all the idea of a centuriated tract of land on the Po or Lower Rhône Valley model. Firstly this is theoretically improbable, because colonial Gloucester's territory almost certainly incorporated, or was even the same as, a tract of land held under the direct control of the Roman military authorities during their 50-year presence in the Gloucester area: it is not certain, but highly probable from evidence for the army elsewhere, that a legion would have a substantial landholding if it stayed in one place for any length of time. It would have controlled farming and other activities on it, so that there was probably a working system for the colonial settlers to take over. Secondly, a series of attempts to look for centuriation on the ground have now shown quite conclusively that it is not there. Recent work, especially by B. Rawes, on sites in the Gloucester area has produced evidence of field boundaries and alignments, but although there are local regularities they quite obviously vary from one site or small area to the next and there is no sign of overall layout (cf. Rawes 1979).

In the earlier account I gave an estimated figure of around 122 sq km (48 sq miles) for the agricultural area of the *territorium*, calculating from an estimated colonial population and multiplying this by the most common landholding unit documented for North Italy (Hurst 1976, 76). This figure was never intended to be taken as a precise statement. Now that the basis for the population estimate has been removed by the reinterpretation of the earliest *colonia* buildings, it is best simply to forget it.

Finberg (1957, 55) was the first to raise the possibility that the tract of land associated with the late seventh-century *civitas* of Gloucester, referred to in the foundation charter of St Peter's Abbey (AD 679), related to the *territorium* of Glevum *colonia*. Following the same line, Heighway (1984, 375) has suggested that this tract of land, described as 300 *tributarii* in the charter, may correspond to the three early hundreds of Dudstone, King's Barton and Gloucester, which became the medieval hundred of Dudstone and King's Barton, covering an area of *c*. 179 sq km (70 sq miles) on both sides of the Severn Valley. This is plausible, as such suggestions of Roman–Saxon correspondences often are, but the two crucial assumptions must be seen clearly: first that the *colonia territorium* remained an unchanged unit to AD 679; secondly that the AD 679 unit precisely became the three Late Saxon hundreds later united into one.

Mrs Clifford long ago drew attention to the distribution of the RPG-stamped tiles as a possible indicator of the *territorium* extent (Clifford 1955). As others have pointed out, building materials are notorious for their ability to 'walk', so that individual finds of the stamped tiles must be treated with caution. But most *RPG* tiles found outside Gloucester in any case occur in the Severn valley just east of the city, in areas which would naturally be assumed to lie within its territory. Finds of stamped tiles are nevertheless known from as far east as Ifold (Painswick), on the Cotswold edge *c*. 8km (5 miles) from Gloucester, and from as far south as Frocester, *c*. 20km (12 miles) from Gloucester. The Ifold find, together with another possible one from the Cotswold edge at Dry Hill, is of interest in the light of comments below.

The discussion can be moved in a new direction by looking at a theoretical military *territorium*, which we have already suggested may have been handed over intact to the civilian authorities, together with the fortress itself, on the creation of the *colonia*. The basis of this would be the land needed to supply the legion's needs for food, basic building materials and equipment, as far as that could be produced locally. It must be admitted that this is hypothetical: others would perhaps see the legions being supplied centrally out of general taxation, but without arguing at length, this would not fit what we know of the working of Roman administration in the early empire (which was generally low-key and uncentralized), while there is some archaeological support for the present hypothesis. Initially, we may imagine the army simply requisitioned what it needed locally, but as time went by the arrangements are likely to have become formalized: in the Gloucester area, for example, the creation of the *civitas* of the Dobunni in the Flavian period would have required the boundary between areas under civilian and military authority to have been established. Two resources the army would probably have exploited directly, which at once give some geographical definition to their area of interest, are iron ore from the Forest of Dean and limestone from the Cotswold edge. As has been noted, later links between the Forest and Gloucester are provided by the increased signs of ironworking and the use of sandstone roofing tiles; on the other hand the *RPG* tiles extended to the Cotswold edge at Painswick, the most likely source for much of the oolitic limestone at Gloucester. Grounds are therefore provided for believing that the *territorium* included some of the Forest on the west and at least the Painswick area of the Cotswold edge on the east.

Between these limits was the prime food-producing area of the Severn valley. How much land would a legion need to feed itself? Calculations of food needs are much in fashion at the present time: Davies (1971, 123) estimated the food needs of a Roman soldier at 3lb (1.36kg) of corn per day, or just under 500kg (1100lb) per annum; this may be compared with the figure of 30 *modii* or 200kg (440lb) per annum given by Garnsey (1983, 118) as the corn dole in Rome. Multiplied by 6000 (full legion plus 500-strong auxiliary cohort or equivalent) this would produce a total annual requirement of some 3000 tonnes (using Davies' estimate). Reynolds' (1976, 61) figures from cultivating einkorn suggest that this amount of grain could be produced in Britain from 1500ha (3700 acres), though as Millett (1984, 71–2) pointed out when using these figures for a slightly different calculation, it is safe to double this to 3000ha (7400 acres) to allow for poor crops, seed corn etc. This is a modest area of land, some 5 × 6km (3 × 4 miles) such as could be found without difficulty in the immediate vicinity of Gloucester. If we increase it by half, to provide food for the inhabitants of the *canabae* and those who actually cultivated the land, and then double the whole area, to provide grazing for cattle (food, tents and armour), sheep (food and clothes) and horses and further areas for pig-farming, vegetable and fruit cultivation, the maximum territory required would be 90 sq km (35 sq miles). In other words, a north-south stretch

of about 10km (6 miles) on the east side of the Severn valley alone (it is not less than 8km (5 miles) wide near Gloucester) would meet the legion's food requirements. Timber was another resource of which the army was a major consumer, but that could have been provided from the Forest, as in the medieval period. These figures show only that a legion based at Gloucester *could* have obtained all that it required locally by controlling quite a modest tract of land. As it turns out, the area of land could have been similar to that of the hundred of Dudstone and King's Barton.

In my earlier account (1976) I suggested that the population progressively left the city to live in the surrounding countryside. We must now ignore the calculations then made of the initial colonial population, though the trend still seems to hold (based on a very small amount of evidence, however). What is known at present of sites in the Severn Valley around Gloucester could be taken as supporting this suggestion, since a short survey of evidence published up to 1985 by Nigel Pollard showed that, of some 30 rural sites known within the area of the hundred of Dudstone and King's Barton, only three have so far produced clear evidence of first-century occupation (cf. Rawes 1984 for map and list, with references, of 16 of the sites). All the others have a main occupation range of the second to fourth centuries. Eighteen of the 30 sites are represented only by surface sherd scatters, so this evidence must not be pressed too hard. However, it does focus on some key questions: for example, given the rather piecemeal look to the start of the *colonia* which we now have, were colonists settling directly in the countryside? Let us hope that over the coming years the chronologies of several more of these rural sites can be established sufficiently well to throw light on their relationship with the *colonia*.

General conclusions

A major change in our understanding of the development of Gloucester and a modification of our general view of the military occupation is proposed here. The army was in the area longer and its physical impact greater than we might previously have imagined. Within the city it is suggested that barrack buildings and, we can surmise, the *principia* and city wall (and presumably a whole range of unexcavated military structures), were taken over for civilian use. The municipal tilery probably followed on from the legionary one and likewise in the countryside the stone quarries and the exploitation of some other resources probably passed directly from the army's control to that of the new *colonia*.

Roman Gloucester was never more than an average-sized Romano–British town, covering some 50ha (12 acres) at its maximum, of which 17ha (43 acres), representing the original legionary fortress, were enclosed by defences. Our picture of it is still liable to be distorted by the imbalance of excavation within the walled and extramural areas, but information we have to date suggests its fortunes were also comparable to those of many other Romano–British towns. It had some impressive public architecture and rich private houses, but it does not look like a thriving commercial centre any more than Silchester, Wroxeter or Cirencester does; its population looks to have diminished through the second–fourth centuries, though this is difficult to quantify. We have suggested that while the army may have given it a head start in terms of its physical fabric, there were social and economic disadvantages inherent in its military origins. Undoubtedly there is a great deal more to learn, but at present the overriding impression is of a modest city belonging to a society where cities only had a modest part to play.

Appendix – The Documents

The following is a list of the principal written documents bearing on Roman Gloucester's military and early civilian occupation, with comments illustrating some of the problems of interpretation that they pose. (For reasons of space full texts and translations are not given, but reference is given to the standard publications: *RIB* = *Roman Inscriptions of Britain, CIL* = *Corpus Inscriptionum Latinarum*.)

(1) Tacitus, *Annals* XII 32, says that in AD 49 the Silures (in South Wales) were out of control and needed to be suppressed. This led to the transfer of the XXth legion on the foundation of the colonia at Colchester. Tacitus uses the phrase *castris legionum premenda* – literally, 'suppressed by the camp of legions', but the words can be used loosely to mean no more than 'suppressed by the army' (Tacitus in particular has a tendency to misuse precise-sounding phrases for rhetorical effect.) Thus there is not necessarily a specific reference here to a base of the XXth legion at Gloucester/Kingsholm or

anywhere else (although, of course, the fact of military activity carries with it the probability that such a base or bases would be built somewhere suitable for activity against the Silures).

(2) A lost tombstone from Wotton Pitch of a soldier of the XXth legion who died while still in the army (*RIB* 122). This has been taken as confirmation of Tacitus' implication that the XXth legion was at Gloucester from AD 49, especially since *VV* (*Valeria Victrix*, thought to be honorific titles awarded after the Boudican revolt of 60–1) is not given with the title of the legion. But even if the dating of *VV* is accepted, it still has to be demonstrated that it is used in all post-Boudican inscriptions of the XXth legion, and therefore has value as negative evidence. The possibility that this could be a later first century inscription cannot therefore be excluded.

(3) The Rufus Sita tombstone of a cavalryman from the first *ala* of Thracians who died on active service (*RIB* 121), also found at Wotton Pitch. Could be from any stage of the military occupation at Gloucester.

(4) A building inscription of the XXth legion, with the abbreviated *VV*, reused in the masonry of Gloucester cathedral (Hassall and Tomlin 1986, 429). If, as is probable, the stone came from a building in Roman Gloucester, it is positive evidence that a whole century of the legion was at Gloucester and actively building something. It is in stone, implying that it came from a stone building, such as the barracks of the second city-centre fortress, dating to AD 87–8 or later. An alternative suggestion, that it was from a stone building, perhaps a bath-house, associated with one of the periods of military occupation in timber buildings at Kingsholm or the city centre, is less plausible because the odds against survival of inscriptions from such a building (if it ever existed at all) are many times higher than from a general period of stone buildings; also would there be inscribed centurial stones on a legionary bathhouse rather than (or in addition to) a more generalized inscription of the whole legion?

(5) A fragmentary centurial building inscription, from King's Walk (eastern defences of city centre fortress (Wright and Hassall 1972, 353). In stone, no mention of legion; otherwise same comment as for 4).

(6) The tombstone of a decurion (member of the town council) of the *colonia* of Glevum (Gloucester) who died at Bath aged 86 (*RIB* 161). This shows that Gloucester was a *colonia*, and that it had the

regular system of self-government. No precise dating.

(7) Tiles stamped *RPG* or with *RPG* followed by one or more names, probably made at the tilery on the site of St Oswald's Priory, Gloucester. Interpreted as standing for *Res Publica Glevens(is/ium)*, *Res Publica* being the corporate body of a self-governing Roman city. The names would be of magistrates holding annual or sometimes quinquennial office. The earliest stratified example of such a tile occurs in a hearth at Berkeley Street which should date to *c*. AD 110–140 (p. 57, above); production of the tiles may have ceased not long after the mid-second century (cf. Heighway and Parker 1982).

(8) The tombstone of a soldier (a *frumentarius*) of the VIth legion from Rome, who gives Glevum as his birthplace (*CIL* VI 3346). *NER* before the word *GLEV* refers to the emperor Nerva (AD 96–98). In this inscription it is used instead of the man's voting tribe, a device sometimes used for cities called after the name of emperors, as was often the case with *coloniae*. Often, but not invariably, the emperor's name referred to the reign in which the city was founded or promoted in status. Honorific titles were, however, sometimes given retrospectively: thus a Hadrianic foundation (AD 118–137) might use Trajan's family name *ULPIA* (Trajan's reign AD 102–118) and so on. On the other hand, Nerva's predecessor, Domitian, suffered *damnatio memoriae* (condemnation of his memory) and it is possible (but unlikely in the present example) that official titles using his name were replaced with that of Nerva. Thus Gloucester is most likely to have been founded in AD 96–98; it might have been later or, just possibly, it could have been earlier.

(9) Tombstone of a veteran of the XXth legion, from the Coppice Corner cemetery (Hassall and Tomlin 1984, 333). The man's name *AURELI*, the ligatured lettering and his dress all suggest a late second to third-century date. We might guess from other Roman colonies in military areas that Gloucester continued to have a large number of military families in its population long after it became a *colonia*, but this is one of only two inscribed civilian tombstones so far found in the city.

Overall information from the documents
The documents imply that at some time part at least of the XXth legion was stationed at Gloucester and they also tell us that the city was a *colonia* founded not later than the early second century. Beyond that we can only deal in probabilities and possibilities. We can infer that the *colonia* was founded in 96–98 since several pieces of independent evidence converge in that direction, but at the risk of seeming pedantic it is dangerous to start with that assumption (see comments above on misinterpreting the rebuild of the fortress at the city centre). Likewise with the fortress and the XXth legion. The most likely context for the building inscription, which is the really useful one for showing that the legion was at Gloucester, is in the city centre fortress rebuild after AD 87–8. Having the legion at Gloucester then makes us review the preceding sequence in a new light and, without going into the arguments, it might encourage thé belief that the legion was in the area previously, and we might even look at Tacitus and Kingsholm more positively. But Tacitus on his own told us nothing specific about Gloucester or Kingsholm, and for years Gloucester's archaeology was distorted because people thought he did.

Acknowledgements

The writer wishes to thank Dr J.R. Timly and Miss J.M. Reynolds for their helpful comments respectively on Roman pottery and on document no 8 in the Appendix.

Bibliography

Atkin, M. 1986 — 'Kingsholm' *Glevensis* 20, 4–12

Bryant, R. 1980 — 'St Mary de Lode Excavations 1978–79' *Glevensis* 14, 4–12

Clifford, E.M. 1965 — 'Stamped Tiles found in Gloucestershire' *Journal of Roman Studies* 45, 68–72

Darling, M.J. 1977 — 'Pottery from early military sites in Western Britain' in Dore, J., and Greene, K. (eds), *Roman Pottery Studies in Britain and Beyond*, *BAR* International Series 30, 57–100

Davies, R.W. 1971 — 'The Roman military diet' *Britannia* 2, 122–42

Finberg, H.P.R. 1957 — *Gloucestershire Studies*, Leicester

Frere, S.S. 1986 — 'Roman Britain in 1986. I, sites explored' *Britannia* 18, 302–59

Fullbrook-Leggatt, L.E.W.O. 1952 — *Anglo-Saxon and Medieval Gloucester*, Gloucester

Garnsey, P. 1983 — 'Grain for Rome' in Garnsey, P., Hopkins, K. and Whittaker, C.R. (eds), *Trade in the Ancient Economy*, London

Garrod, A.P. 1983 — 'Site Reports' *Glevensis* 17, 26–35

—— 1984 — 'Site Reports' *Glevensis* 18, 46–52

—— 1985 — 'Site Reports' *Glevensis* 19, 45–9

—— 1986 — 'Minor Development Sites in Gloucester' *Glevensis* 20, 19–24

Garrod, A.P., *et al.* 1982 — 'Site Reports' *Glevensis* 16, 29–36

Garrod, A.P., and Heighway, C. 1984 — *Garrod's Gloucester*, Western Archaeological Trust

Green, C. 1943 — 'Glevum and the Second Legion, ii; evidence of the pottery, metal objects, etc.' *Journal of Roman Studies* 33, 15–28

Greene, K. 1975 — 'The Romano–Celtic head from the Bonmarché site, Gloucester: a reappraisal' *Antiquaries' Journal* 55, 338–45

Hassall, M.W. and Rhodes, J.F. 1974 — 'Excavations at the New Market Hall, Gloucester, 1966–7' *Transactions of the Bristol and Gloucestershire Archaeological Society* 93, 15–100

Hassall, M.W.C., and Tomlin, R.S.O. 1984 — 'Roman Britain in 1983. II, Inscriptions' *Britannia* 15, 333–56

—— 1986 — 'Roman Britain in 1985. II, Inscriptions' *Britannia* 17, 428–54

Heighway, C.M. 1980a — 'Roman Cemeteries in Gloucester District' *Transactions of the Bristol and Gloucestershire Archaeological Society* 98, 57–72

—— 1980b — 'Excavations at Gloucester. Fifth interim report: St Oswald's Priory 1977–8' *Antiquaries Journal* 60, 207–26

—— 1983 — *The East and North Gates of Gloucester*, Western Archaeological Trust

—— 1984 — 'Saxon Gloucester' in Haslam, J. (ed) *Anglo-Saxon Towns in Southern England*, Chichester

Heighway, C., and Garrod, P. 1980 — 'Excavations at Nos. 1 and 30 Westgate Street, Gloucester' *Britannia* 11, 73–114

Heighway, C.M., and Parker, A.J. 1982 — 'The Roman Tilery at St Oswald's Priory, Gloucester' *Britannia* 13, 25–77

Hunter, A.G. 1963 — 'Excavations at the Bon Marché site, Gloucester, 1958–9' *Transactions of the Bristol and Gloucestershire Archaeological Society* 82, 25–65

Hurst, H.R. 1972 — 'Excavations at Gloucester, 1968–71: first interim report' *Antiquaries Journal* 52, 24–69

—— 1974 — 'Excavations at Gloucester, 1971–1973: second interim report' *Antiquaries Journal* 54, 8–52

—— 1976 — 'Glevum: a *Colonia* in the West Country' in Branigan, K., and Fowler, P. (eds), *The Roman West Country*, London

—— 1985 — *Kingsholm*, Gloucester Archaeological Reports, vol. 1, Gloucester

—— 1986 — *Gloucester, the Roman and Later Defences*, Gloucester Archaeological Reports, vol. 2, Gloucester

—— forthcoming (1) — *The Roman Forum and post-Roman sequence at Gloucester city centre*, Gloucester Archaeological Reports, vol. 3

—— forthcoming (2) — *Excavations at 13–17, Berkeley Street, Gloucester: the Roman levels*, Gloucester Archaeological Reports, vol. 4

Johnson, A. 1983 — *Roman Forts of the 1st and 2nd centuries AD in Britain and the German Provinces*, London

Knowles, W.H. 1938 — 'Gloucester Roman Research Committee Report 1938–39' *Transactions of the Bristol and Gloucestershire Archaeological Society* 60, 165–8

Millett, M. 1984 — 'Forts and the origins of towns: cause or effect?' in Blagg, T.F.C., and King, A. (eds) *Military and Civilian in Roman Britain*, BAR British Series 136, 65–74

Neal, D.S. 1981 — *Roman Mosaics in Britain, Britannia monograph* no. 5

Rawes, B. 1972 — 'Roman Pottery Kilns at Gloucester' *Transactions of the Bristol and Gloucestershire Archaeological Society* 91, 18–59

—— 1978   'Roman Pottery Kilns at Gloucester: a supplementary note' *Transactions of the Bristol and Gloucestershire Archaeological Society* 96, 77–8

—— 1979   'The Possibility of Roman Land Boundaries near Gloucester' *Glevensis* 13, 5–10

—— 1982   'Gloucester Severn Valley Ware' *Transactions of the Bristol and Gloucestershire Archaeological Society* 100, 33–46

—— 1984   'The Romano–British site on the Portway, near Gloucester' *Transactions of the Bristol and Gloucestershire Archaeological Society* 100, 23–72

Reynolds, P.J. 1979   *Iron Age Farm*, London

Richmond, I.A. 1946   'The Four Coloniae of Roman Britain' *Archaeological Journal* 103, 57–84

Rowbotham, F.H. 1978   'The River Severn at Gloucester' *Glevensis* 12, 4–10

Strickland, T.J. 1982   'The Defences of Roman Chester: a note on discoveries made on the North Wall, 1982' *Journal at Chester Archaeological Society* 65, 25–35

—— 1983   'The Defences of Roman Chester: discoveries made on the East Wall, 1983' *Journal of Chester Archaeological Society* 66, 5–11

Wacher, J.S. 1974   *The Towns of Roman Britain* (esp. pp. 137–55 on Gloucester), London

Webster, P.V. 1976   'Severn Valley Ware' *Transactions of the Bristol and Gloucestershire Archaeological Society* 94, 18–46

Wright, R.P., and Hassall, M.W.C. 1972   'Roman Britain in 1972. II, Inscriptions' *Britannia* 3, 352–67

Note: *Glevensis* is the Gloucester and District Archaeological Research Group Review, published annually since 1967.

4 CIRENCESTER
(Corinium Dobunnorum)

Unlike other places discussed in this book, the Roman city of Cirencester was not preceded by a legionary fortress, but in view of the pre-eminence of *Corinium* amongst the civitas capitals of Roman Britain, and its close proximity to legionary bases at Kingsholm and Gloucester, it is constructive briefly to examine the way the change from a comparatively smaller auxiliary fort to the second largest city in Roman Britain took place.

Since the discovery in the nineteenth century of two inscribed tombstones at Cirencester (*RIB* 108 and 109), it has always been assumed that a Roman military establishment existed on the banks of the River Churn. It was usually considered to have been built soon after the conquest in AD 43 and occupied whilst the army was campaigning in the west. Attempts to fit this base into a regional picture have been frustrated by not knowing the type of military installation which existed at Cirencester, although the two units depicted on the tombstones are cavalry *alae*. In addition, our understanding of the disposition of the army in this area was further complicated by not knowing what was happening in and around Gloucester, although this has now to some extent improved (Heighway 1983). More recently the dating evidence for the occupation of the fortress at Exeter (Bidwell 1979), where *Legio* II *Aug* was based, has caused a number of problems in trying to identify the units active in the Cotswolds. A far too simplistic view is often taken about the size and nature of units operating at this time, and the dating evidence for the occupation of a fort or fortress has been frequently based on the excavation of a very small, and not necessarily, representative sample. Needless to say, this is the case at Cirencester, where evidence of the military phase still remains limited.

In addition to the two tombstones (figs. 4.1, 4.2), items of military equipment have been recorded at Cirencester and studied by Dr Graham Webster (1960 and 1982). None of this material has indicated the presence of legionary troops in Cirencester; all the evidence has, in fact, pointed to the presence of auxiliary cavalry units. The first indication of military structures (fig. 4.3) came from Professor J.S. Wacher's excavations in 1961 (Leaholme site) with further observations being made in 1964 (Chester Street) and 1974–6 (Admiral's Walk, St Michael's Field; Wacher and McWhirr 1982).

The pattern of pre-Roman settlement which the Roman army encountered when it made contact with the territory of the Dobunni is not fully understood and has often been clouded by interpretations of excavations which can no longer be substantiated. The major settlement so far identified (fig. 4.4) is at Bagendon, 4.8km (3 miles) north of Cirencester (Clifford 1961), an *oppidum* which Wacher has suggested was 'the capital of the north-eastern half of the Dobunni, whose king Boduocus was one of the first to surrender to Plautius in AD 43' (Wacher 1975, 30). Bagendon was almost certainly Ptolemy's *Corinion*. Two other sizeable settlements existed at Ampney St Peter (Ranbury Ring hill-fort), 5.6km (3½ miles) east of Cirencester, an enclosure of 4.7ha (11½ acres), and at Coates (Trewsbury hill-fort), 4.18km (3 miles) west of Cirencester where a 4.9ha (12-acre) site is known (for details of both sites see *RCHM* 1976). Neither of these hill-forts has been excavated.

Prior to the conquest, the area on which the fort and later city of *Corinium* was built appears to have been purely agricultural. There is some evidence for pre-Roman occupation in the form of a circle of 17 stakes, 2.43m (8ft) in diameter (Wacher and McWhirr 1982, 28) but there are no signs of any large-scale earthworks or concentration of artefacts which might be associated with a major settlement of the Dobunni. Their main centre was indubitably at Bagendon some 5km (3 miles) to the north.

As the Roman army fanned out across the

4.2 Tombstone of *Dannicus*, a horseman of the *ala Indiana* (Corinium Museum).

4.1 Tombstone of *Sextus Valerius Genialis* a cavalry-man from Thrace, height 2.1m (Corinium Museum).

4.3 The fort ditch at Cirencester as revealed by excavations in 1961 (ranging pole in feet, Cirencester Excavation Committee).

country during the early years of occupation, military installations were established for a variety of reasons, and the presence of a large and important native settlement at Bagendon would clearly have attracted the attention of military officials. If as Wacher suggests this area was friendly to Rome, then a small mobile unit based at some distance from the native centre might, in the eyes of the military commanders, have been considered sufficient, since a larger reserve of troops was close at hand at Kingsholm and later at Gloucester (see Chapter 3).

Dr Graham Webster has suggested that Cirencester was part of the Fosse Way frontier zone, and that the road itself was the main military north-east – south-west communication link (Webster 1960 and 1980, 123). Such a frontier occupying a zone some 32–48km (20 or 30 miles) in depth would have been garrisoned by mobile units to maintain contacts with tribes in and beyond the zone. This part of the frontier was bounded by the lower Severn and its estuary and the main threat was from the unconquered tribes on the west bank. It could, therefore, be argued that a unit at Cirencester was there to protect a friendly tribe, possibly with a client relationship. If this may not have been felt necessary under Plautius, the sudden attack by Caratacus across the lower Severn 'into the territory of our allies' (Tacitus, *Annals*

4.4 Cirencester in relation to Bagendon (Cirencester Excavation Committee).

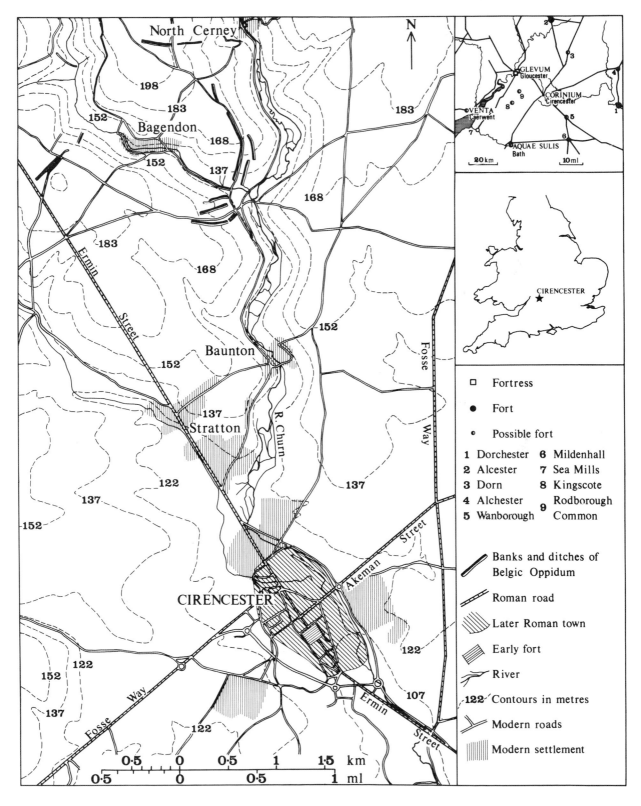

North Cerney

198

183

152

Bagendon

168

152

137

183

168

183

168

Ermin Street

152

Baunton

152

137

Stratton

R. Churn

122

137

137

152

152

122

122

137

122

CIRENCESTER

Akeman Street

Fosse Way

Fosse Way

Ermin Street

107

122

N

CORINIUM
Cirencester

GLEVUM
Gloucester

VENTA
Caerwent

AQUAE SULIS
Bath

20 km   10 ml

CIRENCESTER

□   Fortress

●   Fort

◉   Possible fort

1 Dorchester   **6** Mildenhall
2 Alcester   **7** Sea Mills
3 Dorn   **8** Kingscote
4 Alchester   **9** Rodborough
5 Wanborough   Common

Banks and ditches of
Belgic Oppidum

Roman road

Later Roman town

Early fort

River

122   Contours in metres

Modern roads

Modern settlement

0.5   0   0.5   1   1.5   km
0.5   0   0.5   1 ml

XII, 31) would have made a strong military presence necessary. It is possible that the two early ditches found beneath an intervallum road may belong to a campaign camp relating to this phase of the army's activities (see below).

The site chosen for the fort was carefully selected and avoided the low-lying area against the Churn, which, although a narrow and shallow river at this point, occasionally floods the low-lying land adjacent to its course. The land gradually rises to the west of the river and within 100m or so from the river the ground is well drained and free from flooding; it was here that the army engineers chose to build their fort.

The earliest military features so far identified consist of a pair of parallel ditches found immediately behind the later military rampart, but on the same alignment (fig. 4.5). No secure dating evidence can be associated with the cutting and use of these ditches, although pottery from the subsequent fill of one of them included pre-Claudian or early Claudian forms and fabrics, with some sherds of a late Iron Age tradition. A date in the 40s would not seem unreasonable for this initial phase of activity. The alignment of these two ditches, together with the date of the associated material, makes a military interpretation most likely. It is clear that these two ditches were stratigraphically earlier than the main sequence of military structures found in 1961, as they were sealed by an intervallum road of the later fort. The small size would appear to indicate the presence of a campaign camp or *hiberna* (winter quarters), associated with the earlier years of the invasion and the initial military contact with the area.

The 'campaign camp' was replaced by a fort housing, presumably, a cavalry unit. Ditches and the remains of a turf rampart belonging to this fort were found in 1961. The rampart was 6m (20ft) wide at its base, but over the years it had become compressed to a mere 20cm (8in), however, in that thickness six layers of turf were observed. Contemporary with the rampart were two ditches. The inner ditch lay 2.25m (7ft 4in) beyond the front face of the rampart and was 2.5m (8ft 2in) wide with a total depth of 1.2m (3ft 11in) including the cleaning channel which was placed centrally in the bottom of the ditch. The rampart and inner ditch were located in several trenches over a distance of some 22m (72ft). An outer ditch was deduced from the behaviour of two stone walls of the later civil period which had dramatically subsided into its fill. The area between the inner and outer

ditches seems to have been full of obstacles on the evidence of a number of post-holes and beam slots, beyond which were a number of randomly-placed stake holes. The latter were probably the result of inserting branches as a further obstacle to those intent on penetrating the defences of the fort.

Further sections of military ditches were found 60m to the east of those mentioned above. They were on the same side of the fort, but to the east of the north-west gate and beneath the later basilica, which had encountered difficulties with its foundations because of the loosely compacted fill of the ditches. A further pair of ditches was found in 1964 in Chester Street, but again there were difficulties in completely excavating the site in order to obtain the full profile of both ditches. However, sufficient was recovered to postulate the eastern alignment of the fort.

The excavations at Leaholme and Chester Street indicated two sides of the fort, and an observation to the west of the Leaholme site may indicate a corner, giving an overall dimension of the north-west side of the fort as 165m (540ft). Ermin Street passes through the mid-point of this side, which supports the reconstruction put forward. By considering the evidence of streets and ditches, a possible layout of a fort has been deduced, but it must be emphasized that this is only a working model. It fits the known archaeological facts, and until fresh evidence is produced from the ground must suffice for the present. This reconstructed plan gives a fort, perhaps the second on the site, with an internal area of 1.8ha ($4\frac{1}{2}$ acres) facing east and possibly occupied by a *quingenary ala* (500 men), although to some, despite the evidence of the tombstones and equipment, this might seem rather too small to accommodate such a unit and they would prefer to equate the fort with a *cohors peditata* (i.e. infantry).

No complete plans of buildings from within the fort have emerged from any excavations, but groups of posts and several slots have been noted. At Leaholme, Professor Wacher was able to demonstrate at least three phases of structure and two different methods of construction. In the two earliest phases posts were set in individual pits, but later palisade trenches for timbers were the norm. The change from individual post-pits to foundation trenches was also noted on Admiral's Walk where again three possible phases were noted. Precise dating of the phases of internal occupation is not possible, but the large quantity of pottery

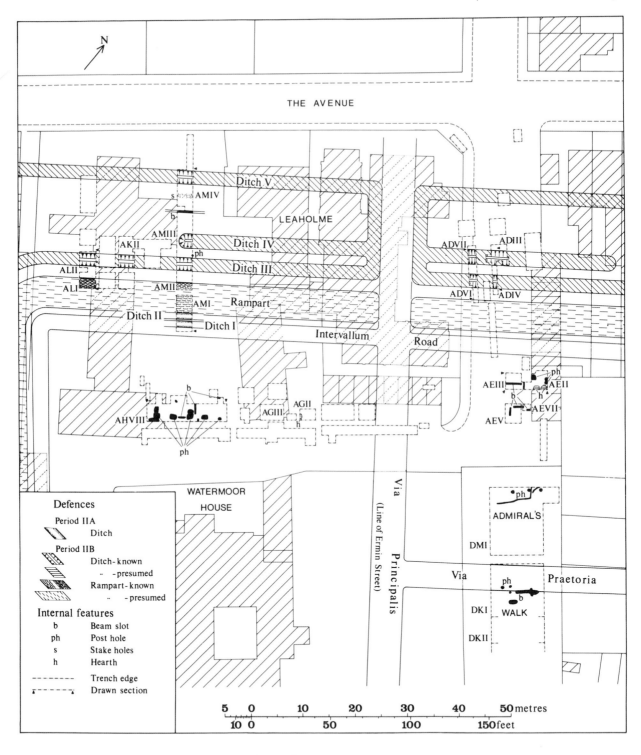

4.5 Excavated features of the Cirencester fort and a possible reconstruction (Cirencester Excavation Committee).

found in the inner ditch and also from the levels that sealed military deposits suggests that the fort was not finally abandoned until the mid 70s.

Associated with the fort was a *vicus*, a cemetery, and possibly one or two annexes. The latter are hinted at by the discovery of two stretches of rampart of military character, one beneath the later city defences close by Trinity Road and the other beside Watermoor Road near the site of the later Silchester Gate. Insufficient is known to be able to reconstruct the outline of these annexes or to date them securely, but the military interpretation of the Watermoor Road rampart is supported by the change in direction of Ermin Street at this point. In addition, the fact that the military cemetery is just to the south of where the rampart meets Ermin Street, seems to indicate that the land between this point and the fort to the north was being fully utilized by the army, and could not therefore be used to bury their dead. The evidence for a military origin of the cemetery comes from the discovery of two cavalry tombstones found in 1835 (*RIB* 108) and 1836 (*RIB* 109) respectively. The first records the burial of Dannicus of the *Ala Indiana* who came from *Germania Superior*, but there are conflicting views as to when the regiment came to Britain. One opinion would allow for the tombstone to be erected at any time between AD 43 and AD 59, whilst the other argues for a date after AD 70 (Hassall 1982). Neither of these views would be inconsistent with the evidence from excavations. The second tombstone was erected to Sextus Valerius Genialis of the *Ala Thracum* which probably accompanied *Legio* XX from Neuss in Lower Germany to Britain in AD 43. If this was the case then, as Genialis had served for 20 years when he died, the stone could have been set up anytime between AD 43 and AD 63. The epigraphic evidence points to two different units being based in Cirencester, but in what order they were there is unclear.

The annexes and cemetery were to the west and south of the fort, but a *vicus* grew up to the north and north-west where Ermin Street and Fosse Way crossed. Glimpses of the nature of the *vicus* have come from a limited number of trenches which have been dug to the necessary levels. For example, in the area which was to become the site for the forum and basilica, there existed foundations for a timber building and a well-metalled street on a parallel alignment to the fort's north-western defences. Another street in the *vicus* was revealed during the excavations in Lewis Lane.

This street, which was later to become one of the city's main streets linking the Verulamium and Bath Gates, may be considered as the original line of the Fosse Way, and the dating evidence indicates that it was contemporary with the fort and again parallel to the north-western defences. Traces of buildings in the *vicus* have come from a number of sites, but too little to offer any evidence of the layout of the *vicus* or the nature of the buildings within it. However, it is possible that we can identify one of those who lived and worked in the *vicus*, for a civilian tombstone found in 1836 in the same area as those described above commemorates 'Philus, son of Cassavus, a Sequanian, age 45' (*RIB* 110). The find spot and the character of the stone itself point to a first-century date probably contemporary with military occupation, and it is quite likely that Philus from Gaul was trading between Britain and the Continent.

Although the fort was not finally vacated until the mid 70s, there is no clear evidence of the subsequent history of the *vicus*. Prior to that date a community existed outside the fort and it would not be surprising if most of the people living in the *vicus* remained and only some of the camp followers and traders followed in the tracks of the army as it moved further north and west. When it was decided to build a city to administer the *civitas*, it was natural to choose a site which was already in the hands of the Roman authorities and, although the fort was small, it is clear from the positions of the cemetery and the annexes that a much larger area had been under army control. It is possible that some 40ha (100 acres) was occupied by the army and the civil settlement was very much smaller.

During the last two decades of the first century the street grid was laid out and the first public buildings erected (fig. 4.6). The transition from *vicus* to city involved clearing away some existing buildings and streets, as we have seen in the area of the forum, but the alignment of the new street grid was based on the existing network of Ermin Street and the Fosse Way. The main central buildings (fig. 4.7), the forum and basilica, were the first of the public buildings to be erected, an enormous enterprise that could hardly have taken place without the co-operation and involvement of the local community, who would have provided the bulk of the labour. The raw materials required included stone, lime, sand, timber, iron, roofing materials, etc., all of which had to be acquired and prepared for building work. Sources of good-

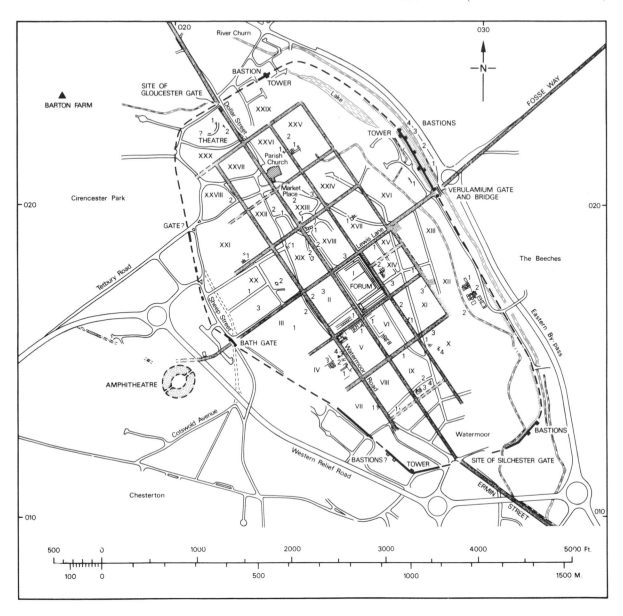

4.6 Composite town plan of *Corinium* from the late first to the fifth century AD (Cirencester Excavation Committee).

quality stone were obviously known earlier to the army as they had used the local oolitic limestone for their funerary monuments. Likewise the army would have sought out supplies of other raw materials, so that when the time came to commence a major building scheme in stone these sources would have been known and already exploited. The quarries which supplied the stone

for the basilica and forum were probably those identified at the Querns just to the west of the city (McWhirr, Viner and Wells 1982). The logistics of securing these supplies was a huge task, but one which would have come as second nature to army engineers. Although we have no direct evidence from Cirencester, it is a possibility that army engineers were seconded to supervise the layout, drainage and basic planning of great civic buildings in the new city. At about the same time the *colonia* at Gloucester was being laid out, and so the demands on supplies and skilled personnel in the

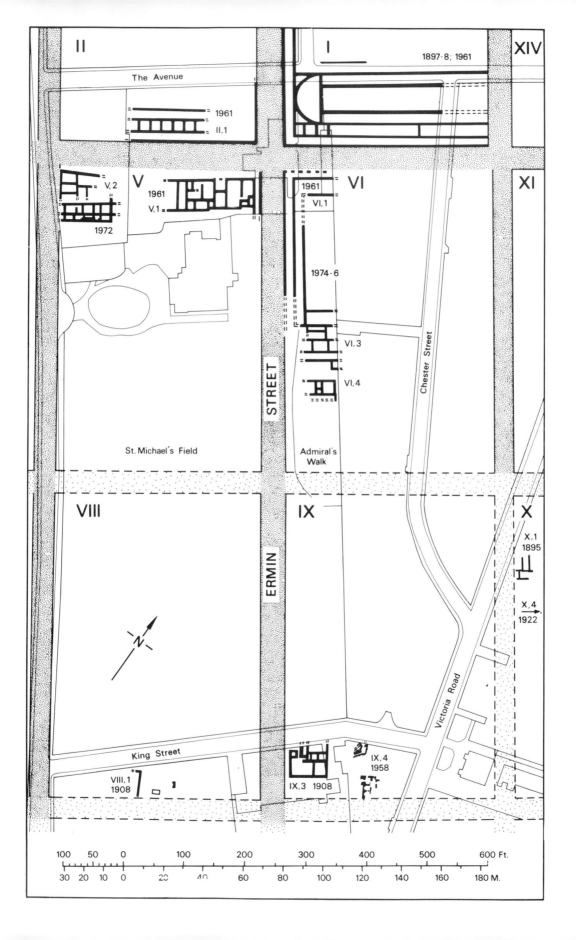

region would have been considerable and have needed careful planning.

The forum and basilica occupied the central *insula* of the city, with the entrance to the forum piazza fronting the main street linking the Verulamium and Bath Gates, the Fosse Way. In plan this civic centre was similar to the other British *civitas* capitals, and from the little that is known of the internal arrangements, does not appear to have been affected by outside influences, as was the case at Verulamium. The cathedral-like basilica was 100m long and must have dominated the townscape. The quality of the masonry was first-rate and the internal appearance with its huge pillars, marble cladding and imposing tribunal was a magnificent symbol of Roman government, which undoubtedly had its impact on the native population and barbarian visitors. It is difficult to understand how the basilica came to be built over the filled-in ditch of the auxiliary fort, but it clearly had an effect on the stability of the building which had to undergo major repairs in the middle of the second century in order to arrest subsidence. It is possible that all traces of the fort vanished when the army levelled the site before departing, so when the city was planned and laid out the location of these earlier ditches may have been forgotten. It may have been assumed that the army would have backfilled and thoroughly consolidated as was its custom. A similar problem arose in London where the great basilica walls sank into back-filled brick-earth quarries in the course of building, which could have been avoided by a little trial trenching.

As stated above, the enormous quantities of stone required for the civic centre probably came from the area known today as the Querns, and when those quarries nearest to the town became exhausted, it is not surprising to find that the city's amphitheatre was built in that derelict landscape. The clay and waste stone was used for the seating banks of the amphitheatre, and the whole structure was finished off with stone walls around the arena and probably outside the bank. The view as one looked along the main street towards the amphitheatre must have been one of the most dramatic in any Romano–British town (figs. 4.8a, 4.8b).

There is little doubt that Cirencester possessed a

4.7 Detailed plan of the central area of *Corinium* as revealed by excavations from 1958–1976 along with earlier observations (Cirencester Excavation Committee).

theatre and evidence for such a building was encountered in *insula XXX* (McWhirr 1981, 37). No temples and shrines have been found during excavations, but the considerable quantity of fine sculpture, architectural fragments and inscriptions indicate that several existed. Of some importance is the inscription found in 1891, thought to have been part of a Jupiter Column (*RIB* 103). This inscription records that the Column was restored by the 'governor of *Britannia Prima*', and this is usually taken to indicate that *Corinium* was the seat of the governor of the province of *Britannia Prima* which was established in the fourth century. Professor Wacher has suggested that fourth-century alterations which he detected in the forum may have resulted from the elevation in the status of the city to that of the capital of one of the provinces of Britain.

The town remained undefended until the end of the second century, when it was surrounded by an earth bank into which had been built stone towers and at least one, and probably two, stone gates (the Verulamium and Bath Gates). During the first half of the third century the earth bank was cut back and a stone wall inserted. Various thicknesses of wall have been noted at Cirencester, and a possible chronological sequence established. It would seem that the first wall to be erected was only 1.2m (3ft 11in) wide, but soon it was found necessary to replace sections with a wider wall, about 3m (10ft) wide, similar in width to those found in other towns and cities in Britain. This sequence of modifications to the town's defences is more like the pattern established at the *colonia* of Gloucester and Lincoln, for example, than in the *civitas* capitals. The final modification to the defences so far noted occurred in the middle of the fourth century, when external bastions or towers were added to the front of the wall.

Discoveries over the past 200 years or so have provided a great deal of information about private housing in *Corinium* (McWhirr 1986), but in very few cases has it been possible to recover complete plans of buildings or to examine areas where more modest housing might be found. The picture that emerges on present archaeological evidence is of a city with well-built and lavishly decorated houses, with no separate accommodation for the less affluent members of society. Is this a reflection of the sample so far examined, or is it a true picture of those who owned houses in Cirencester? Did all those who carried out menial tasks in the city live in the houses of the rich? Only with large-scale

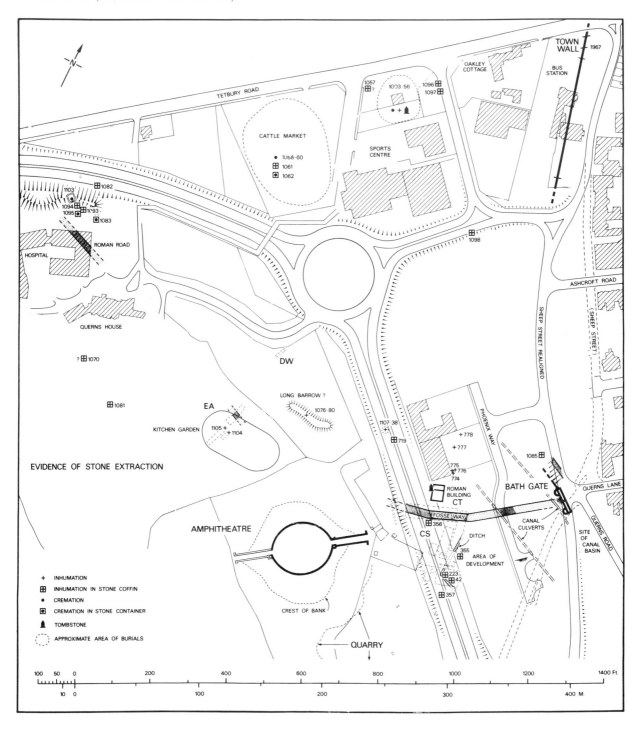

4.8 Extramural features outside the Bath Gate, *Corinium*, including amphitheatre, cemetery and Fosse Way (Cirencester Excavation Committee).

4.8b The Fosse Way as it leaves the Bath Gate, *Corinium* (Cirencester Excavation Committee).

open-area excavations will the answers to such questions be discovered.

In addition to these well-appointed houses, shops have been identified, particularly alongside Ermin Street and in the centre of the town opposite the *macellum*. Some were clearly dealing in the commodities of everyday life, but there is also some evidence for the presence of specialized craftsmen making and selling their wares.

One of the most debated discoveries of the last decade or so is the group of buildings (fig. 4.9) found in the east of the town close to the defences (McWhirr 1986). This area of the town, *insula XIII*, appears not to have been occupied by houses or any other buildings until the second half of the fourth century when this group was erected. Two of them have a distinctly rural appearance and although the evidence might be classed by some as circumstantial, building XII,2 (fig. 4.10) with its 'winged corridor villa' plan must surely be a farm. From unstratified levels above the building came part of an iron coulter and four bone weaving tablets,

whilst in the outbuilding there is evidence of metal-working, just the sort of finds one would expect on a farm. The aisled building (XIII,3), if that is what it was, again looks more at home within the agricultural community than in a provincial capital (McWhirr 1986, 71). There must have been a close association between the city and the tribal territory, especially in the area immediately around it. Such an example of *rus in urbe* may not be so surprising.

The presence of such an important and sizeable city in the Cotswolds had its effect on trade, and local crafts and industries. The demand for stone, lime, sand and gravel has already been referred to, but the buildings of *Corinium* also needed to be roofed and this was done to begin with by using ceramic tiles (*tegulae* and *imbrices*). Later, it seems to have been more economical to use sandstone from the Forest of Dean or elsewhere. Brick and tile were not used extensively in the Cotswolds and yet this is one area in the country where tilemaking seems to have been highly organized, and where the makers were in the habit of stamping their products with their names. There is virtually no evidence of pottery-making in the vicinity of

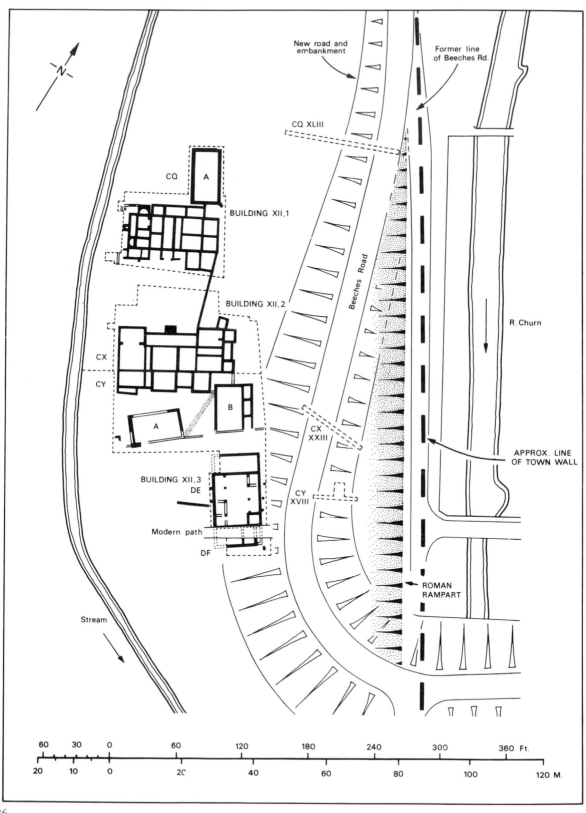

N

New road and
embankment

Former line
of Beeches Rd.

CQ XLIII

CQ

A

BUILDING XII,1

BUILDING XII,2

CX

CY

Beeches Road

R. Churn

B

A

CX
XXIII

APPROX. LINE
OF TOWN WALL

BUILDING XII,3
DE

CY
XVIII

Modern path

DF

ROMAN
RAMPART

Stream

| 60 | 30 | 0 | | 60 | 120 | | 180 | | 240 | | 300 | | 360 Ft. |

| 20 | 10 | 0 | | 20 | | 40 | | 60 | | 80 | | 100 | | 120 M. |

4.10 Details of one of the hypocausts in the group of buildings found in *insula* XII close to the eastern defences (Compare with fig. 6, Cirencester Excavation Committee).

Cirencester, and the bulk of the pottery found appears to have come from centres of production slightly further afield, for example, North Wiltshire and Oxfordshire to name but two.

Estimates of the population of Cirencester have ranged from 5000 to 20,000, but any figures put forward must be no more than guesswork. It may be possible to note that the seating capacity of the town's amphitheatre was around 6–7000, but whether this gives any indication of the city's population is debatable. It is impossible to date individual graves in the cemetery, or to be certain what fraction of the graveyard had been examined, and so the number of burials found cannot be used

4.9 A group of fourth-century buildings close to the eastern defences, *Corinium*, probably connected with agriculture.

to estimate the population (fig 4.12). With considerably less than 10 per cent of the city having been archaeologically investigated, there is no way of deducing a population figure from the density of building within the city.

In conclusion, it is instructive to look at the subsequent development of the town in comparison with others discussed in this volume. If it is accepted that the statement in the *Anglo Saxon Chronicle* indicates that Cuthwine and Caewlin captured three 'cities' – Gloucester, Cirencester and Bath – then it must be assumed that in 577 there was still a sufficiently large population living around the town for the settlement to be considered in this way. Unlike Lincoln, Gloucester or Exeter, Cirencester did not develop into a cathedral city. (A large Saxon church was erected in Cirencester probably in the eighth century, and during the medieval period one of the wealthiest Augustinian abbeys in the country stood in the heart of the town, only to be swept away during the sixteenth-century upheavals of the Reformation.) In the 500 years between the arrival of the Roman

4.11 The 'hare' mosaic found in building XII, 1 (Cirencester Excavation Committee).

4.12 A group of skeletons from the late Roman cemetery in the suburbs between the Bath Gate and the amphitheatre (Cirencester Excavation Committee).

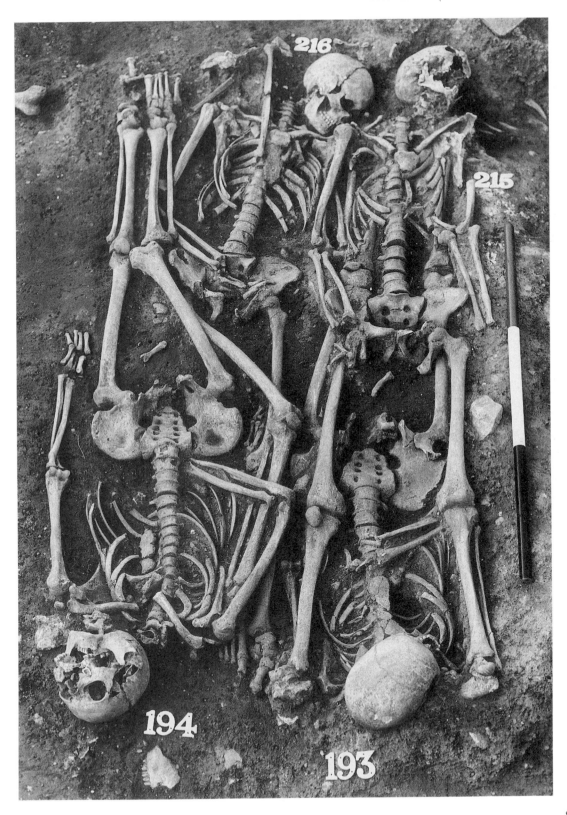

army and the fall of Cirencester at the Battle of Dyrham, it is clear that the settlement had grown from a relatively small and insignificant military installation to the second largest city in Britain, from a small cog in the mighty military machine to the capital of one of the British provinces, *Britannia Prima*.

Bibliography

Bidwell, P. 1979	*The Legionary Bath-House and Basilica and Forum at Exeter*, Exeter
Clifford, E. 1961	*Bagendon: A Belgic Oppidum*, Cambridge
Hassall, M. 1982	'Inscriptions' in Wacher and McWhirr (eds) 1982
Heighway, C. 1983	*The East and North Gates of Gloucester*, Bristol
McWhirr, A. 1981	*Roman Gloucestershire*, Gloucester
McWhirr, A., Viner, L., and Wells, C. 1982	*Romano–British Cemeteries at Cirencester*, Cirencester
McWhirr, A. 1986	*Houses in Roman Cirencester*, Cirencester
RCHM	*Iron Age and Romano–British Monuments in the Gloucestershire Cotswolds*, Royal Commission on Historical Monuments, HMSO 1976
RIB	*The Roman Inscriptions of Britain*, Collingwood, R.G. and Wright, R.P., Oxford 1965
Wacher, J. 1975	*The Towns of Roman Britain*, London
Wacher, J. and McWhirr, A. (eds) 1982	*Early Roman Occupation at Cirencester*, Cirencester
Webster, G. 1960	'The Roman Military Advance under Ostorius Scapula', *Archaeological Journal* 115, 49–98
Webster, G. 1980	*The Roman Invasion of Britain*, London
Webster, G. 1982	'Gazetteer of Military Objects from Cirencester', in Wacher and McWhirr (eds) 1982

5 EXETER
(Isca Dumnoniorum)

The Roman conquest of Dumnonia and the foundation of Exeter

The Second Augustan Legion (*Legio* II *Aug*), the builders of the fortress at Exeter, came to Britain with the Roman army of invasion in AD 43, having previously been stationed at Strasbourg in the upper Rhineland. Suetonius tells us that the commander of the legion, Flavius Vespasianus (later the emperor Vespasian), conquered two warlike tribes (*Divus Vespasianus*, IV, 1); his tour of duty in Britain lasted three or four years (Eicholz 1972). Excavations at Maiden Castle and Hod Hill in Dorset have yielded dramatic evidence for the capture of these hillforts by the Roman army in the 40s, leaving little doubt that the Durotriges were one of the tribes subjugated in Vespasian's campaigns. The identity of the second tribe is less certain but the most likely candidate is the southern Dobunni (Webster 1981, 15 n. 3). It is unlikely to have been the Dumnonii, the tribe who lived in the south-western peninsula to the west of the rivers Parrett and Axe (Thomas 1966, 83), as there is no sign of a Roman military presence in Dumnonia during the early years of the conquest (Bidwell 1980, 10; Maxfield 1987). A Claudian date has been claimed for Hembury in east Devon (Todd 1984, 264). Whilst this is not impossible, the few pieces of samian from the site date from AD 50–70 and so provide no proof of a Claudian foundation. Thus the theory that the zone garrisoned by the Roman army in the aftermath of Vespasian's campaigns extended as far as the Exe estuary is not so far supported by archaeological evidence.

Although a number of Roman forts dating from the 40s are known in Durotrigian territory, no full-size legionary base has been identified. In the 40s and early 50s, prior to the foundation of the fortress at Exeter, the winter quarters of *Legio* II *Aug* may have been divided between two or more 'vexillation fortresses'. At Lake Farm, near Wimborne in Dorset, the 11.7ha (29-acre) base held by the army until AD 60–65 (Ian Horsey, pers. comm.) would have been capable of accommodating at least half the legion, perhaps brigaded with auxiliaries; a second half-fortress may await discovery in or near Dorchester.

The literary sources give no information concerning events in the south-west, so an understanding of the timing and progress of Roman campaigning in the peninsula and of the subsequent military occupation must depend on the relatively imprecise evidence provided by archaeology. The closely-spaced network of forts gradually being revealed by air survey in Devon (Griffith 1984) probably implies Dumnonian resistance to the Roman advance, although this need not necessarily have been the case (Maxfield 1987). The military occupation of Dumnonia apparently lasted for up to 30 years (see below p. 109).

There is at present no indication of Roman military activity in the Exeter area before the foundation of the legionary fortress. The precise foundation date of the fortress cannot be established in the absence of literary or epigraphic evidence. Attempts to push the occupation of the site back to *c.* AD 50 seem unwarranted. The argument advanced by Todd (1982, 54–5) for 'a start to the occupation about (or possibly shortly before) AD 50', based on the earliest date of manufacture of decorated samian ware types from Exeter, takes no account of the full date range of these types. The earliest levels have produced few closely datable finds, but the notable paucity of Claudian samian from Exeter argues against foundation before the mid-50s (Bidwell 1979, 13–16). Further evidence that the occupation commenced no earlier than AD 55–60 is provided by the Terra Nigra pottery, the earliest of which dates from *c.* AD 60. Foundation in the late 50s seems likely, although a case has been made recently for the establishment of the fortress as part of a general reorganization of military dispositions following the Boudican revolt of 61 (Holbrook and Fox forthcoming).

Setting, approaches and environs of the fortress

The fortress of *Legio* II *Aug* at Exeter lies on the east bank of the Exe overlooking the lowest early crossing point on the river, about 5km (3 miles) above the Exe estuary. Earlier speculations that Exeter was founded on the site of an Iron Age hill-fort have not been borne out by extensive modern excavations. Only two or three sherds of pre-Roman pottery have been recovered from the town (Henderson 1984, 1). However, no excavation has taken place on Rougemont Hill, the site of the Norman castle immediately to the north of the fortress, and the possibility remains that this prominent volcanic knoll was occupied in the pre-Roman period. Within a 15km (9.4 miles) radius of the fortress at least eight Iron Age hill-forts overlook the floodplains of the Exe and its tributaries the Creedy, Culm and Clyst; the nearest of these, Stoke Hill Camp, lies 3km (1.9 miles) to the north of the fortress. It is not known which, if any, of the nearby hill-forts were inhabited at the time of the Roman advance into Dumnonia. Aerial reconnaissance by Professor J.K. St Joseph and more recently by Frances Griffith has led to the identification of many smaller settlement enclosures (principally as yet undated) on the fertile lower ground fringing the river valleys in a zone 10km (6¼ miles) to the north and south of the fortress. The few sites so far to yield pottery have dated to the second century AD and later.

Ships of the Roman fleet would have been able to navigate the estuary at least as far as Topsham, about 5.5km (3.4 miles) below the fortress. Above Topsham the river becomes very shallow in places; before weirs blocked the channel in the thirteenth century, the river was probably navigable for small craft as far up as Exeter in certain conditions, but the difficulty of the passage and the frequency of delays in times of drought or spate would have made river transport very unreliable (Jackson 1972, 61; Blaylock and Henderson 1987, 3–4). There must therefore have been an early Roman port on the estuary to handle supplies destined for the fortress at Exeter and the forts in its hinterland. This was almost certainly located at Topsham, where a little-known Roman site, which extends over an area of at least 25ha (62 acres) has

produced finds and buildings of pre-Flavian date (Jarvis and Maxfield 1975, 210).

The principal routeways of the south-western peninsula converge on the lower Exe Valley, making it the natural route-centre of the region. Immediately above and below Exeter cliffs hamper descent to the floodplain, and further downstream the river channel is flanked by expanses of marsh. The fortress lies astride a sloping spur which is thought to have carried a prehistoric ridgeway down to a ford across the river. The Roman army probably built a timber bridge at the crossing, but no trace of this has yet come to light.

The road from Topsham to Exeter heads straight towards the south-east gate of the fortress on almost the same alignment as the *via principalis* within (fig. 5.1). Excavations outside the gate have shown this road to date from the early Roman period (Bidwell 1979, 9–11). Other suburban roads are assumed to be Roman in origin, although only for the upper part of High Street, outside the north-east gate of the fortress, has this been demonstrated by excavation. Towards the river, Stepcote Hill may approximately represent the line of the road leading down from the south-west gate to the edge of the floodplain 25m (82ft) below.

Only the north-east gate, located at the upper end of the spur, 12m (39ft) higher than the south-west gate, is approached across comparatively level ground. On the south-east, towards Topsham, the fortress is flanked by a minor combe, whilst to the north-west lies the deep cleft of the Longbrook Valley. Excavation has demonstrated that no Roman road crossed the valley immediately below the north-west gate (Blaylock and Henderson 1987, 59); it is possible however that Lower North Street, which crosses about 60m (66yds) further to the north-east where the gradient is slightly less severe, dates from the early Roman period. A road on this line would have run up the valley side to join a broad, well-metalled road that has been traced for 175m (191yds) running along the outer edge of the fortress ditch between the head of Lower North Street and the northern corner of the defences (Frere 1985, 303–4).

Relatively few areas outside the fortress have been investigated to date. The shops and houses of the dependent civil settlement (*canabae*) have yet to be located, but several zones of contemporary extramural activity are known. Buildings have been found on both sides of the Topsham road about 230m (251yds) from the south-east gate

EXETER: Roman Legionary Fortress

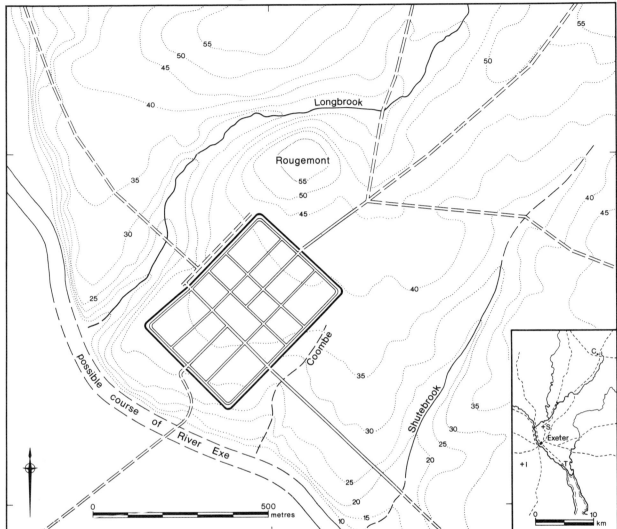

5.1 The setting of the legionary fortress. *Inset*: possible Roman routes and military sites near Exeter: Cullompton fort (C), Ide signal station (I), Stoke Hill signal station (S).

(Bidwell 1979, 9–11). To the north-east of the road a few cremations excavated by Stewart Brown in 1974 were succeeded by a compound containing a group of buildings set around a courtyard. Buildings in a second compound on the other side of the Topsham road produced evidence for metalworking. On a site excavated by Mary Dale in 1974 at Southernhay Gardens, 330m (360yds) to the north-east of this area, two isolated buildings and a well were found (*ibid.*, 11).

Other evidence of military activity occurs over a wide area around the fortress. Deep drainage ditches have been located on several sites near the defences, including two ditches apparently demarcating an annexe or enclosure in the area to the north-west of the south-west gate. Outside the north-east gate various industrial activities are attested: stone was quarried from Rougemont Hill; the clay daub used in the walls of the timber buildings in the fortress was probably dug in this area; and pottery, roofing- and hypocaust-tiles were made here. Elsewhere, a potter making mortaria and flagons operated on a site at Bartholomew Street West excavated by John Thorp in 1974

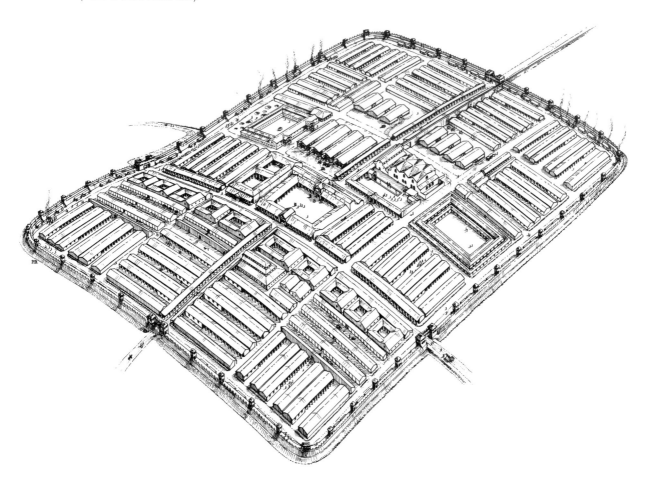

5.2 Artist's impression of the legionary fortress, viewed from the south.

near the western corner of the fortress (*ibid.*, 12).

Apart from the few early cremations discovered next to the Topsham road (above), no burials belonging to the fortress period have yet been found, and no tombstones or funerary inscriptions are known. The cemeteries which would have flanked the other extra-mural roads remain to be identified in excavation.

Discovery, orientation and size

Graham Webster argued for the existence of an early Roman fort at Exeter in a paper read to the conference on Roman towns held at Leicester in 1963 (Webster 1966, 41). The first evidence to be recognized as clearly indicating a Roman military presence at Exeter came to light the following year when Aileen Fox found a mid first-century ditch running south-east to north-west beneath the south-east gate of the later Roman town (Fox 1968, 3–6). This feature was interpreted as the defensive ditch of a Roman fort lying in the area to the north-east of the gate. The ditch is now thought more likely to have bounded a compound or enclosure outside the fortress on the south-west side of the Topsham road.

The fortress proper was first recognized in 1971 when John Collis discovered mid first-century barracks at Goldsmith Street (Bidwell 1980, 35–6) and an excavation by Michael Griffiths, Tony Johnson and Paul Bidwell at the west end of the Cathedral Close uncovered the fortress bath-house beneath the basilica of the later Roman town (*idem* 1979). Since 1971, the Exeter Museums Archaeological Field Unit has undertaken rescue excavations on development sites throughout the city. These have established the full outline of the fortress and permitted a considerable number of internal buildings to be identified.

The defences were first located in 1975 on a site in Rack Street where the ditch at the southern corner of the fortress was found (*idem* 1980, 23). By 1979 three sides of the circuit had been traced with varying degrees of precision, allowing Paul Bidwell to propose a tentative reconstruction of the overall plan of the fortress in his report on the Cathedral Close excavations (*idem* 1979, 8–9). He concluded that the fortress faced north-east, away from the Exe, and this became the accepted view for a number of years. Observations made at Paul Street and Queen Street in 1982 (Frere 1985, 303–4), followed by the discovery of the northern corner of the defences at Gandy Street in 1986 (Blaylock and Henderson 1987, 51) and sectioning of the north-east defences at Catherine Street in 1987, have shown the fortress to be longer than was originally thought, and it is now clear that it faced south-west – towards the Exe rather than away from it. In outline the fortress is a somewhat irregular rectangle about 349m (380yds) wide and 476m (520yds) long, measured from the inner lip of the enclosing defensive ditch. At about 16.6ha or 41 acres, Exeter is smaller than the other full legionary bases in Britain. This is probably accounted for by the necessity to fit the fortress into a restricted spur site. It is roughly the same length as several other broadly contemporary bases but narrower than any of them. As a consequence of its unusually small size, the various types of buildings identified within the Exeter fortress are in general smaller than their counterparts known from legionary bases elsewhere (fig. 5.3).

Garrison and name

Until recently the fortress at Exeter was thought incapable of accommodating a full legion. However, the discovery of its full size and the elucidation of the layout of the barracks (see below) have now placed the matter beyond doubt. The fortress was apparently designed to accommodate a garrison comprising 12 units of quingenary strength. Since in the pre-Flavian period the normal complement of a legion was 10 quingenary cohorts, it follows that two of the units provided for in the fortress layout are likely to have been auxiliaries rather than legionaries. There are indications

that the two auxiliary units were in fact cavalry *alae*.

There is no reason to doubt that the fortress was built and garrisoned by *Legio* II *Aug*. A firm link may be demonstrated between Exeter and the fortress at Caerleon, founded *c.* AD 75, where the presence of *Legio* II is attested by epigraphic evidence (Boon 1972, 20). The link is provided by decorative tile antefixes from the Exeter bath-house which prove to have been made in the same mould as examples of similar pattern from Caerleon. The mould must have travelled to Caerleon as part of the stock-in-trade of a legionary artisan (Bidwell and Boon 1976).

The name of the fortress at Exeter was *Ĭscā*, like that of Caerleon. In each case the name is a latinized version of the Celtic name for the river upon which the fortress was situated, respectively the Exe and the Usk – variants of the British *Isca*, meaning 'water' in the sense of 'river' (Rivet and Smith 1979, 376–8). The name is first recorded in Ptolemy's *Geography*, compiled around AD 140–50, in which *Legio* II *Aug* is placed at *Isca*-Exeter, despite the legion's having left Exeter about three-quarters of a century earlier. There is, however, evidence to suggest that Ptolemy's source map for southern Britain and South Wales was produced in the pre-Flavian period before the foundation of *Isca*-Caerleon (Rivet 1974, 61); hence even had Ptolemy possessed a fully up-to-date list of legionary dispositions, he would probably have placed *Legio* II *Aug* at *Isca*-Exeter, the only place of that name on his source list.

Internal layout and street system

The fortress was the usual 'playing card' shape with rounded corners and a gate in each side of the defences (fig. 5.3). Its planning is now understood in some detail. Precise mapping of excavated buildings and other features has demonstrated that the defences, street system and buildings were all designed and laid out in multiples of the standard Roman foot (*pes monetalis*, here assumed to be 0.2959m (0.9708ft)). The layout nevertheless exhibits many minor irregularities. These probably resulted from the careless use of the *groma* (the instrument employed to establish survey lines at right angles) and from the surveyors' practice of measuring along the ground, which on a sloping site causes a significant contraction in true plan dimensions over longer distances.

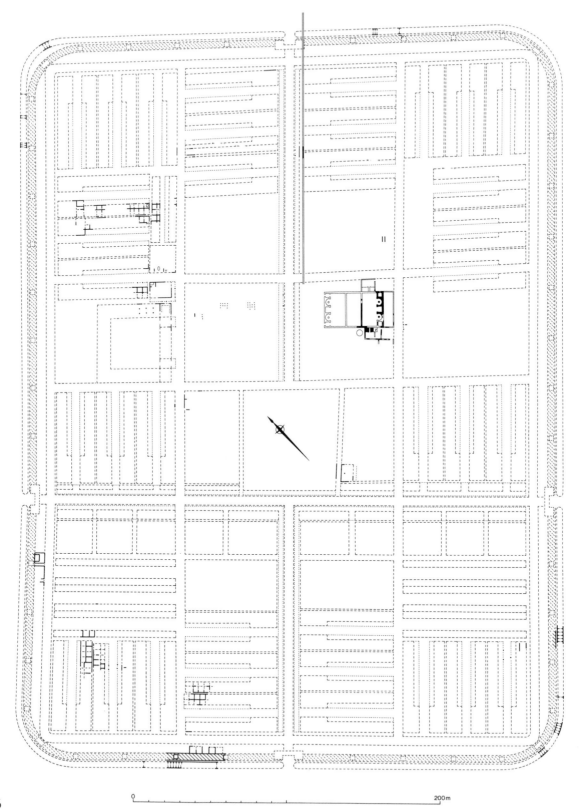

0   200m

5.3 Plan of the legionary fortress, showing excavated features and restored outlines of the defences, streets and buildings.

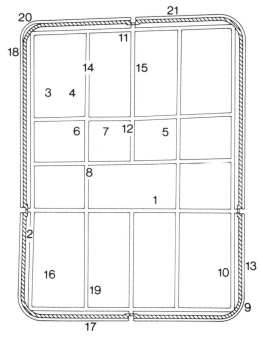

5.1 Key to excavation sites, Exeter legionary fortress: (1) South Street 1945–6; (2) Bartholomew Street East 1959; (3) Goldsmith Street 1971; (4) Goldsmith Street 1971–2; (5) Cathedral Close 1971–6; (6) Trichay Street/Pancras Lane 1972–4; (7) High Street 1972–5; (8) North Street 1974; (9) Rack Street 1974–8; (10) Preston Street 1976–7; (11) High Street 1974; (12) National Westminster Bank 1977; (13) Mermaid Yard 1977–8; (14) Queen Street 1978; (15) High Street 1980; (16) Bartholomew Street East/ Mary Arches Street 1980–1; (17) Friernhay Street 1981; (18) Paul Street 1982–5; (19) St Nicholas Priory 1983–4; (20) Upper Paul Street 1986; (21) St Catherine's Almshouses 1987–8.

The overall dimensions of the street system were apparently intended to be 1100 × 1540 *pedes* (325.5 × 455.7m) measured from the outer edge of the perimeter street on each side. This area was divided into front, middle and rear divisions. The front division was bisected by the front axial street (*via praetoria*) which ran uphill from the front (south-west) gate to form a T-junction with the main transverse street (*via principalis*) running between the two side gates. The middle division lay between the *via principalis* and a second transverse street, the *via quintana*. The rear division was bisected by the rear axial street (*via decumana*), linking the rear gate and the *via quintana*.

The three main streets were 20 *pedes* wide, flanked by drainage gullies for which 2 *pedes* was

allowed to either side of the carriageway. These dimensions may be deduced from an analysis of the fortress plan and in the case of the *via decumana* have been confirmed by excavation. The latter street was lined by porticos with timber posts spaced at intervals of 12 *pedes* along the frontage (High Street site 1980; National Westminster Bank site 1977: Bidwell 1979, fig, 14 and 35). It is likely that similar porticos, aligned on the gateways at the end of the streets, also flanked the *viae praetoria* and *principalis*, defining thoroughfares 24 *pedes* wide. The portico on the south-east side of the *via decumana* was 10 *pedes* wide and fronted a row of store-rooms (*tabernae*) built against the fortress aqueduct. *Tabernae* probably also lined much of the *via principalis*; they are however unlikely to have been present on the *via praetoria* or along other sections of the *via decumana*.

The second-rank streets in the fortress comprised the perimeter streets and the *via quintana*, already mentioned; a transverse street in the rear division; and a pair of lateral streets running the full length of the fortress equidistant from the long axis. Although all nominally 20 *pedes* wide, they were in most cases narrower than this, owing to minor encroachments by buildings and the intrusion of eavesdrips and drainage gullies at their margins. All the streets described so far were metalled, the makeup of river gravel and quarry stone being up to 0.4m (1ft 4in) thick at the crown. The third-rank streets ranged in nominal width from 8 to 20 *pedes* and were relatively thinly metalled or, exceptionally, unmetalled.

The principal non-residential buildings

With the exception of the bath-house, described in the next section, the buildings in the fortress were all constructed in timber, wattle and daub, and were in most cases probably roofed with wooden shingles. At the centre of the fortress stood the headquarters-building (*principia*), which fronted on the *via principalis* at the head of the *via praetoria* (fig. 5.3). The largest building in the fortress, the *principia* would have presented an imposing sight to a visitor ascending the *via praetoria*. The south-east side of the *principia*, bounded by a minor street, was located by Aileen Fox in 1945–6 (Fox 1952, 31–7). The carved body of a bird discovered in 1972 in a late first-century pit next to Waterbeer Street, probably came from the *principia*. Carved in Purbeck marble, it is believed to have belonged to a life-size figure of an eagle, possibly an adjunct to a statue of Jupiter or an emperor in Jupiter's guise. A likely setting for such a statue would have been the legionary chapel of the standards (*sacellum*), situated in the centre of the *principia* rear range (Bidwell 1979, 130–2).

Behind the *principia*, four large plots in the zone beyond the *via quintana* were reserved for major buildings with a variety of functions. On the north-west side of the *via decumana*, opposite the baths, stood a group of granaries raised upon foundations of driven piles (*idem* 1980, 37; cf. Manning 1981, 168ff for driven piles at Usk). In the fortress at Inchtuthil space seems to have been allowed for at least 10 large granaries, although only six of these had been built by the time the base was abandoned three years or so after its foundation (Pitts and St Joseph 1985, 117–22). At Exeter there are several unexplored plots that could have contained other granaries.

To the north-west of the granaries, fronting on the right lateral street, stood the *fabrica*, the building which housed the legionary workshops (fig. 5.3). Although only its eastern corner has been excavated, it is possible to suggest that the *fabrica* took the form of a large square courtyard building very similar in layout to the workshops erected 20–25 years later at Inchtuthil (*ibid.*, 105–15). If, as seems likely, the *fabrica* extended as far as the *via quintana*, it would have been about 52m (57yds) square, compared with about 60m (66yds) square in the case of the Inchtuthil workshops. In both buildings the front range seems to have contained carpenters' shops and storage lofts, access to the latter being gained from wide internal loading bays, of which there were probably two at Exeter but only one in the Inchtuthil *fabrica*. At the eastern corner of the Exeter *fabrica*, next to the north-east entrance and loading bay (partly exca-vated in 1972), there was a carpenters' shop furnished with work-benches. Behind this room an aisled hall 30 *pedes* wide contained much metal-working debris – including slag, metal offcuts and crucibles – associated with hearths and other industrial emplacements used in blacksmithing and particularly bronze-smithing (Bidwell 1980, 31–5). Similar aisled halls probably occupied the other two sides of the courtyard as at Inchtuthil, where three interconnecting halls were found to have been used for blacksmithing, notably in the manufacture of nails. The bronze-smithing carried out at Exeter represents a more mature stage in the life of a legionary *fabrica* than was reached at

Inchtuthil. Once construction-related require-ments had been satisfied, operations in the *fabrica* would have diversified into the more varied manu-facturing activities – such as the making and mending of armour – necessary to service the legion in the longer term.

The plot behind the *via quintana* on the north-east side of the fortress is likely to have contained the hospital (*valetudinarium*), which would have occupied a large site near the baths. Only a short section of the north-west frontage of this plot has been explored to date (*idem* 1979, 26–7).

The baths and aqueduct

The legionary baths, erected *c.* AD 60–5, occupied a plot about 65m (71yds) square at the rear of the *principia* on the corner of the *viae decumana* and *quintana* (fig. 5.3). In their layout, aspect and design the baths are remarkably similar to the fortress baths at Caerleon, built by *Legio* II *Aug* 10 to 15 years later. In both cases the long, tall bath-house lay near the eastern corner of the plot, with the exercise yard (*palaestra*), which was probably enclosed by porticos, occupying the sunny south-west side. At Exeter there were presumably en-trances into the *palaestra* from the *via quintana* and the *via decumana*. Only a small area in one corner of the *palaestra* has been excavated, next to the *caldarium* furnace-house of the bath-building. Here the compacted sand surface preserved the outline of a circular enclosure (fig. 5.5) identifed as a cockfighting pit (*ibid.* 42–3).

The bath-house was the only stone building in the fortress. The excavations to the west of the Cathedral in 1971–6 uncovered about half its length, including the hot room (*caldarium*) and part of the warm room (*tepidarium*) (*ibid.* 22ff). It can be shown that design considerations similar to those recently demonstrated by David Zienkiewicz in the planning of the Caerleon fortress baths (Zienkiewicz 1986, 96ff) also governed the planning of the Exeter bath-house, whose full ground plan and design dimensions may be reconstructed with some confidence. Although there are important differences between the two buildings, the core architectural elements thought to be indicative of cross vaulting in the Caerleon fortress baths were already present a decade or more earlier in the Exeter bath-house. The Caerleon building is none-theless the larger and more elaborate of the two and clearly represents a marked advance over the design of its predecessor.

5.5 The *palaestra* of the fortress baths looking north-east; probable cockpit in centre, furnace-house wall in foreground, and robbed south-west wall of bath-house on right (2m scale).

The intended dimensions of the Exeter bath-house, excluding service adjuncts, are thought to have been 132 × 81 *pedes* (39.06 × 23.97m). The building would probably have been entered through one of the doorways in the north-west end wall. Once inside, the bather found himself in the *frigidarium*, which has not been excavated but is likely to have contained a cold-water bath and two large, pedestalled basins (*labra*). He would then have proceeded to the *tepidarium*, in the middle of the building, which was provided with a thick concrete floor supported on tile stacks to form a hypocaust (underfloor heating system) through which circulated hot gases drawn from the hypocaust of the *caldarium*. The *caldarium* (fig. 5.6) contained two hot plunge-baths and two *labra*

occupying semi-circular recesses (fig. 5.7). Furnaces at either end of the *caldarium* heated the hypocausts as well as boilers supplying hot water to the plunge-baths and *labra*.

The stone used in the bath-house was a type of basalt known as 'trap' which outcrops in Rougemont Hill next to the northern corner of the fortress. The demolition rubble from the two excavated rooms contained many fragments of decorative materials used in the building. Purbeck marble from Dorset was employed in carving the *labra*, as well as for veneers lining the doorways and the plunge-baths. Triassic sandstone from the east Devon coast was used for architectural details such as the pier bases flanking the recesses on the south-east side of the *caldarium*. The floors were paved with square stone tiles laid in simple chequerboard fashion: white lias limestone tiles from Somerset and grey Carboniferous mudstone ones quarried locally. Small fragments from a figured polychrome mosaic were recovered – the earliest

5.6 The *caldarium* of the fortress baths looking south-east; the south-west wall of the *curia* of the town basilica is on the right (2m scale).

examples of this technique known from Britain. Various types of ceramic tiles were used in the building. Antefixes of two patterns decorated the eaves of the tiled roofs covering the concrete vaults. The more common pattern bears a female face, probably of Medusa (fig. 5.8). The other design, represented by two fragments only, and depicting two dolphins flanking a rosette, is identical with examples from Caerleon (see above).

The baths consumed an estimated 70,000 gallons of water each day. The source of the aqueduct built to supply them is thought to have been a copious spring which existed down to early modern times next to the medieval St Ann's Chapel, about 900m (984yds) beyond the rear (north-east) gate of the fortress. The aqueduct was identified inside the

5.7 Model of the fortress baths showing the *caldarium*; Purbeck marble *labra* occupy apsidal recesses and a cockfight is taking place in the *palaestra*. (This reconstruction of the bath-house does not incorporate cross vaulting.)

fortress in 1980 running along the south-east side of the *via decumana* 6m (20ft) from the street in a basement excavated by John Pamment at 41–2 High Street (Henderson 1984, 23–5) (fig. 5.3). It took the form of a substantial stone wall which would have carried a raised water channel with a gradient of perhaps 1 in 200. Where the channel crossed the defences or major streets it probably consisted of a wooden launder. Assuming the aqueduct entered the fortress at a height about 3m (10ft) above ground level (just below the rampart walkway but well above the *via sagularis*) it would have been about 6m (20ft) high at the point of delivery into the main reservoir tower, presumably sited somewhere near the northern corner of the baths plot. From here lead pipes conveyed the water to the plunge-baths, boilers and *labra* of the bath-house, and a secondary system of wooden pipelines carried a supply to other parts of the fortress including the *fabrica*.

Residential buildings

The praetorium *and senior officers' houses*
In legionary fortresses the legate's residence (*praetorium*) was sometimes sited behind the *principia*. At Exeter, however, this area was taken up by the baths and a group of granaries (see above). The *praetorium* therefore probably lay to one side of the *principia*, as was usual in auxiliary forts. To the left (south-east) of the *principia*, part of a building containing a hearth was excavated by Aileen Fox in 1945–6 (Fox 1952, 31–7), whilst on its right (south-west) side, the northern corner of a substantial building was located at North Street in 1974 by John Allan and Jon Hunn (fig. 5.3). The walls of the latter were framed on timber posts set in foundation trenches up to 1.2m (3ft 11in) deep, suggesting a building of exceptional height (Bidwell 1980, 38). It remains uncertain which of the buildings flanking the *principia* was the *praetorium*.

The zone in a fortress known as the *scamnum tribunorum*, lying in the front division adjacent to the *via principalis*, was usually reserved for the houses of the senior officers of the legion, probably seven in number (Pitts and St Joseph 1985, 136–7). At Exeter, the street grid allowed for a row of 10 building plots in this zone ranged across the breadth of the fortress, five to either side of the *via*

5.8 Terracotta antefixes from the roof of the fortress baths at Exeter (height 20cm).

praetoria. It is possible that two of these plots were intended for the houses of the commanders of auxiliary units stationed in the base (see below). Foundation trenches probably belonging to two officers' houses were glimpsed by Stewart Brown in 1974 at Mary Arches Street on a development site which straddled the right lateral street. Nothing else is known of the buildings in this zone.

The legionary barracks

By far the most common type of building in a legionary base was the barrack accommodating an infantry century under the command of a centurion. The barracks belonging to a cohort of six centuries were normally grouped together in a compact block. Parts of barracks in seven such blocks have been excavated at Exeter to date, and both their internal layout and disposition within the street system are now understood in some detail (fig. 5.3).

The barracks in a legionary base were usually distributed so that four 'cohort blocks' occupied either end of the fortress and a further two lay on the flanks of the middle division. Most commonly, the individual barracks lay parallel with the long axis of the fortress: those in the eight blocks at the extremities having their centurial quarters fronting on the end perimeter streets, those belonging to the two blocks in the middle division lying with them facing the *via principalis*. Exceptionally, as at Inchtuthil, the barracks in the blocks at the four corners of the fortress lay transversely with their centurial quarters fronting on the side perimeter streets.

At Exeter there appears to have been space for 12 cohort blocks, of which 10 were distributed in the usual pattern described above. Within this pattern, however, the arrangement of the barracks at either end of the base differed from that known elsewhere in one important respect: the barracks of the four inner blocks (i.e. those nearest to the long axis of the fortress) lay transversely with their centurial quarters facing towards the axial streets. The advantage gained from rotating some barracks through 90 degrees was that they took up less space across the breadth of the fortress, a consideration of some importance at Exeter which was restricted in width by its spur location. The designer's decision on whether to rotate the barracks in the corner blocks or those in the inner blocks would have been influenced by requirements for space elsewhere, particularly in the middle division, the *scamnum tribunorum* and in the front plots of the rear division. Another factor was probably a desire to maintain an uninterrupted line from one end of the fortress to the other for the two lateral streets. In the pre-Flavian period the retention of a regular street grid was perhaps accorded a high priority in the preparation of fortress designs. Colchester and Neuss may have possessed continuous lateral streets, and other examples will probably be identified elsewhere. Once the space allotted to the first cohort was increased in the fortresses of the later first century, as at Gloucester, it would have been difficult to retain symmetrically-disposed continuous lateral streets.

Certain members of the legion who performed special duties were probably allocated separate accommodation in barracks not forming part of a cohort block. In the rear division of the fortress, on the eastern corner of the plot containing the *fabrica*, stood a house with porticos on two sides which may have accommodated the officer in charge of the workshops (Bidwell 1980, 35, 37). On the corner site across the street to the north-east of this house another officer's house, or more probably two conjoined centurial houses, apparently belonged to a pair of barracks lying parallel with the right lateral street (*ibid.*, fig. 21).Because the plot occupied by these barracks was rather narrow, it appears that only the south-east barrack possessed a portico. These barracks may have housed the *fabri*, specialist craftsmen attached to the *fabrica*. Another pair of barracks was perhaps provided for the medical orderlies in an equivalent position near the hospital, possibly with a separate house nearby for the legionary doctor.

The street system of the fortress was laid out to encompass cohort blocks of standardized size designed in multiples of the Roman perch of 17 *pedes* (5.03m; for the Roman perch see Fernie 1985, 250). The use of the perch in the design of barracks appears to be widespread. Examples include the Lion Walk barracks at Colchester, the Berkeley Street barracks at Gloucester, and the barracks on the north side of the *via praetoria* at Wroxeter. The barracks of a full cohort were usually arranged in three maniples, each consisting of a pair of barracks facing onto a street which at Exeter was nominally 20 *pedes* wide. The standard Exeter cohort block occupied a compact rectangle measuring 12 × 16 perches, proportions of 3:4. The standard barrack in such a block was nominally 12 perches long by 2 perches wide: a ratio of 6:1. The building was planned longitudinally in 17 modules

of 12 *pedes*, five being assigned to the centurial quarters, 60 *pedes* long, the remainder to the men's quarters comprising 12 pairs of rooms (*contubernia*) 144 *pedes* in overall length. Flanking the *contubernia*, which were nominally 24 *pedes* deep, was a portico 10 *pedes* wide. (It should be noted that these dimensions include the thicknesses of the walls, assumed to have been 1 *pes*.)

Cavalry barracks and stables

As observed above, the design of the fortress at Exeter apparently anticipated a garrison occupying barracks comprising 12 cohort blocks of standard size, two more than would have been required to accommodate the normal legionary complement of 10 infantry cohorts. Space for two extra blocks of barracks was provided in the middle zone of the rear division, which was deeper than would otherwise have been necessary (fig. 5.3). Presumably two of the 12 quingenary units catered for in the fortress layout must have been auxiliaries rather than legionaries; hence the question arises whether their barracks can be recognized amongst the buildings that have been excavated.

A case may be made for the occupation of the block of six barracks in the western corner of the fortress by an auxiliary cavalry unit (*ala*). Parts of three barracks in this block have been excavated (Frere 1983, 324, fig. 24). In one of these a row of six *contubernia* was exposed at the end of the building (figs. 5.3, 5.9). It is reasonably clear that although this barrack probably contained 12 *contubernia* in all, no more than eight full-size inner rooms were provided, the inner rooms belonging to the four *contubernia* at the end of the building being smaller than the others. Hence the accommodation provided appears inadequate for a normal infantry century housed eight men to a *contubernium*. It would however have been appropriate for two *turmae* (comprising 32 men each) of a cavalry *ala*, with their decurions being housed in the 'centurial' quarters. The four *contubernia* at the end of the building were perhaps partitioned to form eight storage rooms of roughly equal size.

The barracks in a standard Exeter cohort block contained a total of 72 *contubernia*. The troopers belonging to a cavalry *ala* made up of 16 *turmae* required accommodation in 64 *contubernia*, leaving eight pairs of rooms potentially available for storage – one room perhaps being allotted to each *turma*. In the case of the Bartholomew Street barracks, it may be suggested that the 'maniple' in the western corner of the fortress housed four

5.9 Cavalry barracks at Bartholomew Street East with probable stable range lying transversely at the far (north-east) end of the site. Figures stand in the inner rooms.

turmae and contained eight pairs of storage rooms. If so, the remaining barracks in the block would each have possessed the usual 12 *contubernia*, making them indistinguishable from standard legionary barracks. Sufficient of the north-west barrack in the middle maniple was excavated to suggest that store rooms were probably not present at the end of this building. A distinctive element in the layout of the barracks of the middle maniple

was the provision of a narrow passage within the outer (equipment) room of each *contubernium* which gave access from the portico to the inner (dormitory) room. This feature is likely to have been present also in the barrack to the north-west, where evidence for it would not have been preserved. It is assumed that the partitions between the outer rooms of adjoining *contubernia* were founded on timber sills which have left no trace. The use of such sills can also be postulated in the barracks at Goldsmith Street and Pancras Lane (see below). The passages in the Bartholomew Street barracks are only recognizable because post-trench wall foundations mark the lines of partitions within the outer rooms rather than the divisions between the rooms as would normally be the case. It is therefore quite possible that such passages were provided in other barracks in the fortress.

If the Bartholomew Street barracks are accepted as belonging to a quingenary *ala*, it remains to ask: where did they put the horses? The question whether cavalry mounts were stabled inside Roman forts or kept at pasture outside has been the subject of recent discussion (Wells 1977). At Exeter, the large plot to the north-east of the Bartholomew Street barracks provided ample space for the stables of the whole *ala*. This plot has been little explored but parts of two possible stable ranges in this area were excavated next to Mary Arches Street in 1980 by John Pamment and Peter Weddell (Frere 1983, 324, fig. 24). An unmetalled footway 8 *pedes* wide separated the Bartholomew Street barracks from a range of rooms 4.7m (15½ft) wide which faced onto a street or long yard containing a urine-stained drain. No 'stable pits' or drains were found in the two fully excavated rooms in this range but the floors had a rather dirty 'disturbed' character as though the ground had been churned up during the life of the building. Perhaps the rooms were occupied as loose-boxes without fixed stalls. If stalls were provided they would probably have been set against one of the cross walls. A second building about 9m (30ft) wide which lay on the other side of the yard is thought possibly to have contained two rows of rooms placed back-to-back, giving a width for the yard of about 7m (23ft). The whole plot was notionally 170 *pedes* deep, affording just sufficient space for three such yards flanked by stable ranges lying transversely (fig. 5.3). It is assumed that each room in the stables measured about 11 × 14 *pedes* internally and accommodated four horses. On this basis the troopers and officers of the *ala* would have required a total of 132 rooms for their mounts. There is space in the plot for exactly this number assuming a range contained 22 rooms. In this case each stable would have accommodated the horses of half the men occupying a *contubernium*, and presumably the horses of four decurions would have shared one stable. If the stable ranges were nominally 272 *pedes* long (the design width of the adjacent block of barracks) there would have been 8 *pedes* spare for an access way, separating each range into two equal lengths.

Evidence that horses may have been present in the western quarter of the fortress is provided by the discovery of two pieces of horse gear from the Bartholomew Street/Mary Arches Street site. A horse pendant and a harness buckle were found in a demolition deposit overlying the military buildings. These are the only items of horse equipment known from the fortress, although a terret ring found in a late Roman context at Mermaid Yard, in the southern quarter of the base, may also be early Roman in date.

In view of the symmetrical layout of the fortress it is likely that its southern quarter likewise contained the barracks and stables of a cavalry *ala*. The end *contubernium* of the barrack next to the south-east perimeter street was excavated by Colin Tracy at Preston Street in 1976–7 (fig. 5.3). It proved to be of normal layout, as might be expected since this building is in the sinistral maniple of the block and would therefore probably have housed the most junior *turmae* in the *ala*; on analogy with the Bartholomew Street barracks, eight pairs of store-rooms would have been located in the maniple housing the four most senior *turmae*, on the dextral north-west side of the block.

The fortress defences

The defences occupied a zone up to 20m (66ft) wide beyond the perimeter street. They comprised the intervallum, the rampart, a berm and a single defensive ditch. The intervallum – the space at the back of the rampart – has been sampled by excavation on three sides of the fortress. At Friernhay Street it was about 22 *pedes* wide, occupied initially by small blocks of storerooms (*tabernae*) and subsequently by successive cookhouses containing ovens of early Flavian date. Similar store-buildings and ovens were found by Aileen Fox in the intervallum at Bartholomew Street East in 1959 (Fox 1966, 50, fig. 9; Holbrook and Fox forthcoming). Here an initial period of smithing activity preceded both the laying down of the *via sagularis* and the erection of the buildings.

The rampart generally survives to a height of about 0.9m (3ft). In its dimensions and method of construction it was very similar to the rampart at Gloucester (Hurst 1986, 100–103), being about 16–18 *pedes* wide at the base, founded on a corduroy strapping of logs and branches (Rankov 1982, 382–3) (fig. 5.11). The core consisted of layers of coarse stony clay dug from the ditch and held between revetment cheeks of turf and fine clay.

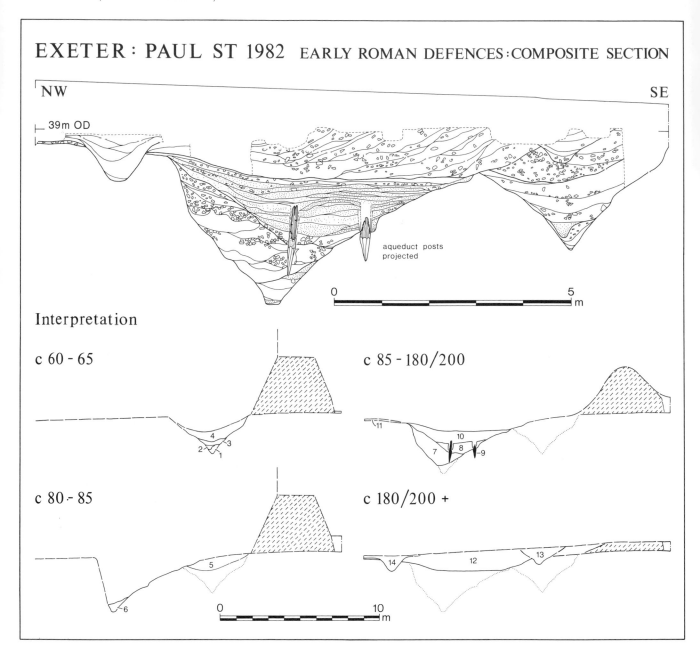

EXETER: PAUL ST 1982 EARLY ROMAN DEFENCES: COMPOSITE SECTION

NW

SE

39m OD

aqueduct posts
projected

0   5
                      m

Interpretation

c 60 - 65

4
3
2   1

c 85 - 180/200

11
10
7   8   9

c 80 - 85

5

6

c 180/200 +

14   12   13

0   10
                      m

5.10 Section through the successive defensive ditches on the north-west side of the legionary fortress and early Roman town. The restored rampart profiles are based in part on evidence from the site excavated at Friernhay Street in 1981. *First ditch*: (1) Silts (2) Erosion rill (3) Clay with oak offcuts (4) Rampart material (5) Gravel from digging 2nd ditch. *Second ditch*: (6) Silts (7) Slump (8) Silts (9) Aqueduct post *c* AD 100/101 (10) Silts. *Later*: (11) Metalling (12) Levelled rampart clay (13) 3rd-cent. ditch (14) 4th-cent. ditch.

5.11 Remains of log corduroy foundation of the fortress rampart at Friernhay Street (2m scale).

At Friernhay Street the remains were found of two timber towers set into the rampart. The fully excavated example was about 3m (10ft) square, supported on four corner posts held in foundation pits sealed beneath the basal corduroy (*ibid.*, 383, fig. 21). The posts presumably supported an observation platform at a level higher than the rampart walkway. The towers were sited about 30m (100ft) apart, which implies a total of 44 towers in the full circuit of the defences including one at each corner. A further rampart tower was found by Mark Knight and Jon Dunkley at Catherine Street in 1987 (fig. 5.3). No fortress gate has been available for excavation at Exeter. The planning of the defences allowed for gateways 24 *pedes* wide flanked by nine-post towers 6m (20ft) square similar to those known or inferred at Lincoln, Inchtuthil and Gloucester.

The fortress was provided initially with a V-shaped defensive ditch which reached a width of 4–5m (13–16ft) and a depth of 2m (6ft 6in) (fig. 5.10). This was filled in *c.* AD 60–65 and replaced by a new ditch a little further out (*ibid.*; Frere 1983, 321, fig. 22). The rampart was probably refurbished at this time, since on all four sides of the fortress the silty lowest fill of the first ditch was overlain by layers of material identical to the turf and fine clay used in the rampart revetment. This deposit was capped off with clean clay dug from the replacement ditch. The original ditch seems to have grown in size through weathering and clearance to a point where it threatened to undermine the rampart. In order to minimize erosion towards the rampart the second ditch was dug further out and provided with a Punic profile. Its inner face had a relatively gentle slope not liable to serious weathering; by contrast, the nearly vertical outer face would have suffered severe erosion each winter. Hence the ditch must have required frequent clearance during the 20–25 years it was kept clean. It eventually reached a width of almost 10m (33ft) and a depth of over 3m (10ft).

Flavian occupation of the fortress

Most of the buildings excavated in the fortress display just one or two major constructional phases and have produced only pre-Flavian finds from their construction levels. However, the *fabrica* and the baths continued in use during the early 70s, and a number of other buildings can be shown to have been erected or reconstructed after AD 70. The quantity of early Flavian pottery and coins recovered both from the fortress and the extra-mural compounds to the south-east indicates that the military occupation continued in strength down to the mid-70s (Bidwell 1979, 15–19). After about AD 75, however, most of the buildings in the fortress stood empty or had been demolished, although the base apparently remained in military hands into the early 80s (see below).

Within a decade of its erection, major modifications were made to the fortress bath-house which resulted in the creation of a smaller suite of heated rooms (*ibid.*, 60–66). The *tepidarium* hypocaust was filled in and covered by a mortar floor; this room now functioned as the *frigidarium*. The *caldarium* hypocaust was blocked along its midline, allowing the two halves to be heated to different temperatures; presumably the room was partitioned to form a *caldarium* (on the south-west side) and a *tepidarium*. At the same time the cockpit in the *palaestra* was removed to make way for a corridor or portico on the south-west side of the former *tepidarium*.

The contraction in the heated area of the baths would have reduced running costs and perhaps freed the old *frigidarium* for other purposes. The

changes must have been effected at a time when the garrison of the fortress had undergone a permanent reduction in strength. Nevertheless, even in their modified form the baths were large enough to serve several thousand men, and it must be assumed that they were still intended to cater for a sizeable garrison. For this reason it is likely that the alterations to the bath-house were made sometime in the late 60s or early 70s, before the full-scale military withdrawal attested around 75. These alterations are not well dated, but the few finds recovered from deposits certainly associated with them include no Flavian material (*ibid.* 64–5).

From the evidence discussed above it emerges that a major reduction in the size of the garrison at Exeter probably occurred within a few years of AD 70. This is about the period when the legionary fortress at Gloucester was established, probably in the late 60s (Hurst 1986, 4). The building of Gloucester has usually been attributed to *Legio* II *Aug*, although two other legions have also been suggested as possibly being responsible for its foundation. For both of these there are difficulties, however, in accepting the presence of the legion at Gloucester in the late 60s or early 70s: *Legio* XX is believed to have been stationed at Wroxeter at this period and *Legio* XIV spent only one year (69–70) in Britain at this time. *Legio* II *Aug* thus remains the most likely founder of the fortress at Gloucester.

Assuming therefore that the legion did move to Gloucester in the late 60s, it remains to examine the nature of the military occupation at Exeter after 70. There seems no doubt that the fortress continued to be used on a significant scale, with several army units probably having their quarters in the base. It is possible that down to about AD 75, at which period the fortress at Caerleon was founded by *Legio* II *Aug*, the men of the legion were divided between Exeter and Gloucester. However, Gloucester is a full legionary base and a more likely explanation for the continuing activity at Exeter in the early 70s is that a number of auxiliary units were stationed there after the legion had moved to Gloucester.

Two blocks of barracks at Exeter are known to have been occupied in the early 70s. The block lying on the right side of the fortress behind the *fabrica* has been extensively explored (Bidwell 1980, 35–6). Parts of five barracks fronting on the north-west perimeter street were excavated at Goldsmith Street and Pancras Lane in 1971–4 in advance of the construction of the Guildhall Shopping Centre. At least two of these were rebuilt in the early 70s in a form which differed from that of the standard Exeter barrack in a number of respects. Although roughly the normal length, the rows of *contubernia* in two adjoining back-to-back barracks at Goldsmith Street probably contained 13 pairs of rooms instead of the usual 12, each *contubernium* being about 1 *pes* narrower than normal. The additional pair of rooms is thought to have housed a junior officer, since in both barracks the inner end room was furnished with a clay floor, whilst the outer end room contained a latrine pit. Laid clay floors and latrines have been found elsewhere in the fortress only in officers' accommodation. The distinctive plan of the Goldsmith Street barracks and their continued occupation into the 70s suggest the possibility that in their final period of use they may have been occupied by an auxiliary unit.

A number of cookhouses containing large ovens were built in the early 70s on the site of two blocks of *tabernae* behind the rampart at Friernhay Street. This may indicate that the nearby St Nicholas Priory barracks, excavated by John Allan in 1983–4, were occupied at this period – possibly even for the first time.

Repairs were still being made to the defences in the early 70s. The rear posts of both rampart towers at Friernhay Street were replaced subsequent to the erection of the early Flavian cookhouses behind the rampart. The front posts were not affected, so possibly the repairs were occasioned by a fire originating in one of the cookhouses.

The third and final chapter in the life of the fortress commenced around AD 75, from which time the base was apparently almost deserted. The bath-house may have continued in use after AD 75 but at some point in the period AD 75–80 furnace ash and refuse ceased to be cleared from the south-west furnace-house, marking the disuse of the building. The deposit of ash outside the bath-house *caldarium* contained a group of samian ware closing around AD 80 in association with a large group of coarse pottery. It is probable that refuse was dumped on the ash heaps for regular disposal while the baths were in use, but that this practice ceased on their closure.

With one possible exception, no evidence of building activity or occupation during the late 70s or early 80s has been recognized in any other building in the fortress. The exception is a substantial post-trench building, situated on the south-east side of the right lateral street at the back of the *retentura*, which could have been erected late in the life of the fortress (Bidwell 1980, 55, *Insula* X (1)).

The final withdrawal of the Roman army from Exeter is signalled by the digging of 'demolition pits', particularly widespread on the Guildhall Shopping Centre sites, which contained pottery dating from the period AD 80–90. The defences show signs of neglect from about this time. The regular cleaning out of the fortress ditch ceased upon the departure of the army. In a length of the ditch sectioned by John Pamment and Barbara Jupp at Paul Street in 1982 a massive wedge of clay had slipped down from the steep outer face, probably in the first winter after the military withdrawal (Fig. 5.10); whilst at the southern corner of the defences at Rack Street silt in the bottom of the ditch was overlain by refuse containing pottery of AD 80–90 (Bidwell 1980, 46).

The pottery from the bath-house furnace-ash deposit contains none of the distinctive coarseware types that made their first appearance in the early 80s. These types do however occur in the rubbish thrown into the fortress ditch at Rack Street and in the demolition pits dug on the sites of military buildings in the area of the *fabrica* and the Goldsmith Street barracks. Similar wares are also present in a large group of pottery from the defensive ditch outside the west gate of the fort at Bolham, near Tiverton, excavated recently by Dr Valerie Maxfield (Frere 1986, 415–16). It seems reasonable to suppose that the fortress at Exeter and the Tiverton fort were given up simultaneously by the Roman army in a military withdrawal from the South-West in the period 80–5.

Stages in the military occupation at Exeter, *c.* 55/60–80/85

To summarize, it is possible to distinguish three main stages in the occupation of the fortress. The following sequence is proposed as a provisional framework:

(1) For around a decade or more after its foundation in the late 50s Exeter was the main base and headquarters of *Legio* II *Aug*, containing winter quarters for the whole legion and two auxiliary cavalry units. A large territory in the south-west under the control of the legion was administered from Exeter.

(2) In the period AD 65–70, the legion moved its

headquarters to Gloucester where a new fortress was established. A number of auxiliary units continued in occupation at Exeter, perhaps under the command of a senior officer of the legion, and possibly accompanied by a legionary detachment including administrative and specialist staff. The fortress bath-house was modified to suit the smaller garrison at this time.

(3) About AD 75 the garrison was further reduced, with perhaps one unit now remaining, or more probably a skeleton staff on care-and-maintenance duties. By AD 80 at the latest the bath-house was no longer in use, but stood intact in its modified form. This final stage closed in the period AD 80–85 with the full withdrawal of the army from the south-west, signalled at Exeter by the usual indicators found on abandoned Roman military sites: rubbish deposited in the defensive ditch and demolition pits dug on the sites of buildings in the interior. The town *Isca Dumnoniorum* was probably founded on the fortress site as soon as the army departed (see below).

The foundation and layout of the town *Isca Dumnoniorum*

The decision to found a town on the site of the fortress had probably already been taken by the time the Roman army was preparing to leave. This is suggested by the fact that the defences and the bath-house were not demolished when the army left (see below). Most of the other buildings in the fortress may already have been demolished at an earlier stage. It is unknown whether any were left standing after the withdrawal of the army, but the adaptation and continued use of former military buildings on the scale attested in the *coloniae* at Colchester and Gloucester can be excluded (cf. Crummy 1984, 9–10).

The street system of the legionary fortress was easily adapted to create a regular grid of streets defining 23 rectangular plots. The *viae praetoria* and *decumana* were joined up so as to bisect the *principia* site. A new transverse street, found by Peter Weddell next to Mary Arches Street in 1980, followed the line of one of the long stable yards in the western quarter of the fortress. This street subdivided the front division of the fortress to form eight plots: a group of four plots 200 *pedes* wide to the south-west of the *via principalis*, and a further four about 290 *pedes* wide adjoining the south-western defences. A second transverse street was

probably introduced to subdivide the north-east part of the rear division, but this has yet to be confirmed.

The siting of the new civic centre was determined by the position of the legionary bath-house, several of whose main walls were incorporated into the basilica (civic hall), saving on building costs. The civic centre occupied a double plot with maximum dimensions of about 66m by 142m (72 × 155yds). This took up the whole of the fortress baths site and extended across the line of the *via quintana* to take in almost half of the *principia* site as well as the plot adjoining it to the south-east. The three principal elements in the civic centre were the basilica, the forum-piazza – an enclosed market place in front of the basilica surrounded by ranges of shops and offices with porticos – and an external market place, perhaps for livestock, lying between the forum-piazza and the former *via principalis*. The public baths of the new town were eventually built on a plot to the south-east of the forum; no other public buildings have so far been identified.

The rampart and ditch of the fortress defences were retained, probably to define the formal limits of the new town, but it is not known whether any of the gates survived into the early civil period. The north-west entrance to the early Roman town may have been situated about 60m (200ft) to the north-east of the fortress gate. This would account for the location of the later town gate at the head of Lower North Street (Frere 1985, 304, fig. 26). It is possible, however, that the position of the entrance was changed at some later period.

The town founded within the dismantled fortress at Exeter in the early 80s was intended to serve as the administrative and commercial centre of the Dumnonian tribal *civitas* or canton. A clear indication of its status as a tribal *civitas*-capital, as opposed to a *colonia* inhabited principally by army veterans, is given by its name, *Isca Dumnoniorum* (Rivet and Smith 1979, 376–8).

The temporary civic centre

The partial demolition of the legionary bath-house marks the start of work on building the civic centre of the new town, since the gutting of the baths and the construction of the basilica apparently represent two stages in a single building operation. The south-west furnace house was levelled at this time and the main baths building reduced to a shell retaining just the major walls. The side and rear walls were destined to be incorporated into the basilica. The front (south-west) wall was not

EXETER: Development of Forum Area

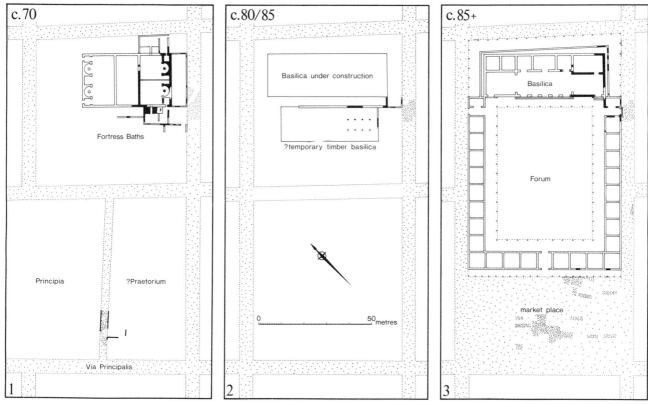

5.12 Plans showing stages in the development of the forum area: (1) fortress baths as modifed *c*. AD 70; (2) temporary basilica and forum *c*. AD 80–85; (3) forum, probably completed late 80s.

ultimately to be retained but was left standing during the construction period, to be demolished only on the completion of the new building 5m (16ft) to its rear (Bidwell 1979, 67–73).

The basilica probably took several years to build. During this time the *palaestra* of the fortress baths, and possibly the whole of the area eventually occupied by the forum, is likely to have been used as an interim market place. The front wall of the old bath-house, now free-standing and presumably reduced in height, formed a boundary between this 'proto-forum' and the building site to the north-east. Against this wall a substantial timber building was erected whose south-east wall was founded on a sleeper beam 0.25m (10in) thick. A row of pits spaced at *c*. 3.3m (10ft 10in) intervals is thought to have held timber posts forming an aisle 4.75m (15ft 7in) wide next to the retained

bath-house front wall. This building is assumed to have been an aisled hall erected to serve as a temporary basilica while the permanent civic centre was under construction (*ibid*. 72–3). The aisled hall tentatively reconstructed in fig. 5.12 measures 144 × 48 *pedes*. This building differs from the Flavian timber basilica at Silchester (Fulford 1985, 46–9) in having been built as an interim provision while work was in progress on the stone basilica. Fulford (*ibid*., 58) has suggested that the Exeter stone basilica may date from the end of the first century or early in the second. Although such a date cannot be entirely excluded, it seems unlikely in view of the absence from the construction levels of pottery types current at the end of the first century. The Silchester basilica was built in timber presumably as an economy measure and because there was a shortage of easily obtainable building stone of good quality near the town. Upon completion of the Exeter stone basilica, the timber hall and the old bath-house front wall were demolished and their foundations covered over by the mortar surface of the forum-piazza.

The basilica and forum

The surveyor who designed the civic centre of the new town had to work within the constraints imposed by the layout of the pre-existing military bath-house and street system, to produce a design that utilized the available space efficiently, providing a functional building whose appearance conformed to established architectural conventions. Analysis of the plan of the basilica and forum shows how well this was achieved.

The basilica was situated on the north-east side of the forum plot. Its rear and south-east end walls, retained from the fortress bath-house, were set back from the street frontages next to the eastern corner of the building by up to 9m (30ft). Had the building been erected *de novo* on a vacant site, no doubt its design would have been better tailored to the plot, perhaps with the main outer walls positioned along its margins. Previous discussion of the forum layout has assumed a basilica of asymmetrical plan whose north-east end wall lay on the street frontage of the former *via decumana*. It seems reasonable, however, to anticipate a building planned symmetrically about its short axis, with the latter coincident with the long axis of the forum. Fig. 5.12 shows the ground plan of the basilica restored in this manner, with overall dimensions of 19m × 53m (62ft × 58yds).

Only the south-east end of the basilica has been excavated. A large rectangular room in the eastern corner of the building was probably the council chamber (*curia*). This took up the north-east end of the former baths *caldarium* and was entered through a doorway near the southern corner of the room. The remainder of this part of the basilica was occupied by an extension of the main hall, reached from the south-east forum-portico by means of a flight of steps leading up to a doorway at the southern corner of the basilica (fig. 5.13).

The central section of the basilica occupied the full width of the former *frigidarium* and *tepidarium*. The main hall is thought to have possessed an arcaded facade probably containing five arched openings; this was approached from the forum-piazza up a flight of steps. The hall would have been lit by windows at first-floor level. There were probably three rooms to the rear of the main hall: a central rectangular room flanked by two square ones; the central room would have contained the *aedes* or civic shrine. Other rooms in the rear range probably included the record-office and the treasury.

The north-west end of the basilica was built as an addition to the fabric of the military bath-house. It would have contained an extension to the main hall, probably with two offices at the rear and an apsidal tribunal or magistrate's dais in an axial position at the end of the building.

The eastern corner of the forum-piazza, together with a small portion of the south-east forum range – containing shops or offices and including an entrance from the adjacent street – were excavated in the early 1970s. The range of rooms at the front (south-west) end of the forum was found by Aileen Fox in 1945–6; a wall in front of this range probably carried a portico facing the external market place (Fox 1952, 38–40). Analysis of the forum plan suggests that the forum-piazza was intended to measure 140 × 210 *pedes*, the proportions of 2:3 recommended by Vitruvius (Book V, 1, 2). The original design included porticos on three sides of the forum-piazza but none at the front of the basilica. This is made clear by the presence of a stylobate gutter block next to the base of a column flanking the flight of steps leading up into the basilica at the north-east end of the south-east forum-portico (fig. 5.13), showing that the portico originally abutted the basilica facade. There is evidence, however, that a portico or corridor was added to the basilica facade during the final stages of building the forum (Bidwell 1979, 74).

As we have seen, the rear and side walls of the basilica were set back from the adjoining street frontages. The strips of vacant ground remaining next to the streets were filled in by three narrow ranges which were probably built as interconnecting porticos, although later they were subdivided to form shops. The portico at the rear of the basilica lay on an alignment slightly different from that of the main building (fig. 5.12.3). This is because it was set out along the edge of the adjoining street, which was itself incorrectly aligned by the military surveyors who laid out the streets of the fortress. A short length of wall belonging to this portico was found near the northern corner of the forum-basilica in 1977 during excavations in the vaults of the National Westminster Bank next to High Street (Bidwell 1979, fig. 35, 42). The three external porticos running around the rear and sides of the basilica were exactly half the width of the ranges enclosing the forum-piazza, so that a continuous roof-line along the full length of the forum-basilica was seen from the adjoining street.

5.13 Steps at the front of the basilica at the end of the south-east forum portico; column base and gutter block to left (30cm scale).

Public baths and town aqueduct

The public baths occupied a plot measuring about 73 × 83m (80 × 91yds) which adjoined the defences to the south-east of the forum (fig. 5.14). This area is now crossed by South Street. Finds of massive masonry and tessellated pavements were made on a number of occasions in the early 19th century, in the course of building works and the laying of services. In 1932 digging by the Exeter Excavation Committee in the Deanery Gardens uncovered part of a pool (*piscina*) 16.75m (54ft 11in) long and a little over a metre (3ft 3in) deep. The pool was surrounded by a pavement of sandstone slabs 2.5m (8ft 2in) wide which is thought to have carried a free-standing decorative colonnade. Aileen Fox discovered a number of walls belonging to the public baths on sites excavated in advance of post-war rebuilding. However the layout and date of

EXETER : EARLY ROMAN TOWN   AQUEDUCT AD 100/101

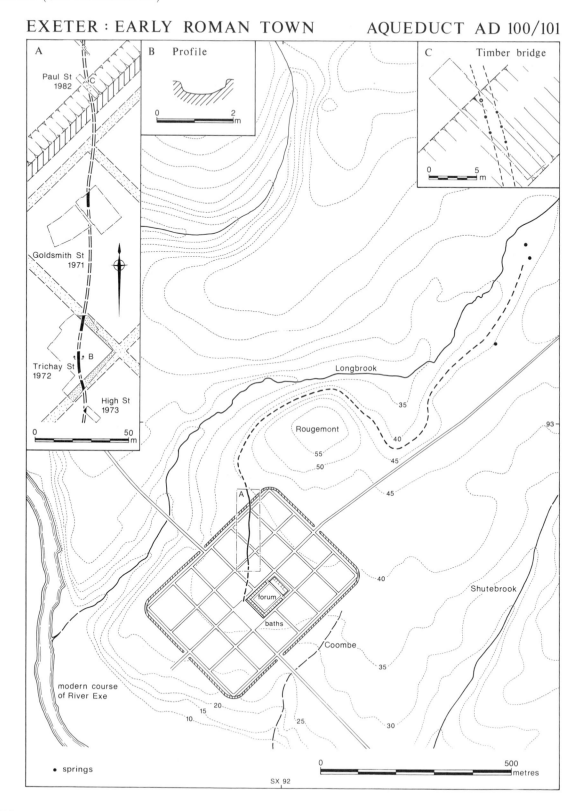

A
Paul St 1982
C
Goldsmith St 1971
Trichay St 1972
B
High St 1973
0   50
m

B Profile
0   2
m

C Timber bridge
0   5
m

Longbrook
35
40
45
93
Rougemont
55
50
45
A
45
40
forum
baths
Shutebrook
Coombe
35
40
35
30
25
modern course
of River Exe
20
15
10

• springs

0   500
metres

construction of the main bathing-suite remains to be established (*ibid.*, 121–3). Construction of the public baths is likely to have commenced only upon the completion of the basilica and forum. The baths are thus unlikely to have been started before AD 90.

The baths would have required an abundant water supply. The fortress aqueduct seems to have gone out of use when the military baths ceased operation: the digging of two wells in the late 70s or 80s in the area to the north-east of the legionary *fabrica* indicates that the supply had probably been discontinued by that time. In AD 100/101 an aqueduct was built to bring water to the market place in front of the forum and thence probably to the new town baths. This tapped a source on the Longbrook Valley, probably a spring in the vicinity of Well Street where two of Exeter's medieval aqueducts drew their supply (fig. 5.14). The water was conveyed in an open contour leat running along the valley side and around the northern flank of Rougemont. It entered the town at a point next to Paul Street where the remains of a timber bridge, crossing the partly infilled defensive ditch at an oblique angle, were discovered in 1982 (figs. 5.10, 5.15). The bridge was about 1.2m (3ft 11in) wide, supported on six driven oak posts, and presumably carried a wooden launder bringing the aqueduct channel across the ditch and through the rampart. Four of the posts from the bridge have been dated by dendrochronology (tree-ring dating) by Jennifer Hillam of Sheffield University. They proved to have been felled in the winter of AD 100/101 and may be assumed to have been used in the bridge very soon afterwards. Within the town the aqueduct was located on several sites in the area of the Guildhall Shopping Centre in the early 70s (Frere 1983, 320–23). When first built it took the form of an open leat, but at least part of the channel was subsequently backfilled when a wooden pipeline was laid in it. The aqueduct seems to have continued in use for only a few years. By the mid-second century its course had been lost and houses overlay it at several points. This aqueduct was probably re-routed in the second century.

Houses in the early town

Our picture of the early development of the town is at present far from clear. Little excavation has been possible in the building plots adjoining the

5.14 Plan of early Roman town showing probable course of aqueduct built *c.* AD 100/101.

basilica and forum, which would have been built up at an early stage. In the outer areas, for example in the plots adjacent to the defences on the north-west side of the town, few traces of first- or early second-century occupation have come to light, and as we have seen (above), it was still possible around the year AD 100 to dig an open leat diagonally across the plots in this area. The first- and second-century buildings that have been found were all constructed in timber, in most cases founded on sill-beams laid on the ground or set in shallow trenches. Some post-built structures were also erected. No full building-plan has been recovered from the early Roman town but the impression gained from the somewhat fragmentary remains is of simple rectangular buildings of the type familiar from other towns at this period (Bidwell 1980, 53–6). Little is known of the character or extent of suburban occupation. A building dating from around AD 125–50 was found in 1985 by John Pamment and Paul Patch immediately outside the probable site of the north-west entrance to the town (see below). This building may have fronted on a road leading across the Longbrook Valley and was bounded on its south-east side by the external perimeter street (Frere 1985, 303–4).

The early town defences

Most of the cantonal capitals of Roman Britain were undefended in the first and earlier second centuries. Although at Exeter the fortress defences were retained to mark the boundary of the new town, it seems unlikely that the rampart and ditch were maintained in a defensible condition, since there is no evidence that the ditch was ever cleaned out or recut. On the other hand, despite this apparent lack of maintenance, almost no rubbish was dumped into the ditch, which suggests that the town authorities discouraged activities that would have hastened the deterioration of the defences.

Excavations on several sites have shown that the ditch was allowed to silt up naturally in the late first and early second century. In the length of ditch excavated at Paul Street in 1982 layers of sand and silt – probably in part eroded from the rampart – accumulated gradually during the late first century. An indication of the rate of deposition at this period is given by the position of the six aqueduct posts driven into the ditch fill around AD 100/101, when the silts had reached a depth of 0.4–0.5m (1ft 4in–1ft 8in) (see below). Thus in the 15 to 20 years between the departure of the army and the

5.15 Oak posts of aqueduct bridge built *c.* AD 100/101 across the partially infilled fortress ditch at Paul Street.

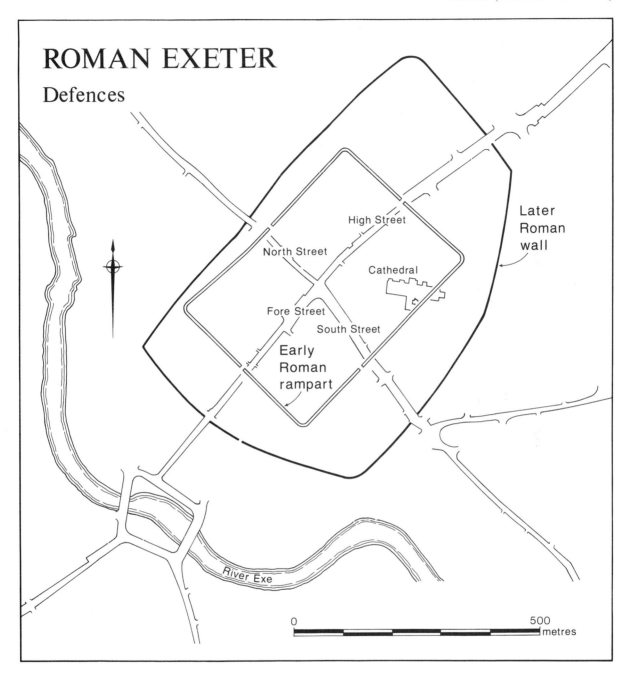

ROMAN EXETER

Defences

High Street

North Street

Cathedral

Later Roman wall

Fore Street

South Street

Early Roman rampart

River Exe

0   500 metres

5.16 The line of the early Roman defences shown in relation to the town wall built *c.* AD 180–200.

construction of the aqueduct the average rate of silting (disregarding the initial slumping) was in the order of 30mm (1.2in) per annum in the centre of the ditch. Silting continued through the second century, until by the last quarter of the century the silt deposit accumulated in the ditch had reached a total thickness of about 1.5m (5ft).

At the Friernhay Street site, near the western corner of the defences, the ditch likewise silted up gradually, but here the lowest fill was waterlogged, indicating that the ditch had contained standing water in the period *c.* AD 85–120. The wet conditions preserved a variety of organic materials which shed some light on environmental conditions at the edge of the early town. In addition to aquatic plants and insects, samples taken from the ditch contained cereal chaff from Spelt wheat and a specimen of the grain weevil *Sitophilus granarius*, thought to have been introduced to Britain in the early Roman period (Straker *et al* 1984).

The end of early Roman Exeter

The defences of the Roman fortress and early town were finally demolished towards the end of the second century. For a brief period the old fortress ditch became an 'official' rubbish tip, with large quantities of domestic refuse – including food bones, oyster shells and pottery – being dumped into it. Excavations on all four sides of the early defences have shown that the fortress rampart was thrown down around the end of the second century, with the material from it being spread over the largely infilled ditch to seal off the noisome

rubbish deposits. The stone wall which surrounded the late Roman town (fig. 5.16), enclosing an area of 37.5ha (93 acres), was probably already under construction at this time. With the demolition of the early defences there remained in the urban landscape little trace of the Neronian legionary fortress other than the lines of a few of its streets.

Acknowledgements

In writing this chapter I have benefited greatly from the assistance of past and present members of the Exeter Museums Archaeological Field Unit of Exeter City Council. The drawings were prepared by Sandy Morris, Mike Dobson, Penny English, Jane Brayne, Erich Kadow, Piran Bishop and Barbara Jupp. David Garner, Bruce Sinclair, Bob Turner, Nigel Heard and Adrian Daley produced the photographs and Pam Wakeham and Jannine Juddery assisted with the preparation of the manuscript. I am grateful to Paul Bidwell and Neil Holbrook for their comments on the dating of the pottery from Exeter and Tiverton and to Dr Valerie Maxfield for permission to refer to the Tiverton material in advance of publication. Drafts of this chapter were kindly read by Graham Webster and Frances Griffith. Many hundreds of people, of whom a number are acknowledged in the text, have worked on excavations in Exeter over the last 60 years. It is as a result of their efforts that we now possess so much detailed information about the origins and development of early Roman Exeter.

Bibliography

Bidwell, P.T. 1979 — *The Legionary Bath-House and Basilica and Forum at Exeter*, Exeter

—— 1980 — *Roman Exeter: Fortress and Town*, Exeter

Bidwell, P.T. and Boon, G.C. 1976 — 'An antefix type of the Second Augustan Legion from Exeter' *Britannia* 7, 278–80

Blaylock, S.R. and Henderson, C.G. (eds) 1987 — *Exeter Archaeology 1985/6*, Exeter

Boon, G.C. 1972 — *Isca, the Roman Legionary Fortress at Caerleon, Mon.*, Cardiff

Crummy, P. 1984 — *Colchester Archaeological Report 3: Excavations at Lion Walk, Balkerne Lane, and Middleborough, Colchester, Essex*

Eicholz, D.E. 1972 — 'How long did Vespasian serve in Britain?', *Britannia* 3, 149–63

Fernie, E.C. 1985 — 'The "Northern" System, the Perch and the Foot', *Archaeological Journal* 142, 246–54

Fox, A. 1952 — *Roman Exeter (Isca Dumnoniorum): Excavations in the War-damaged Areas, 1945–7*, Manchester

—— 1966 — 'Roman Exeter (*Isca Dumnoniorum*) Origins and early development' in (ed) Wacher, J.S. *The Civitas Capitals of Roman Britain*, 46–51, Leicester

—— 1968 'Excavations at the South Gate, Exeter, 1964–5' *Devon Archaeological Society Proceedings* 26, 1–20

Frere, S.S. 1983 'Roman Britain in 1982. I. Sites Explored' *Britannia* 14, 280–335

—— 1985 'Roman Britain in 1984. I. Sites Explored' *Britannia* 16, 252–316

—— 1986 'Roman Britain in 1985. I. Sites Explored' *Britannia* 17, 364–427

Fulford, M. 1985 'Excavations on the sites of the amphitheatre and forum-basilica of Silchester, Hampshire: an interim report' *Antiquaries' Journal* 65, 39–81

Griffith, F.M. 1984 'Roman Military Sites in Devon: Some Recent Discoveries' *Devon Archaeological Society Proceedings* 42, 11–32

Henderson, C.G. 1984 *Archaeology in Exeter 1983/4*, Exeter

Holbrook, N. and Fox, A. forthcoming (1987) 'Excavation at Bartholomew Street East, Exeter, 1959' *Devon Archaeological Society Proceedings* 45

Hurst, H.R. 1986 *Gloucester, The Roman and Later Defences*, Gloucester

Jackson, A.M. 1972 'Medieval Exeter, the Exe and the Earldom of Devon', *Report of the Transactions of the Devonshire Association* 104, 57–81

Jarvis, K. and Maxfield, V.A. 1975 'The Excavation of a First-Century Roman Farmstead and a Late Neolithic Settlement, Topsham, Devon', *Devon Archaeological Society Proceedings* 33, 209–65

Manning, W.H. 1981 *Report on the excavations at Usk 1965–1976. The Fortress Excavations 1968–1971*, Cardiff

Maxfield, V.A. 1987 'The army and the land in the Roman South West' in Higham, R.A. (ed) *Security and defence in South-West England before 1800*, Exeter

Pitts, L.F. and St Joseph, J.K. 1985 *Inchtuthil: the Roman Legionary Fortress*, Britannia monograph ser., no. 6

Rankov, N.B. 1982 'Roman Britain in 1981. I. Sites Explored' *Britannia* 13, 328–95

Rivet, A.L.F. 1974 'Some Aspects of Ptolemy's Geography of Britain', in Chevallier, R. (ed), *Littérature Gréco-Romaine et Géographie Historique (Melanges offerts à Roger Dion)*, 55–81, Paris

Rivet, A.L.F. and Smith, C. 1979 *The Place-Names of Roman Britain*

Straker, V., Robinson, M. and Robinson, E. 1984 'Biological investigations of waterlogged deposits in the Roman fortress ditch at Exeter' *Devon Archaeological Society Proceedings* 42, 59–67

Thomas, C. 1966 'The character and origins of Roman Dumnonia' in (ed) Thomas, C. *Rural settlement in Roman Britain*, 74–98

Todd, M. 1982 'Dating the Roman Empire: the contribution of archaeology' in (ed) Orme, B., *Problems and Case Studies in Archaeological Dating*, 35–56, Exeter

—— 1984 'Excavations at Hembury (Devon), 1980–83: A Summary report', *Antiquaries Journal* 64, 251–264

Webster, G. 1966 'Fort and town in early Roman Britain' in Wacher J.S. (ed), *The civitas capitals of Roman Britain*, Leicester

—— 1981 *Rome against Caratacus*

Wells, C.M. 1977 'Where did they put the horses? Cavalry stables in the early empire' in (ed) Fitz, J. *Limes: Akten des XI Internationalen Limeskongresses*, Budapest

Zienkiewicz, J.D. 1986 *The Legionary Fortress Baths at Caerleon. I. The Buildings*, Cardiff

6 WROXETER
(Viroconium)

The Site of Viroconium

The choice of this site was entirely a military one (fig. 6.1). Although there is a scatter of British farmsteads along the Severn Valley, there is no evidence of any large settlement on or near the site. The local Celtic chieftains lived in their heavily defended hill-forts; the largest in the county is Bury Walls (Haverfield and Taylor 1908, 357–8), $18\frac{1}{2}$km ($11\frac{1}{2}$ miles) due north of *Viroconium*. It is a heavily defended promontory fort with an internal area of *c*. 95ha (235 acres). Some trenches were cut at various places in 1930 by E.W. Bowcock but the account is not very informative (Bowcock 1931: although a plan and sections are referred to, they are not published in the article), and no further investigations have been attempted.

Virconium is dominated by a small hill-fort perched on the top of the Wrekin, a craggy hill of hard igneous rock. Excavations by Kathleen Kenyon in 1939 (Kenyon 1943) and Dr Stanford in 1972 (Stanford 1973) have shown that it was of two main periods. Even in its expanded form, the quality of life was distinctly low, judged from the finds recovered. The final destruction by fire has been dated to the mid-first century AD by the Carbon 14 method. It is probable, however, that the Roman troops stripped the site and its inhabitants of any valuables before the huts were fired. This attack on the hill-fort appears to have been part of the heavily-armed reconnaissance at the outset of the Scapulan campaign against Caratacus, briefly described above in the Introductory Chapter. No doubt the Britons who had resisted the Roman advance were enslaved, leaving the peasants to continue to till the fields to produce grain and fodder for the army. The military site most likely to be connected to this incident is the large fort of 8ha (20 acres) at Eye Farm (St Joseph 1973, 214; Webster 1975, 24) on the crossing of the Severn on the ancient north-south trackway (Chitty 1953, 105). Although this fort has been investigated by Dr A.W.J. Houghton, no dating evidence has been retrieved.

The plateau above the flood plain in a bend of the river is a glacial deposit of clay, sand and gravel. The Eye Farm fort is mainly on clay and, at a later stage of the conquest, when Scapula was planning his new frontier, the great strategical importance of this site of *Viroconium* would have been evident. It blocked the main access into central Wales by the Severn Valley, and also controlled the north-south route from the Dee to Severn Estuary. Also it was soon appreciated that any permanent fort in the new system must be at a river crossing where the main north-south road had to cross the river and continue towards the south-west. The sub-soil near the edge of the flood plain was also more sandy and better drained. An auxiliary fort was established to control the crossing, which was most probably by means of a wooden bridge. The fort and its defence trenches were excavated by Professor St Joseph in 1945, from which he recovered a few scraps of pre-Flavian pottery (St Joseph 1953a, 54–6). The size of the fort, 2.29ha (5.66 acres), is suggestive of cavalry and it may be significant that a tombstone of a trooper of a Thracian *cohors equitata* (*RIB* 291) was found in 1783 near the blacksmith's forge, which is now the village post office. It is most unfortunate that the edge of the tombstone has been eroded where the number of the cohort would have been given. It had evidently been re-used as a building stone so its original provenance is not known. Bushe-Fox in his 1912 excavations found an early cremation burial with a melon bead on the west side of the subsequent main north-south street of the Roman city (Bushe-Fox 1913–16, 12). This could have been in a small cemetery of this unit on a road leading from the fort.

The strategic importance of *Viroconium* during the Scapulan and subsequent campaigns can be judged by the 15 campaign camps found by aerial

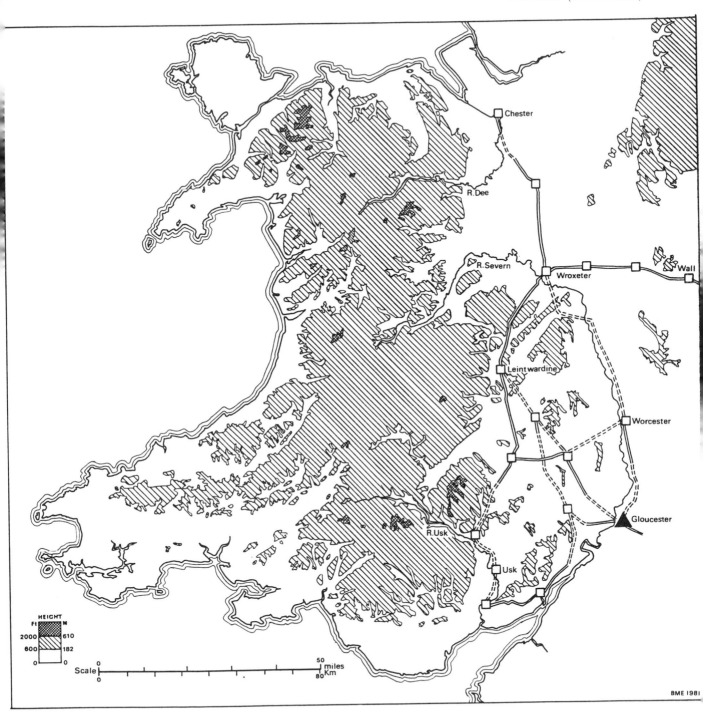

6.1 Map showing the position of Viroconium in relation to the Welsh foothills.

Wroxeter (*Viroconium*)

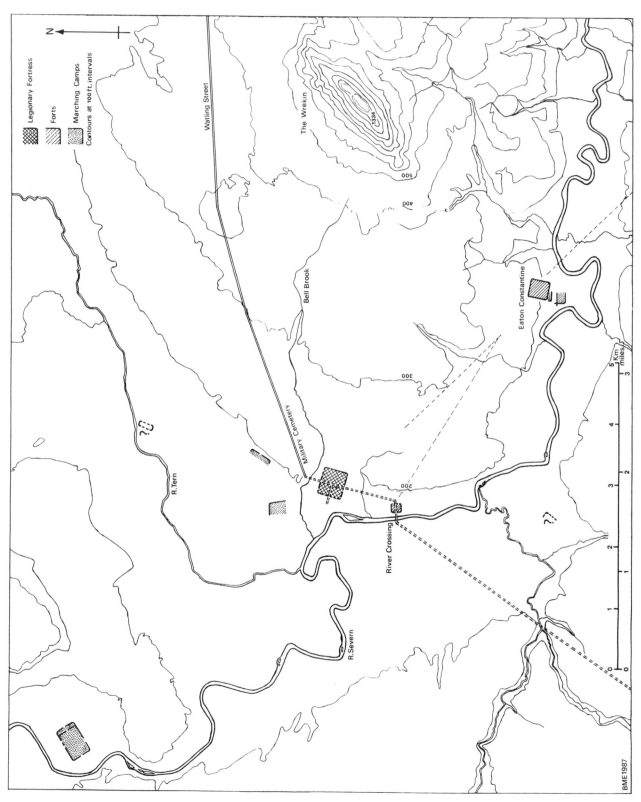

N

Legionary Fortress
Forts
Marching Camps
Contours at 100 ft. intervals

Watling Street

The Wrekin

1334

500

400

Bell Brook

300

Eaton Constantine

200

Military Cemetery

R. Tern

River Crossing

R. Severn

Km
miles

BME 1987

reconnaissance within a few miles of the site, but it did not reach its apogee until the decision of Nero to conquer the whole of Wales. The able governor selected for this task, Q. Veranius, used two legions as his main task force, *Legio* XX from Gloucester and *Legio* XIV stationed at Mancetter in north Warwickshire. This latter legion was moved forward to a new base more suitably placed for the advance and *Viroconium* was the obvious choice.

The legionary fortress (fig. 6.2)

The precise position of the fortress was not known until Arnold Baker recognized a line of military ditches on the north side of the fortress on one of his aerial photographs in 1975 (NMR Air Photograph Library SJ 5608 1242–4). In the same year, while emptying the deep Victorian back-fill in an excavation in the westernmost of one of the cell-like areas in the north range of the *macellum*, the top of the reduced turf rampart and its backface were found. This established the line of the western side of the fortress defences. Again in 1975 Dr Stephen Johnson carried out a series of excavations on behalf of the Department of the Environment, to determine the state of preservation of the eastern line of the civil defences with a view to planning public access (Johnson 1975: 1977, 20–1). Part of the work involved a re-examination of the excavations of Kathleen Kenyon in 1936 (Kenyon 1940). She had found, below the later civil defences, earlier ditches and a turf-revetted rampart which was then interpreted as the civil defences of the early city, dating to the first century. The military character of the turf rampart was clearly revealed in the 1975 cuttings and the V-shaped profile of the ditches with a central shovel slot also explained. Kathleen Kenyon had observed that the early defences were turning westwards at a point which would link them securely to the east-west alignment on Arnold Baker's photographs.

Thus, the north-east corner of the fortress became known, also the western alignment. The same miraculous year of 1975 was very dry at the time, suitable for optimum crop differentials which show in such clarity the buildings and features buried below the plough level. This set of photographs, together with those from other years,

6.2 Plan of the environs of the legionary fortress and other military sites near *Viroconium* (drawn by Barrie Ecclestone).

enabled David Wilson to plot a much more detailed plan of *Viroconium* than had been possible hitherto (Wilson 1984, 117–120, 224, Pls. XIV–XVI). The resulting plan shows elements of the military layout and other features. The line of the eastern defences is buried below the later civil system, but the full length of its inter-vallum road is visible, and also a line of narrow buildings with stone foundations along its eastern edge. Excavations in the *macellum* have revealed a sequence of cook-houses, ovens, and other buildings in this position on the west side, and in the latter phases, some of these have stone walls at the lower part of the structures. The same is also true of the south side, where the road and buildings are also seen. Thus the whole perimeter of the fortress became known, measuring, from the front of the ramparts, east-west axis *c.* 462m (1516ft) and north-south 402m (1317ft) and the area *c.* 19ha (46 acres), comparable with Inchtuthil (Ogilvie and Richmond 1967, 69).

With the outline of the defences known it was possible to establish the position of the gates, but this was dependent on the layout of the road system (fig. 6.3). It is possible to identify the *via principalis* which passed through the fortress in a north-south alignment, since lengths of it survive in the civil pattern of the *insulae*. This is most clearly shown in the 1984 plan (Wilson, D. 1984), although at the time this origin was not appreciated. This road extends northwards to join the road passing round the north side of the Wrekin. To the south the road is directly aimed at the river crossing projected at an earlier phase of the Scapulan frontier by the auxiliary fort. Only the central section has been obliterated by the central civil *insulae* 5 and 6 from 9 and 10, and this was confirmed in 1985, with the discovery of the north side of the north gate tower of the *porta praetoria*, from which the line of the *via praetoria* could be projected. The only other military roads inside the fortress which have been recorded as parch-marks are the *intervallum* roads to the south and east sides. On the outer side of these roads there are also some of the cook-houses, six on the east side, and probably three on the south. They presumably show so clearly because they have stone foundations and lower courses, like those excavated below the civil *macellum* in insula 5. There appears, however, to be little indication of the east gate and its approach road. Information about internal buildings can only be expected with those of stone construction. This is so far very slight, but the air photographs show a fine buttressed stone granary

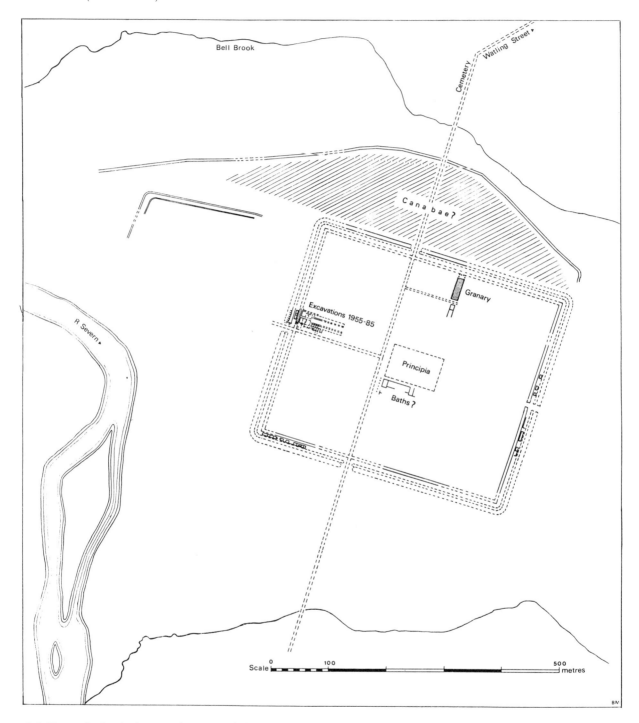

6.3 Plan of the legionary fortress of Viroconium (drawn by Barrie Ecclestone; copyright English Heritage).

on the north side in a north-south alignment with an entrance from the intervallum road. To the south it is probably another building with a narrow street between them.

The only other building in the air photographs which may belong to the fortress is aligned to the *via principalis* in Insula 10. A row of six columns on a north-south axis could have been along the eastern edge of the road. The crop-marks appear to indicate the northern wing of a larger building: there are, however, parch-marks which must demonstrate the presence of stone-work. The only other building of the fortress likely to have been in stone is the legionary bath-house, following the discovery of that at Exeter (Bidwell 1979) of about the same period. But this is the usual position of the *praetorium* and the only example of a bath-house here is at *Novaesium* (Lehner 1904, 111–12) where the *praetorium* is at the rear of the *principia*. The normal position for the bath-house is at the junction of the *via principalis* and *praetoria*, as at Caerleon, *Vindobona*, *Lauriacum* and Chester. These two buildings were never built at Inchtuthil, but there are some spaces where the *praetorium* should be placed on the *via principalis*, and, at the rear of the *praetorium* where the bath-house would be convenient, adjacent to the hospital (*valetudinarium*). At *Novaesium*, however, these placings are reversed. The matter must remain open, especially as the more massive stone-work of the heated rooms should also have shown as parch-marks. The absence could be the result of total robbing. Furthermore, a complete stone bath-house would surely have been a great asset to the inhabitants of the new city. Had this been the case, it may have been then robbed to provide stone and tile for the Hadrianic baths in their new central position.

The defences

These have been studied in detail on a short length below the southern part of the west portico of the baths insula (fig. 6.4). The sections cut by Kathleen Kenyon at the north-east corner of the fortress indicate the presence of two military ditches (Kenyon 1940, Pl. LXX, section 6) which is normal for legionary fortresses. It is difficult, however, to interpret the crop-marks on air photographs as two separate ditches. The restrictive space in the west portico allowed an examination only of part of the inner ditch which was excavated to a depth of *c.* 0.8m (2ft 7in) before it continued under the stylobate wall. Circumstances did not allow the extension of the trench on the west side of the stylobate and below the sequence of the civil streets. Traces of clay on the side of the ditch showed that the whole had been originally deliberately clay-lined. The profile of the ditch when extended coincided with the base of the rampart front, thus allowing for no berm. The rampart (fig. 6.5) was found to survive to the height of about a metre (3ft 3in). It was built of layers of turf with the usual concentration at the front and had been laid out in Roman feet (*pedes Drusiani*, each = 33.5cm = 13.19in) in units of 5, its width being 15 feet and its height projected to 10 feet (fig. 6.6). There was no evidence of any timber vertical revetment at the front in the form of large post holes for supporting uprights, but there were the remains of a clay base, 48cm (19in) wide. It is suggested that the function of this was to support massive horizontal timbers into which verticals could be held by mortice and tenon joints. No remains of this had survived since the whole of such a structure would have been removed when the fortress was dismantled. After about 35 years of occupation, it can be presumed that the timbers were still in a reasonable enough condition to be worth recovering for reuse. The evidence for this was the state of the clay base which had clearly been much disturbed by the removal of the timber and to the underside of which it had become attached. There were also clear indications of spade cuts along the rampart front, made by soldiers freeing the timbers to enable them to be extracted. A scatter of charcoal for the burning of small timbers clearly indicated the extent of the demolition (see section figs. 6.5, 6.7).

Running through the width of the rampart 20cm (8in) from the base was a series of transverse timbers spaced out at distances of 5 Roman feet (*pedes Drusiani*). It was clear how this had been achieved: as each timber had been laid on the rampart at that height and a rod was placed along the rampart abutting it and the next timber laid abutting the other end, and so on, so that the width of space between the timbers was 5 feet. These timbers must have been attached to the front upright, probably by diagonal braces, which suggests that the vertical posts were spaced along the front at the same interval. When during demolition the rampart front had been cut back to free the timbers, these transverse timbers had been sawn off at a distance *c.* 40cm (16in) from the inner edge

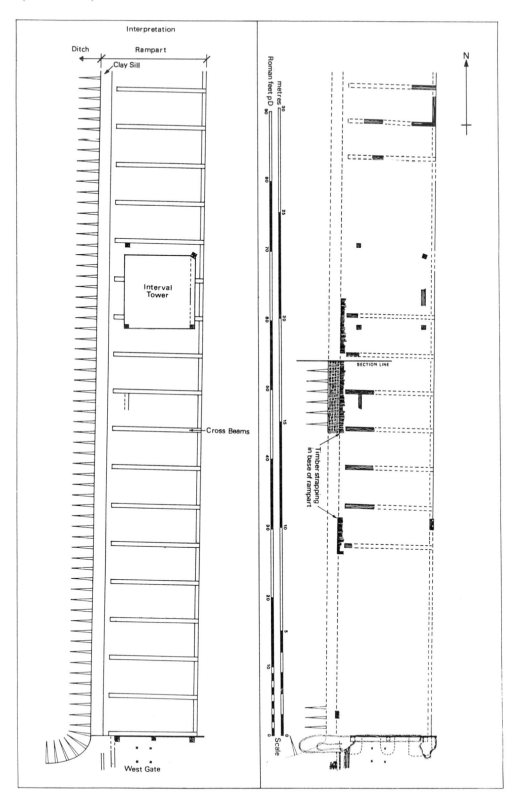

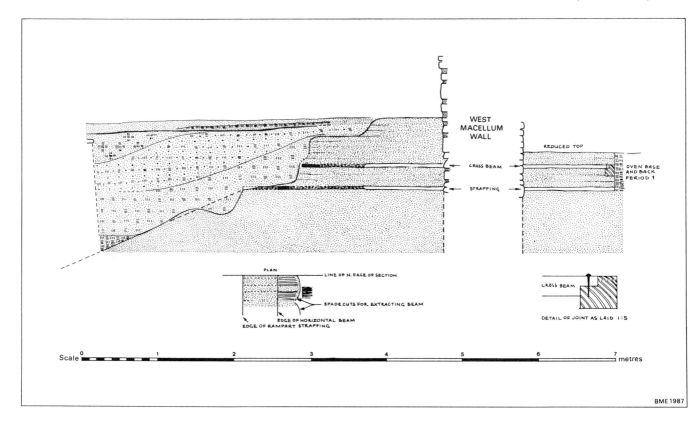

WEST
MACELLUM
WALL

REDUCED TOP

CROSS BEAM

OVEN BASE
AND BACK
PERIOD 1

STRAPPING

PLAN — LINE OF N. FACE OF SECTION

SPADE CUTS FOR EXTRACTING BEAM

EDGE OF HORIZONTAL BEAM
EDGE OF RAMPART STRAPPING

CROSS BEAM

DETAIL OF JOINT AS LAID 1:5

Scale 0 1 2 3 4 5 6 7 metres

BME 1987

6.5 A section across part of the western legionary defences below the west portico of the *macellum* (*mens*. G.W. *delt*. B.E.; copyright English Heritage).

of the clay base. At the back of the rampart each transverse beam was attached by a half-joint to a horizontal timber placed lengthwise at the back of the rampart. These horizontals along the back were buried in the rampart, indicating that there had been no vertical revetment at the back. It is possible that there were other transverse timbers, possibly a medial one, also supporting a diagonal brace to the front vertical. The vertical back face of the rampart survived almost to a height of 2 Roman feet, and against it were the solid clay backs of ovens in the first intervallum period, and of the timber cookhouse in the later periods. It has been assumed that the original height of the rampart back was at least 5 Roman feet.

6.4 Plans of a length of the western legionary defences, as excavated and as reconstructed (drawn by Barrie Ecclestone; copyright English Heritage).

The four post-pits and post-voids of an internal tower were found sealed below the rampart (3.75 × 3m (12ft 4in × 9ft 10in) from the external faces of the posts). The tower front had been set back 1.16m (3ft 10in) from the rampart front, providing an uninterrupted patrol track (fig. 6.8). Another important discovery in the extreme south-west corner of the excavation was the north side of the *porta praetoria*. This consisted of three posts, the centre one being smaller (16.5 × 10cm; $6\frac{1}{2}$ × 4in) than the two outer ones, presumably the same size as those of the interval tower (28 × 18cm; 11 × 7in). In the demolition it was considered that the two corner posts were the only ones worth robbing for reuse. Their positions were thus only determined by their robber trenches which cut into the post-holes originally dug for the posts. The post-pits were sealed by the rampart, showing, as in the case of the interval tower, that the gate had been erected prior to the building of the rampart. Inside the gate tower the floor level was determined by a thin spread of charcoal under which were several stake holes, no doubt to support internal fittings. Outside, at the front, was a thin scatter of pebbles from the road passing through

127

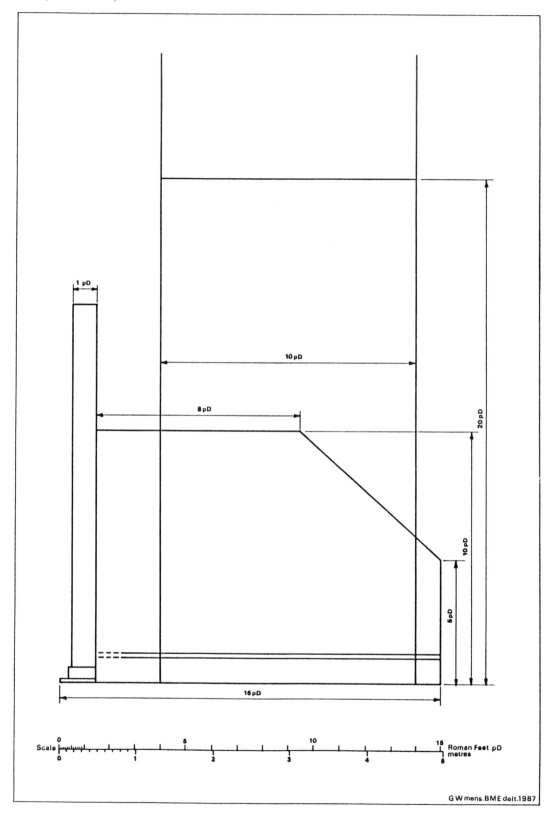

6.7 The front of the legionary rampart showing the slope of the inner ditch, the 48cm clay platform, which is presumably the base for the timber beam supporting the vertical revettment and to which abuts a layer of logs which acted as a foundation for the turf rampart, which is seen above it.

the gate. Packed against the outer east face of the tower was the clay-base of an oven of period 1, with a clay and wattle wall on its inner face, showing a strange disregard of fire risk. The ditch at the front was reduced to a butt-end to allow for the *via praetoria* to pass through the defences.

The intervallum area (fig. 6.9)

This ran between the back of the rampart and the west end of the centurial blocks, and had a width of

6.6 A reconstruction of a section through the rampart in *pedes Drusiani* (drawn by Barrie Ecclestone; copyright English Heritage).

50 Roman feet. It was occupied on the east side by the intervallum road, between which and the rampart back was a succession of seven periods of ovens and cook-houses. The intervallum road was found to have seven distinct phases, the first of which was merely a scatter of gravel of the construction period (fig 6.10). On the final road surface, a scatter of broken pottery, mainly of *amphorae*, had been trampled into it (cf. a similar find at Inchtuthil: Pitts and St Joseph 1985, p. 180) representing the final dismantling of the fortress. The seven phases were matched by the cook-houses. In the first phase, as noted above, the ovens were open and built against the rampart back, as at Chester (1953). The mess rooms of this period were small, narrow timber buildings. In the next phases the ovens were built into larger timber buildings (fig. 6.11). Finally, there were two stone phases, but these buildings appear to have been offices with fire-places, probably associated with the *porta praetoria*.

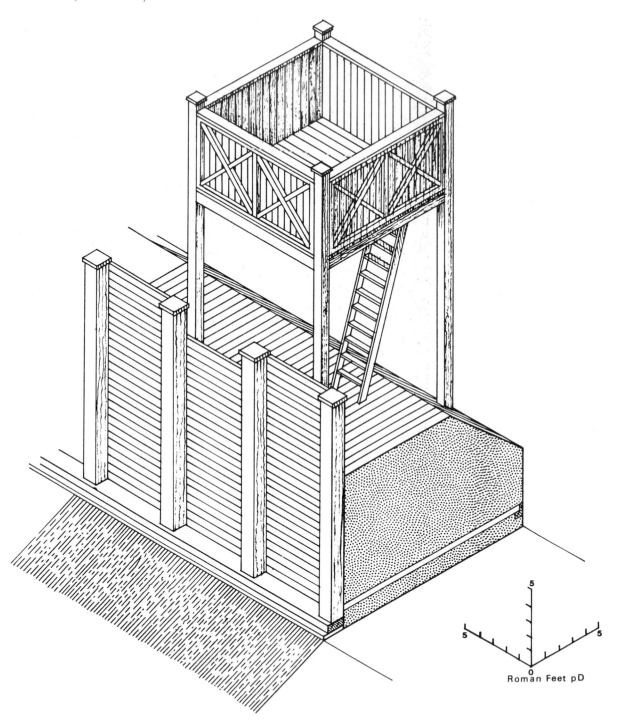

6.8 A suggested reconstruction of the legionary rampart (omitting internal supporting timbers) and an interval tower (drawn by Barrie Ecclestone; copyright English Heritage).

Roman Feet pD

6.9 A general view of the military structures inside the *macellum*. In the distant left are the walls of a stone building thought to have been an office at the back of the rampart (see its plan in the early civil buildings, fig. 11). The diagonal trench in the centre is an abortive Hadrianic foundation trench intended for the medial wall of the western range of the projected forum. This trench has exposed the surface of intervallum road 6. To the left is the final surface of road 7 with a strew of pottery trampled into it.

The barrack blocks

East of the defences there was a pair of barrack blocks in an east-west alignment. These buildings had undergone so many internal changes that it is difficult to extract from a large number of structural elements a convincing plan of any one phase (fig. 6.12). A major difficulty has been the presence of the Hadrianic *piscina* which has prevented any excavation of the military levels below it, since it was decided to preserve this structure intact. This has left a large gap in the plan in a critical area

where the two centurial quarters join the pair of barrack blocks. The suggested reconstruction (fig. 6.13) is based on the outline plans of the centurial buildings, which are slightly clearer than those of the barracks. Between these barrack blocks and the *via praetoria* was a long building *c.* 8.5m (27ft 11in) wide and at least 40m (44yds) long, its north wall was shared with the adjacent barrack-blocks; the complications of the internal divisions are probably due to a sequence of alterations. The *via praetoria* was usually bounded by rows of regular cell-like compartments. Sir Ian Richmond identified them at Inchtuthil from the scatter of sherds of pottery and glass on the road, as stores (Ogilvie and Richmond 1967, 71, 73). Harald von Petrikovits, however, has put forward another possibility, that they were for horsemen and their mounts on duty call (von Petrikovits 1975). There is a building at Haltern along the *via principalis* which is similar in plan to that at Viroconium and also 40m (von Schnurbein 1971, 132–6) long. It is divided lengthwise in a similar manner, but is not compartmentalized.

6.10 A cutting showing the intervallum road sequence, the final road, No. 7 has been removed at this point.

There was a final phase of the fortress buildings when the barrack blocks were demolished and the site cleared for a large building, of which only the large robber trenches in its south-east corner remained (fig. 6.11). It appears to have been a large open building (*c.* 26m (85ft) wide) with a surround 6m (20ft) wide (from the centre of the robbed trenches) on the east side. Its west side has been removed by the construction of the walls and main drain of the Hadrianic building. The evidence is too sparse for a positive identification, but in crude terms it is about the size and shape of the *Basilica Exercitoria* at Inchtuthil (Pitts and St Joseph 1985, Fig. 28 and 124.8). Why it should be necessary to build a cavalry drill-hall while the greater part of the legion was in Scotland is difficult to speculate, and it was most probably another type of building.

This major change may indicate the transfer of the fighting strength of the legion to a new base in the North, possibly Carlisle, at the time of Agricola's campaign into Caledonia. Viroconium may have become a base for administration, training and stores. Also Domitian removed a considerable legionary *vexillatio* for his campaign against the Chatti (*ILS* 1025 and 9200).

The military area round the fortress (fig. 11.3)

Around all legionary fortresses was an area under strict military control (Webster 1985, 207–13). This is a factor often overlooked by excavators who have concentrated their efforts on the space within the defences. The external areas would have been divided into enclosures with specific functions, such as waggon parks, compounds for building stores, including timber stocks, industrial activities (metal working, glass manufacture, tile and pottery workshops) for military specialist craftsmen and for civil contractors. In cutting a section through a city street in the south-west part of the city, Dr A.W.J. Houghton found evidence of iron

6.11 The tile base of a bread oven inside a military bake-house in the intervallum area. Traces of the wattle and daub walls of the building can be seen to the right.

working associated with armour and weapons and a glass-house in the earliest levels (Houghton 1973, 287; 1974, 429; and forthcoming). Donald Atkinson found traces of what he interpreted as the manufacture of melon beads 'just above the natural soil' under the east range of the forum (Atkinson 1942, 234). There were also *prata*, the grazing grounds for horses and baggage animals, and camping spaces allocated for units in transit. Legionary fortresses were invariably situated on navigable rivers with access to the seas, and this required extended military areas for harbour and wharfage, with warehouses. Finally, there were the *canabae* outside the main gates to provide the troops with the essentials needed by all fit and active men; food, drink, sex and entertainment. *Canabae* were under the direct control of the *primus pilus*, who was responsible for discipline and regular medical checks. Outside traders were allowed to take out five-year leases for shops, brothels, and places of entertainment, renewable at each *lustrum*.

There is, at present, very little archaeological evidence for these different compounds. Two ditches turning a right-angled corner were discovered by Professor St Joseph in the early 1950s in the north-west of the forum (St Joseph 1955, 88 and Pl. XIX), clearly of a military type, and they are covered by later civil buildings. However, if their alignment was projected 146m (160yds) to the south-west, it would meet the river escarpment. This would indicate that these ditches are the corner of a small enclosure. Another ditch system which probably had a military origin is that to the north of the fortress and south of the Bell

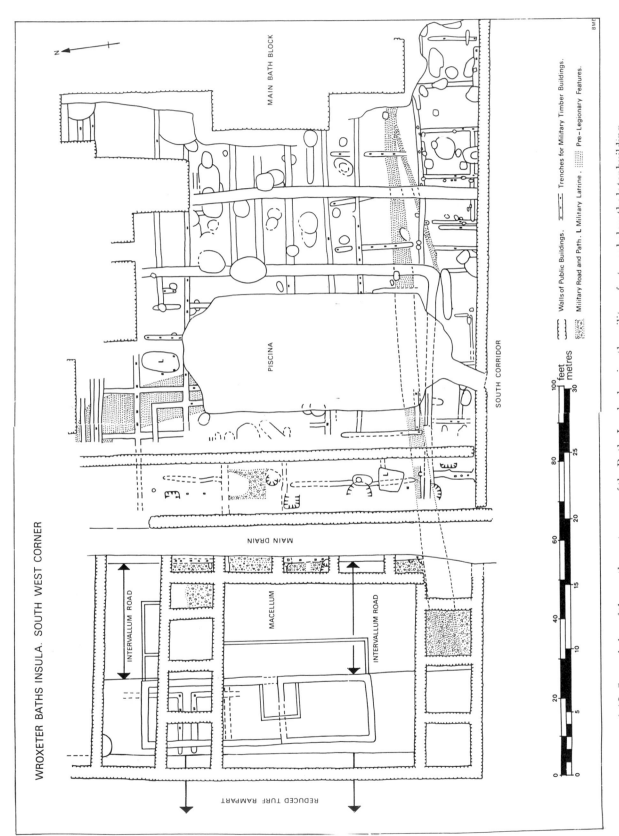

6.12 General plan of the south-west corner of the Baths Insula showing the military features below the later building (drawn by Barrie Ecclestone; copyright English Heritage).

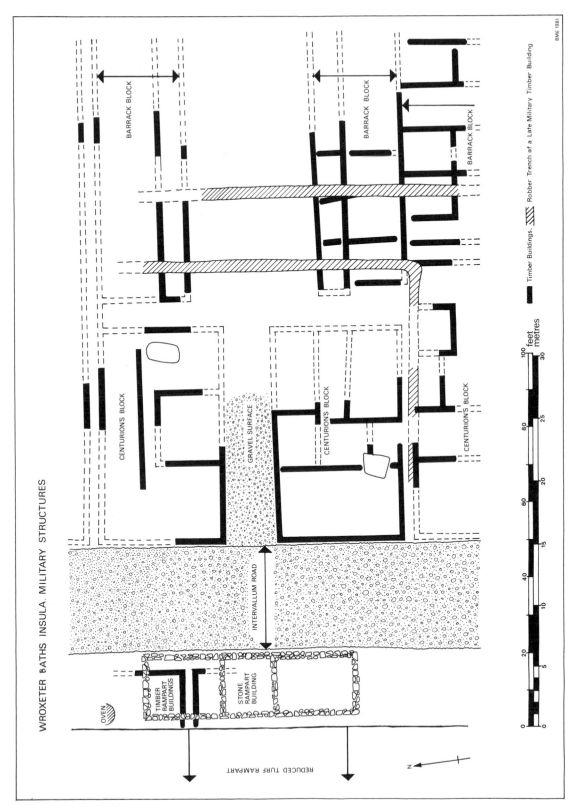

6.13 Plan of selected features to show the pair of barrack-blocks (drawn by Barrie Ecclestone; copyright English Heritage).

Brook. In the absence of any excavation, its character can only be a matter of conjecture, but it is mainly a ditch and bank, the latter clearly visible up to the 1960s, until it was levelled by the farmer with a bulldozer to facilitate ploughing. It has been identified by David Wilson as part of the second-century town defences (Wilson 1984, 120 and Pl. XVI) and this view has been accepted by Professor Frere (Frere and St Joseph 1983, 164 and Pl. 99). However, it had been established by Arnold Baker that the second-century defences coincide with the late alignment north of the Bell Brook (Baker 1971, 200 and Pl. XII) and this has been acknowledged by David Wilson in a postscript to his paper (Wilson 1984). The most likely explanation of this defensive line is that it is military, and that it defined the area under the direct control of the army. It is noticeable that it leaves a space north of the north gate of the fortress where one would expect the *canabae* to have been situated; also the east end turns as if to join the ditches at the north-east corner of the fortress (fig. 6.3). There is an interesting parallel to this from Inchtuthil, known as the western vallum, which cut off an area of the promontary leaving a space outside the *porta praetoria* (Pitts and St Joseph 1985, 244–5 and Fig. 2B), the only feasible area for the *canabae* when the fortress had been completely and fully occupied, which in fact never took place.

The civil settlement

Beyond these military control zones there would have been the civil settlement where retired veterans settled with their families, and traders could come and go freely (Mócsy 1974, fig. 22, gives details of the system on the Danube). These settlements sometimes grew into large independent cities, with the honourable status of *coloniae* as in Britain at York and *municipiae* (as *Municipium Aelium Carnuntum*: Swoboda 1964, I, 83–181). Unfortunately it is not yet known where the civil settlement at *Viroconium* was situated, since no indications have yet been found. A reasonable guess would be the area now occupied by the medieval and modern village, to the south of the church. This would have been well clear of the zones under direct military control, and on the road from the fortress to the bridge near the Severn, which had at an earlier phase been protected by an auxiliary fort.

The legionary base was retained until *c*. AD 90, by which time it had ceased to have any military importance, as Wales had been thoroughly subdued, and the northern frontier advanced into Scotland. *Legio* XX was honoured by the titles *Valeria Victrix* (Valorous and Victorius) following the part it played in the defeat of Boudica.

The early city

When the outline of the legionary fortress became known in 1975 it led to a reassessment of the plan of the city *insulae*. The regular and independent arrangement of the block of *insulae* 5 to 14 had been recognized as being of some historical significance in 1964 (Webster & Stanley 1962–3, 112–31). Once the outline of the fortress had been plotted on the city plan it was immediately evident that this block had been built over the area of the fortress. The inference of this is that there had been an earlier period of the city before the building of the Hadrianic city centre; that this early city had been built soon after the military demolition; and that it had been much smaller than the later city.

As indicated above in the description of the legionary fortress the basic outline of the military street plan survives in the early city. The *via principalis* has, however, been overlayed to conform with city planning which required a dominant centre insula for the forum; traces of this military street do however survive. The *via praetoria* however survived as a city street. Unfortunately, the buildings of the early city were mainly in timber and replaced by later more substantial stone structures, and have thus left no remains which can be recovered as crop-marks in air photographs.

During the excavations of the *piscina* area where the military barracks were found, no traces were recognized of an interface between military demolition and Hadrianic construction levels. This appeared to indicate an occupation gap of about 35 years which was difficult to explain. It was only when the excavation was extended to the west to include the *macellum* that the missing levels were found. However, the first indications of buildings of the early city had been found by Donald Atkinson under the east range of the forum (Atkinson 1942, 7–12 and fig. 5), although not recognized as such. These consisted of a clay floor (under E Room 4) with burning on the surface, another in Room 1, several examples of timber sills, a 'concrete floor'

6.14 A length of a two-period early civil building in the west portico. The earlier wall is of palisade trench construction.

and other features of an indeterminate nature. These structures would appear to be similar to the houses of the early city found during the 1955–85 excavations in the south-west corner of the baths insula. Similar traces were found by Kathleen Kenyon in her 1952–3 excavations in the insula south of the baths (Kenyon 1981, 11–12). Here there were three periods of lath and daub buildings, but one was said to be covered by a thick layer of burnt red clay. The burning is shown in sections G-H in association with clay floors which in the more recent excavations are of the early city (see below), in fact it can be said that no clay floors have been found in military buildings so far investigated.

The early city houses

Remains of the early city were first recognized in the west portico, south corridor and the north corridor of the *macellum*. The fragments of timber walls recovered belong to a sequence of buildings and rebuilding, probably of three periods. Several different methods of construction are represented, the earliest of which is by palisade trenches (fig. 6.14). This was the normal military building method, whereby long trenches were cut for the main walls into which vertical posts were set at regular intervals, lined up and the trenches filled and hard-packed. Unit frames were then quickly attached by nailing them to the posts. The essence of this method was speed, so essential to the army, since it averted the elaborate joinery necessary in the later sill-beam construction.

Another important factor of the earliest civil phase is the possible re-use of some of the military buildings, especially those of more durable materials, like stone and tile. An obvious candidate for this treatment would have been the bath-house, a very large and elaborate building. The pragmatic Roman mind would have seen the sense in keeping intact a building which would have been much needed by the new inhabitants. This building usually occupied a central position in the fortress, just as it would have done in the city. There is a hint of its presence in the *via principalis* from the air photographs, as suggested above and there is no indication of such a building elsewhere in the fortress area.

Another building, the walls of which appear to have been re-used, is the stone-built office in the intervallum area uncovered below the *macellum*. Two palisade trenches of the timber walls of the earliest civil phase have butt-ends at the north-west and south-west corners of this building, which strongly suggests that the west wall may have been used as a sill-beam for the east wall of the early civil building (fig. 6.15). There is no evidence inside this building of its continuity; the floors appear to have been of wood in the military period and these could have been replaced without leaving any archaeological traces. A reasonable conclusion is that the building may have been re-used, or, at least, that its western wall was incorporated into the earliest civil building.

A feature of the buildings which were standing at the time of Hadrian's expansion was their destruction by fire to make space for the new city centre. The houses were cleared of all portable furniture

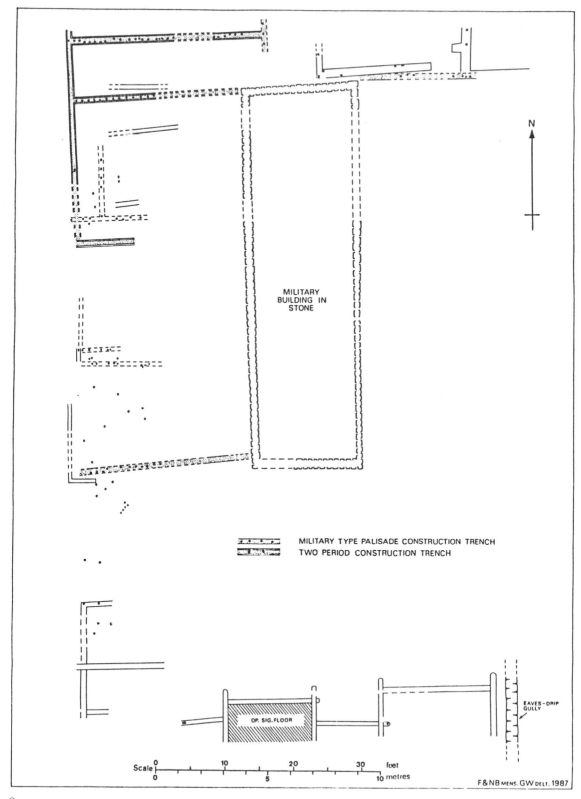

MILITARY
BUILDING IN
STONE

N

MILITARY TYPE PALISADE CONSTRUCTION TRENCH
TWO PERIOD CONSTRUCTION TRENCH

OP. SIG. FLOOR

EAVES-DRIP
GULLY

Scale 0   10   20   30   feet
      0   5   10 metres

F & N B MENS. G W DELT. 1987

6.16 A length of the foundations of an early civil building showing the use of local stone as a base for a sill-beam.

and goods, demolished for their timber, and finally the destruction material was removed and the site levelled, leaving only a layer of burning and the carbonized timber sill-beams.

The plans of the early city buildings are fragmentary, and only tentative suggestions about their planning and character can be offered. A preliminary study appears to indicate that they were most probably private houses with an alignment almost identical to that of the fortress. The only common feature appears to be the western boundary where walls of all periods were found in a north-west alignment. This suggests that a north-south street

6.15 Plan of the early civil buildings at Viroconium showing also the continued use of a military stone building (*mens*. F. & N. Ball, *delt*. G. W.).

of the newly-enlarged city was laid down at this period over the legionary ditches, which in the Hadrianic expansion was to become the main street of the city. It is unfortunate that the section cut by Donald Atkinson through this street is only in diagramatic form in the 1942 report (fig. 3). His description of the lowest road is 'a thin layer 1–3 inches of gravel resting on undisturbed soil'. The road above this which includes fragments of sandstone is presumably associated with the Hadrianic building programme. This road alignment may not have been entirely new, as a military road may have existed to the west of the ditches to enable travellers to reach the bridge without going through the fortress.

The earliest period of the early civil buildings is distinguished by palisade-trench construction, but this is confined to the north part of the site (fig. 6.14). The building of this type appears to have been E-shaped, continuing to the north beyond the limits of the excavation. At a later period there were considerable alterations and new clay and daub walls were built, in some cases over the earlier palisade construction trenches. Walls of later periods were built on sill-beams, according to the normal civil practice. Some of these beams were found in a carbonized state following the Hadrianic destruction of the houses by fire. Another feature of later periods was the laying of flat stones as a foundation to the sill-beams (fig. 6.16): that of the west wall of the north building were of red sandstone, including part of a quern. In the south building the stone used for this purpose was a kind of millstone grit, found locally in the Telford series.

There may have been a space between the north building and the one in the south; however, this is far from certain and the area in question included a latrine, consisting of a long trench with slight evidence of other structural elements. The trench itself had a layer of lime, commonly used at later periods as a purifying agent. The north house had an internal latrine which had been treated in the same way.

The south building was found mainly in the south corridor of the baths insula. It consisted of an east-west wing of a building fronting the street built over the military *via praetoria*. Its eastern limit was marked by a wall with an external gully or eaves drip. A door led into an open area which included a number of large rubbish pits, presumably of this period. One of the most interesting features was an old door or a piece of furniture placed over the eaves drip to facilitate access to the open area. In the destruction by fire this wooden construction had been completely carbonized: it was skilfully removed for permanent consolidation and eventual display in the site museum. One of the rooms of this house had a well-preserved *opus signinum* floor. Further traces of this house were found at the south end of the west portico, but the walls are unfortunately difficult to relate to the rest of the building since there has been considerable interference by later pits.

The new city of Hadrian

Viroconium underwent a dramatic change under Hadrian as part of his Imperial economic policy for the frontier areas of the empire was implemented. Although the sources of the life of Hadrian are very scanty, consisting of the suspect *Historia Augusta* (Syme 1968), the later epitome of Cassius Dio (lxix) and the surviving traces of laws the Emperor enacted (Riccobono 1940–3). It is possible to add to the sketchy accounts of Hadrian's activities, through archaeological evidence from the ground and epigraphy. It becomes evident that while serving as chief-of-staff to Trajan, Hadrian realized the futility of acquiring the enormous desert areas brought into Roman control by Trajan's eastern conquests. He resolved to set limits to the empire by building massive stone or timber walls for all to see and understand as an indication where the frontiers were fixed. In the passage relating to the building of his great wall in Britain, its purpose is stated with great clarity, *qui barbaros Romanosque divideret* (i.e. 'to divide the Romans from the barbarians', *HA*. Hadrian XI, 2). There was a far-reaching corollary to this statement which the pragmatic emperor clearly understood. Within the well-defined Imperial boundary was the Roman way of life, the outward indication of which was the great urban centres linked by an efficient communications system, all dependent on a healthy economic growth (Birley 1956). In other words, Hadrian's plan was to bring urban civilization right up to the frontiers, and with it a determined drive towards the spread of trade, industry and efficient land use.

Hadrian's main achievement was the effective improvement to Imperial administration and government, which he regarded as a personal task, however minute and tedious the detail (Garzetti 1976, 402–10). With this went the clarification of the laws for which the best jurists of the day were employed. The emperor also introduced new legislation aimed at improving the standards of justice and also intended to develop the economy. Fragments which survive include laws, allowing the occupation and development of lands uncultivated for ten years within Imperial domains (Riccobono, 490–5) and others applying similarly to disused mineral resources (Lewis and Rheinhold 1955, ii, 188). He made all rivers free for traffic with access to the banks for moorings (Sanders 1900, 91–2; *Dig.* i, 8, 5). He also improved the lot of soldiers, with laws concerning their wills and inheritances; there was even a law whereby soldiers were exempt from responsibility for injuring civilians when practising throwing javelins in a place allocated for such exercises (*ibid*, p. 413; *Dig.* ix, 2, 9, 4).

Hadrian was a great traveller, and everywhere he went in the frontier zones he founded new cities and breathed new life into old ones. The practice of founding *coloniae* for retired veterans had become rare since there was no longer the need with the large extension of citizenship and Romanization (Garzetti 1976, 425). Some of the large military settlements near his old fortresses on the Danube and in North Africa received municipal status. Hadrian merely accepted this natural development but extended and regularized it. This process is well exemplified in Britain at *Viroconium*, where the early city built over the demolished legionary fortress was now virtually doubled in size.

The archaeological evidence for this development has been accumulating over the last 60 years (Webster 1979; Hanson and Keppie 1980, 241–96). The first intimation came in the excavation of the forum by Donald Atkinson in 1923–7 (Atkinson 1942) and in particular the discovery of a large inscription (*RIB* 288; now in the Rowley House Museum, Shrewsbury) which had collapsed and shattered over the street. This was a dedication to Hadrian dated to AD 128/9 by the *Civitas Cornoviorum*. This date which indicates the completion of the work would fit reasonably well with the visit of Hadrian to Britain in AD 122, when the scheme was probably initiated. The excavation produced a surprise in the form of an uncompleted bath-house below the forum. It was dated by Atkinson, on the basis of residual pottery, to the late first century, but work on the other large insula on the east side of the main street, also

6.17 Plan of the Baths Insula at Viroconium (drawn by Donald Mackreth and reproduced by his kind permission).

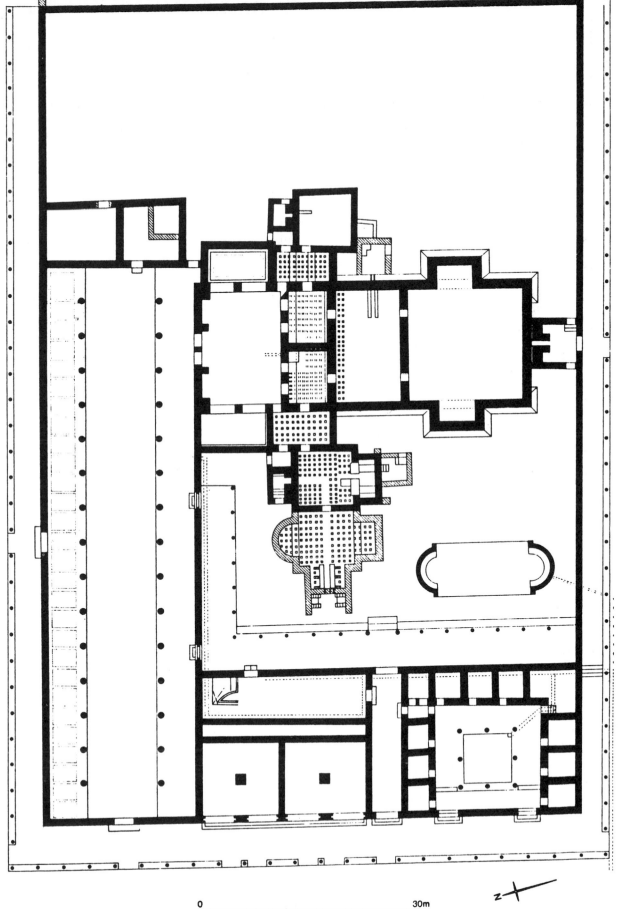

0   30m

z

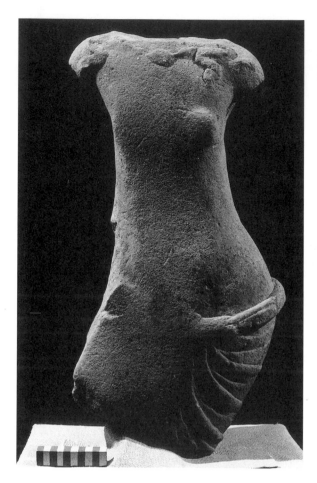

6.19 The water jar held by the right hand of the nymph. The palmette pattern and concentric rings on the base clearly indicate that it was a copy of a metal prototype.

6.18 A much-damaged sculpture of a water nymph found with her water jar (fig. 19) in the Hadrianic levelling. The wear on one side suggests its use as a doorstep in the early civil period. It was presumably for a fountain in the legionary *principia* or the *praetorium*.

designed for civic buildings, has demonstrated that there was a change of plan during construction. This involved the functions of the two insula being interchanged: instead of a bath-house on the west side and a forum on the east, the revised plan was for a forum on the west and a bath-house on the east insula. Below the Hadrianic structures on the east insula, unused foundation trenches intended for a forum and walls of two periods have been found.

The extension of the city to the west and north required a transfer of the civic centre, presumably from the central area of the fortress to a new

location on the western side of the early city. This gave Hadrian an opportunity to plan a monumental scheme in the large insulae, the total area of which is 2.93ha (7.23 acres), one of the largest civic planning projects in Britain, comparable only to Londinium. (The second forum was *c*. 170m square or *c*. 3ha (186yds square or 7.4 acres) and may also have been the work of Hadrian: the dating has tended to be by residual pottery (Merrifield 1983, 68–72 and Fig. 9).)

The east insula included a bath-house in the east range with a large basilican *palaestra* which had originally been intended for the forum basilica on the east-west axis. The west range consisted of public buildings of unidentified purpose and at the south end there was a *macellum*, a small specialist market. The open space in the centre of the insula intended in the original scheme as the forum market became a colonnaded walk round the *piscina* (fig. 6.17). The area of the enlarged city is difficult to assess without any evidence from excavation, but the street pattern as shown by aerial archaeology would suggest that it extended up to the Bell Brook on the north side, to the edge of the river escarpment to the west and to the small stream to the south. This area would have been approximately 56ha (138 acres) whereas the early city was *c.* 22ha (54 acres). If this crude estimate approximates to the truth, Hadrian more than doubled the size and presumably also the number of inhabitants by settling veterans and attracting artisans, craftsmen and traders to this much increased market potential. Only large-scale excavation will reveal the extent of the emperor's plan and the degree of its success or failure. There is already evidence of growing prosperity, and it would seem to have been a remarkable and far-sighted venture to bring such economic expansion up to the very edge of the barbarian world.

Bibliography

Atkinson, D. 1970   *Excavations at Wroxeter 1923–27*, Birmingham Arch. Soc. 1942, reprinted 1970

Baker, A. 1969–70   'Aerial Reconnaissance over Viroconium and military sites in the area in 1969', *Trans. Shrops. Archaeol. Soc.* 59, 24–31

Baker, A. 1971   'Viroconium: An Aerial Study of the Defences', *Trans. Shrops. Archaeol. Soc.* 58 (1971) 197–219

Barker, P. 1974   *Excavations on the Site of the Baths Basilica at Wroxeter, 1966–1973*, an interim report

Barker, P. 1975   'Excavations at the Baths Basilica at Wroxeter 1966–74: interim report', *Brit.* 6 106–17

Bidwell, P. 1979   *The Legionary Bath-House and Basilica and Forum at Exeter*, Exeter Archaeol. Soc. Rep. No. 1

Birley, E. 1956   'Hadrianic Frontier Policy', *Carnuntina: Vorträge beim internationalen Kongress der Altertumforscher, Carnuntum* ed. E. Swoboda

Bowcock, E.W. 1931   *Trans. Shrops. Archaeol. Soc.* 46, pp. 57–9

Bushe-Fox, J.P. 1913–16   *Excavations on the Site of the Roman Town at Wroxeter, Salop.* 1st Report 1913, 2nd Report 1914, 3rd Report 1916, Research Reports of the Soc. of Antiq. Nos. 1, 2 and 4

Chitty, L.F. 1953   'Prehistoric and other early finds in the borough of Shrewsbury', *Trans. Shrops. Archaeol. Soc.* 64, 105

Fox. G.E. 1897   'Uriconium', *Archaeol. J.*, 123–73

Frere, S.S. and St Joseph, J.K. 1983   *Roman Britain from the Air*, 164 and Pl. 99

Garzetti, A. 1976   *From Tiberius to the Antonines: A History of the Roman Empire AD 14–192*, Univ. paperback

Haverfield, F. 1899   'The Founding of Viroconium' *Archaeol. J.*, 46, 65–67

Haverfield, F. and Taylor, M.V. 1908   'Romano–British Shropshire', *VCH Shrops.* 205–78

Houghton, A.W.J. 1973   *Brit.* 4, 287

—— 1974   *Brit.* 5, 429

ILS, 1892–1916   *Inscriptiones Latinae Selectae*

Johnson, S. 1977   *Archaeological Excavations in 1976*, HMSO

Kenyon, K.M. 1940   'Excavations at Viroconium 1936–37', *Arch.* 88, 176–228

—— 1943   'Excavations on the Wrekin, Shropshire, 1939', *Arch. J.* 99, 99–109

—— 1981   'Excavations at Viroconium in Insula 9, 1952–3', *Trans. Shrops. Archaeol. Soc.* 60 5–73

Lehner, H. 1904   'Novaesium', *Bonner Jahrbuch*, 111–12

Lewis, N. and Reinhold, M. 1955   *Roman Civilisation* ii

Merrifield, R. 1983   *London, City of the Romans*

Mócsy, A. 1974   *Pannonia and Upper Moesia*

Ogilvie, R.M. and Richmond, I.A. 1967   *De Vita Agricolae*

Petrikovits, H. von 1975   *Die Innerbauten römischer Legionslager während der Prinzipatzeit*

Pitts, L. and St Joseph, J.K. 1985   *Inchtuthil*, *Brit.* Monograph Ser. No. 6

RIB 1965   *Roman Inscriptions of Britain*, i

Riccobono, S. 1940–1943   *Fontes Iuris Romani Antejustiniani*, 2nd ed.

Sanders, T.C. 1900   *The Institutes of Justinian*

Schnurbein, S. von, 1974   'Die römischen Militärenlagen bei Haltern', Bericht über die

Wroxeter (*Viroconium*)

St Joseph, J.K. 1953   Forschungen seit 1899, *Bodenaltertümer Westfalens*, 14 *Germania* 49, 132–6
'Roman Forts on Watling Street near Penkridge, and Wroxeter', *Birmingham Archaeol. Soc. Trans.* 69, 50

—— 1953/77   Evidence from air photographs, *JRS* 43 (1953), 84, 88, 89 and Pl. XI 2, XII; 45 (1955), 88 and Pl. XIX; 48 (1958) 95, 97, 98 and Pl. XIII; 63 (1973), 234, 235, 244 and Pl. XVII, i; 67 (1977), 145, Fig. 12, 156, 157, Pl. XV, 2.

Stanford, S.C. 1973   *W. Midlands News Sheet* No. 16, 9–10
Swoboda, F. 1964   'Carnuntum', *Römische Forschungen in Niederösterreich*
Syme, Sir R. 1968   *Ammianus and the Historia Augusta*
Webster, G. 1953   'Excavations on the Legionary Defences at Chester, 1948–52 pt. ii', *Chester Archaeol. Soc. J.*, 1–23

—— 1962   'The Defences of Viroconium (Wroxeter)', *Trans. Birmingham Arch. Soc.* 78, 27–39

—— 1975   *The Cornovii*, London
—— 1980   'A note on new discoveries at Viroconium (Wroxeter) which may have a bearing on Hadrian's frontier policy in Britain', in *Roman Frontier Studies 1979*, ed. Hanson, W.S. and Keppie, L.J.F. 1980, BAR: 291–6

—— 1985   *The Roman Imperial Army*, 3rd ed.
Webster, G. and Stanley, B. 1962/3   'Viroconium: a Study of Problems', *Trans. Shrop Archaeol*, 75.2 (1962–3), 112–31

Webster, G. and Woodfield, P. 1966   'The Old Work at Public Baths at Wroxeter', *Antiq. J.* 46, 229–39

Wilson, D. 1984   *Antiquity* 58, 117–20 and 224
Wright, T. 1872   *Uriconium*

7 LINCOLN
(Lindum)

The setting

In a landscape commonly (but inaccurately) known for its flatness, the modern city of Lincoln appears as a prominent hilltop feature, enhanced by the huge scale of its medieval cathedral. From its origin, however, there was an important downhill element to the town, for its site occupies a glacial gap through the Jurassic ridge, known hereabouts as the Lincoln Edge.

This gap constituted a favourable location for a legionary base, with excellent prospects, later fulfilled, for land and water communications, and met the requirements laid down by Vitruvius for a town site (*de archit* I.iv). Yet neither valley floor nor hilltop nor hillside was free from difficulties when it came to establishing a settlement: much of the valley is marshy, the clay hillside full of natural springs and also requiring special attention to drainage; while providing fresh water and moving supplies to the hilltop demanded much investment and effort. These difficulties must have been outweighed by strategic, and perhaps political, considerations – as they had been by similar factors at the Gallic towns of Amiens, with its marshy river crossing, and Lyons, on top of a steep bluff (Baynard and Massey 1983; Drinkwater 1975).

Successive modern accounts of the legionary occupation of Lincoln have discussed its topographical and historical context (Richmond 1946, 26; Webster 1949; Whitwell 1970, 12–20; Jones 1985), yet our appreciation of such factors is constantly being modified by new information from excavations. Furthermore, an understanding of the wider topography is necessary as a background to the earliest settlement. The Jurassic Ridge running north–south was the natural line for the main east-coast route, and the crossing of the Witham gap a natural communications junction. The 2km (1.2 mile) wide gap itself is glacial in origin, having been created by an early course of the River Trent in the Pleistocene period and later occupied by the Witham (Fig. 7.1; May 1976, 16). The river system here is slow-moving, still unstable and complicated by the existence of the Brayford Pool at the point where the Witham, not tidal quite up to Lincoln in historic times, turns through the gap. The exact origin of the Pool is still uncertain, but is more likely to be geological than man-made.

To the south and east of the Pool was much marshy ground. The confinement of the modern watercourse to a narrow canal represents only the latest stage in a long-term development, begun in the Roman period, but still leaving the lower part of the town at risk from flooding. The southern end of the gap is marked by a series of gravel terraces. Between these and the river the ground was apparently cut by meres, and large-scale settlement would have been impossible without extensive reclamation.

Origins

Knolls of higher ground did occur, and it was probably on these that a late Iron Age settlement developed in the first century BC. The existence of pre-Roman occupation at Lincoln has been suggested by a number of scholars, but most have looked to the hilltop. The rich settlements of the eastern Corieltauvi, however, tended to be low-lying (May 1984). It was in 1972 that excavations produced evidence for a round-house and associated features, accompanied by pottery and finds dating to between *c*. 100 BC and the conquest (Jones 1981; Jones and Darling forthcoming). The size and extent of the settlement can only be established by further excavations, but it is now clear that *Lindon*, 'the place by the pool' (Rivet and Smith 1979, 393), occupied an important nodal position in native communications. Much of the land to south and east was fen, and a river crossing at Lincoln or a little to its east was necessary to reach eastern parts of the tribal lands of the Corieltauvi (originally known as the Coritani, see Tomlin 1983; May *loc. cit.*, fig. 1).

The attitude of the tribe to the Roman conquest is not known. Its geographical and political location in relation to the Iceni, Catuvellauni and Brigantes – all basically allies of Rome – the nature of the terrain, and the speed of conquest make it unlikely that more than token resistance was offered. There is, however, no real evidence that they willingly cooperated. Until recently, most known military sites have lain along the lines of Ermine Street and the Fosse Way, with the exception of the temporary camps and 'campaign fortresses' (Webster 1980a, 162–5). The area east of the Jurassic ridge had hardly been considered in terms of the early conquest period, but the existence of a recently discovered fort at Kirmington (Riley 1977) at a gap in the Wolds does not necessarily mean that some show of force, even if only the army's presence, was required. Nor does it hint at resistance from the eastern part of the tribe – the army was disposed at strategic points in case of trouble. Yet it would be useful to fill out the details of the garrisoning of this region. The fluidity of the military campaigning in these early years means that a number of temporary or semi-permanent bases could have preceded the known legionary base in Lincoln, as at Wroxeter (q.v.) and at Neuss in the Rhineland (Chantraine 1984). One cannot rule out an auxiliary fort among the various possibilities.

The question of the disposition of *Legio* IX *Hispana* in the early years of the conquest is similarly confused. Excavation of the 'vexillation fortress' at Longthorpe (Frere and St Joseph 1974) seems to confirm that the Legion was divided in the period before the Boudican revolt of *c.* AD 60, and similar sites at Newton on Trent and Rossington Bridge could have had garrisons of this sort. All these sites were away from the developed military road system and therefore presumably pre-dated it.

The construction of both Ermine Street and the Fosse Way, meeting at Lincoln, was also an early development and a Claudian military presence can be postulated on other grounds. Negative results from excavations on the hilltop have made it less

likely, but not inconceivable, that an earlier, smaller base underlay the known fortress, while the evidence of legionary cemeteries in the lower part of town, *c.* 2km (1¼ miles) from the Neronian site, may indicate an adjacent base (fig. 7.1). Work in 1982 revealed several first-century cremations and a mausoleum at Monson Street, confirming that the finds of gravestones made last century did in fact indicate a cemetery on this site. Some of the tombstones of the Ninth Legion have no *cognomina*, but this does not definitely prove that they are Claudian in date (*RIB* 254, 255, 257; Birley 1979, 83; cf. Webster 1981, 49). The recent discovery of what may have been Ermine Street diverging from the Fosse Way (fig. 7.1) several hundred yards north of the modern junction also complicates matters (cf. Webster 1949, fig. 2). Further excavation is desirable here, as well as geophysical survey, if we are to prove that in the Roman period two distinct roads running obliquely were carried over the low-lying ground.

The question of an earlier fortress at Lincoln like that at Kingsholm, Gloucester (Hurst 1985 and this volume), on a low-lying site, must therefore be reserved. Systematic observation of the potential sites has yet to take place, and if, as at Kingsholm, the earlier site was abandoned for a more favourable river crossing, then we must extend our inquiry of Lincoln accordingly.

The fortress

Certainly the fortress whose existence was first established by Graham Webster in the 1940s has still to yield many secrets, not the least of which is a precise date for its foundation. Study of both the coins and samian pottery to date (the pottery from the excavations of the 1970s has yet to be studied in detail) suggests that the fortress was not built before *c.* AD 60, and possibly not till a decade or so later (Hartley 1981; Reece and Mann 1983). On historical grounds, a date of *c.* 61–2, associated with the post-Boudican reorganization (as Frere 1978, 87, 113), or of *c.* 66–7 at the time of the withdrawal of *Legio* XIV (introduction, above) seems more likely than an early Flavian context. The discovery of the fortress by Webster immediately beneath the *colonia* took place, fortuitously, at the only point where the legionary defences lay immediately beneath the modern surface (Webster 1949). The evidence for timber features is nonethe-

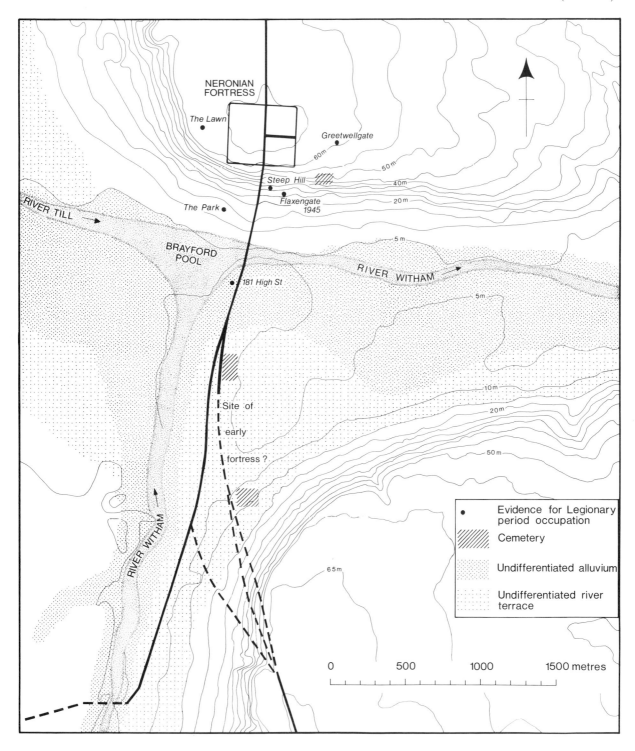

7.1 Map showing topography of Lincoln area, early
finds and roads.

Labels within the map:

NERONIAN FORTRESS

The Lawn

Greetwellgate

60 m

50 m

Steep Hill

40 m

The Park

Flaxengate 1945

20 m

RIVER TILL

BRAYFORD POOL

RIVER WITHAM

5 m

181 High St

5 m

10 m

20 m

50 m

RIVER WITHAM

Site of early fortress ?

65 m

Legend:
- Evidence for Legionary period occupation
- Cemetery
- Undifferentiated alluvium
- Undifferentiated river terrace

0   500   1000   1500 metres

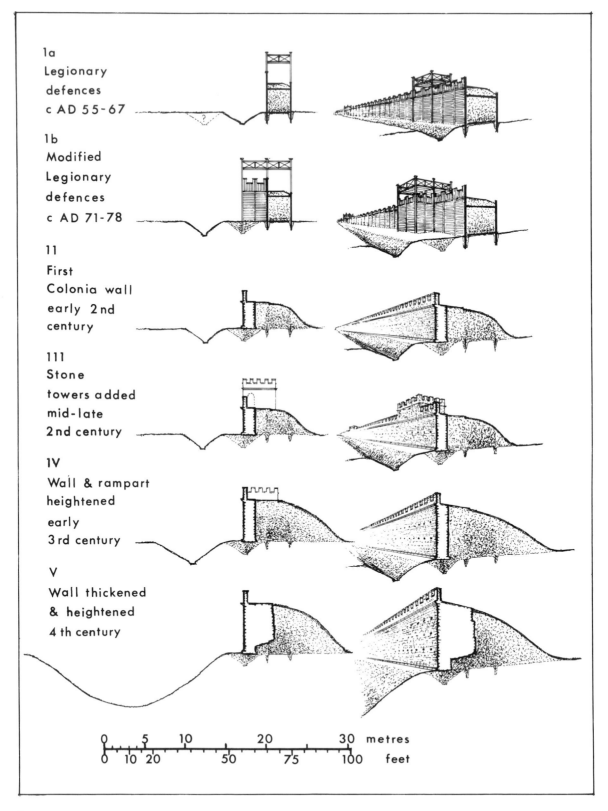

1a
Legionary
defences
c AD 55-67

1b
Modified
Legionary
defences
c AD 71-78

11
First
Colonia wall
early 2nd
century

111
Stone
towers added
mid-late
2nd century

1V
Wall & rampart
heightened
early
3rd century

V
Wall thickened
& heightened
4th century

0 5 10   20   30 metres
0 10 20   50   75   100 feet

less difficult to identify, with fills of sandy or clayey material often barely distinguishable from the underlying subsoil.

The defences have been located and investigated on all four sides (fig. 7.2; see Jones 1980 for recent synthesis). The legionary rampart was formed of the local subsoil – variously sand, sandy clay, and stony clay – based on a 'corduroy' of timbers of various sizes. It now seems probable that turf was intended as the revetting material for the rampart front, as with most forts in Britain, but was abandoned as being unsuitable at an early stage during the construction process. The alternative in such cases was timber boarding revetted by vertical timbers. At the front, posts were set at intervals of 5 Roman feet (*c.* 1.5m) in a palisade trench, but at the rear of the bank, *c.* 10 Roman feet (*c.* 3m) wide, were driven straight into the ground. There is only slight evidence to suggest that the whole structure may have been held together by a framework of transverse timbers. The rear of the rampart was vertical for at least 2m (6ft 6in), again a common feature, and it might be expected that the full height was 10–12 Roman feet (3–3.6m). On top of this a parapet *c.* 5 Roman feet (1.5m) high would have provided extra protection for soldiers on the walkway.

Beyond a narrow berm was at least one V-shaped ditch, *c.* 12 feet (3.6m) wide and *c.* 5 feet (1.5m) deep. A second ditch beyond may only have been dug at a later period (see below). Four-post towers were probably provided at intervals of *c.* 100 Roman feet (*c.* 30m) but only one of the 40–50 examples has been uncovered to date. That tower, at Westgate School, had a further two posts projecting beyond the original rampart, an unusual feature for this period (Webster 1949). It seems likely, on analogy with other fortresses, that the projections belonged to the second phase; otherwise the inner ditch into which their post-pits were dug makes no sense.

The suggested sequence here agrees well with that at the East Gate, the only legionary gateway to have been investigated at Lincoln (Thompson and Whitwell 1973). This comprised a double carriageway flanked by large towers which also received a projecting front in a second phase of construction. The obvious historical context for such modifications was the arrival of *Legio* II *Adiutrix* in AD 71 to replace the Ninth, but close

dating has not yet been possible and other contexts are not out of the question. Hartley (1981, 42) has even suggested that the changes belonged to the early *colonia* period: the early dating of the stone wall might argue against this (and cf. Hurst's reinterpretation of the early *colonia* stone period at Gloucester, this volume).

Little is yet known of the interior of the fortress (fig. 7.3). Excavations before 1968 were either aimed principally at defining the outline of the fortress, and therefore concentrated on its fortifications, or met with poor survival of legionary structures. The *via sagularis* (*intervallum* road) and sometimes the buildings to its rear have been uncovered on the north side (in excavations at North Row in 1946 and at East Bight in 1981) and probably on the south side (Old Bishop's Palace 1955; though identified here as the early *colonia* street). Its position on east and west can be reasonably predicted, set back several metres from the legionary rampart to allow space for 'rampart buildings' or cookhouses. The circuit defines an area *c.* 450 × *c.* 360m (490 × 390 yds), or perhaps 1500 by 1200 Roman feet (*pedes monetales*: 1 p.m. = 0.296m = 11.7in) on which the interior may have been planned (fig. 7.3; cf. Crummy 1985). These dimensions are closely, but not exactly, comparable with Exeter and Gloucester.

Fragments of timber structures were identified at Cottesford Place in 1957, east of Bailgate in 1968, at Westgate School in 1973, on East Bight in 1981, and on the Chapel Lane Corporation Depot in 1985 – all in the northern half of the fortress. At the two last mentioned, there were two periods of military construction. Yet in every case, the area uncovered or the amount of structural detail surviving was unfortunately too small for the plan to be identified. We may presume that most, lying close to the defences, were barracks. At East Bight a rampart building of palisade-trench construction was noted immediately to the rear of the rampart, and such structures were no doubt common.

The investigation of a larger area in the centre of the fortress in 1978–9 was therefore potentially of great significance – not least because the position of the north and south gates of the *colonia*, if overlying those of the fortress, suggested that this may have been the site of the *principia*, or headquarters building. Here too was an important *colonia* building-complex (discussed below).

Interpretation of the Roman features underlying the remains of the Church of St Paul-in-the-Bail was to some extent bedevilled by the

7.2 Reconstruction drawing of legionary and *colonia* defences.

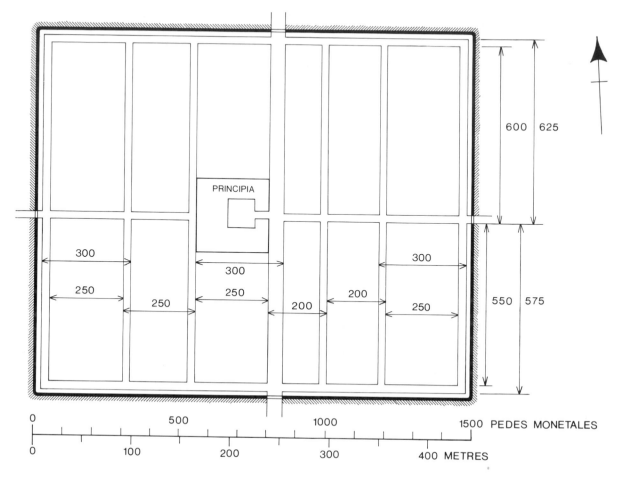

600 | 625

PRINCIPIA

300

300

250

250

300

250

250

200

200

250

550 | 575

0   500   1000   1500 PEDES MONETALES

0   100   200   300   400 METRES

7.3 Plan of legionary fortress, with hypothetical arrangement of street grid according to Crummy's model.

disturbance of the earlier levels by graves. As a result, the legionary period ground surfaces hardly survived and no floors were found, although a layer of pebbles and sand was found in places in areas which were later interpreted as external. In contrast, structural features which had been cut into the stony clay subsoil were abundant. They included large post-pits, postholes, and wall trenches (figs. 7.4, 7.5). The plans of two separate periods were disentangled, consisting principally of three rows of post-pits running north–south – an aisled hall – and a row running eastwards from the northern end (Jones and Gilmour 1980, 63–5). The posts measured 12 by 8 Roman inches (30 × 20cm). The courtyard area to east and south was surrounded by a verandah, and contained a trench for

water supply – perhaps serving a fountain. There were also rectangular areas of rubble foundations for water tanks or other features, and the well found to the east may date from this period. Behind the cross-hall was a plank-lined water tank.

It became obvious from their plan that the excavated remains, lying in a central location within the fortress, could only represent the north-western part of the *principia*: those elements uncovered included the northern part of the basilica, or cross-hall, and the southern margin of the north range. Although the full extent of the building can only be estimated at about 50–70m east–west by 60–75m north–south, the full plan can be reconstructed approximately (fig. 7.6). Its closest parallel is the early first-century example at Haltern (Schnurbein 1974, 56–9).

The discovery confirmed that the fortress faced east, so that the east gate, excavated in the 1960s, formed its *porta praetoria*. The scale of this gate in

7.4 Crosshall of *principia* under excavation.

both legionary and *colonia* periods shows it to have been more important than the west gate, which apparently consisted of only a single portal (Thompson and Whitwell 1973, 194–200). Yet few areas now survive – in a part of town largely covered by historic buildings – where there is a possibility of the large-scale investigations which are necessary if we are to advance substantially our knowledge of the fortress. In particular it would be useful to know the size of the barrack-blocks and of their *contubernia*, so that we might be able to estimate whether a whole legion could be accommodated.

As for the street plan, while only the positions of the *viae praetoria, principalis*, and *sagularis* are known, it is possible using Crummy's method based on the use of units of *pedes monetales* (Crummy 1985) to attempt an outline reconstruction (fig. 7.3). This supersedes previous attempts by the writer and by Crummy (1982, fig. 2), but remains highly speculative, particularly since it is dangerous to assume too much about length units (Millett 1982). Although we have little direct evidence for streets, the finding of buildings eliminates some possibilities for their lines, and there is a chance that some *colonia* streets (see below) followed their military predecessors. Much depends, however, on the lengths of the barrack-blocks, and whether most of the usual buildings were provided. Unfortunately no parallel is well enough known to help fill the huge gap in our knowledge.

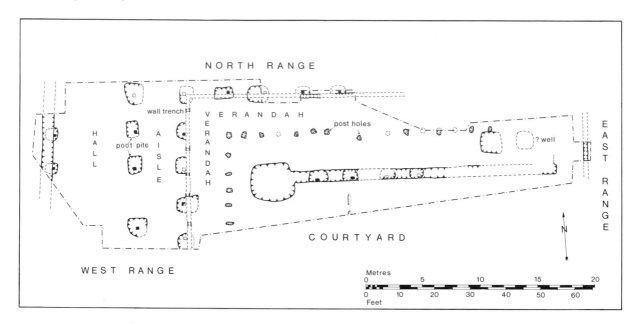

7.5 Plan of *principia* features as excavated, phase I.

Extra-mural occupation

The legionary presence and its influence did not of course stop at the fortress walls. A large area above and below the hill and including the riverside was in use, and would have been purchased or commissioned from the native owners (fig. 7.1). How much land beyond was taken over is an open question (Whitwell 1982, 52–8; see also Hurst, this volume), but this would have included space for grazing animals, for industrial works, and for stockyards. In addition to the land needed for grazing (*prata legionis*), a *territorium* was normally requisitioned, to provide food for the garrison. The increased demand for food could have also stimulated local production and thereby affected the trading and agricultural pattern, and in turn the prosperity, of the local community (cf. Jones 1984). Some new traders would have been attracted, although the legion brought along its own potters, employed already at Longthorpe, to produce fine wares (Darling 1981; Dannell and Wild 1987).

To the south the original cemetery continued in use at least during the 70s, for tombstones of soldiers of the IInd *Adiutrix* were found there, and it may also have served a nearby civil settlement, normally found at some distance from the military enclosures. An area of the hillside to the south-east of the fortress may also have been taken into use for burial. Traces of late first-century occupation have come to light at several points uphill, on the hillside and close to the river (fig. 7.1). The finds from the site of 181–3 High Street, south of the river, suggest occupation associated with military presence rather than a continuation of native settlement.

As a whole, the discoveries indicate extra-mural occupation on a large scale. While too little is known of the plans of these structures (mainly because of disturbance by later features), those immediately to the west and south of the fortress could contain the *canabae*. The area east of the fortress might also be thought a more favourable location, but the only discovery here to date is an extensive metalled surface, possibly for military parades. Trial excavations west of the fortress since 1984 have brought to light only slight remains of structures, but much ceramic evidence which may even indicate another pre-Roman focus (Jones and Darling forthcoming). These structures did not survive beyond the end of the legionary period. In the early second century stone quarrying took place here before commercial development of the land adjacent to the west gate later in the century. Further excavations are planned, and this is a possible site for the amphitheatre (*ludus*) which catered for the essential performances of religious rituals and weapon training. In contrast, though also fragmentarily surviving, the traces of early occupation on the hillside did form the basis for settlement which continued into the life of the *colonia*.

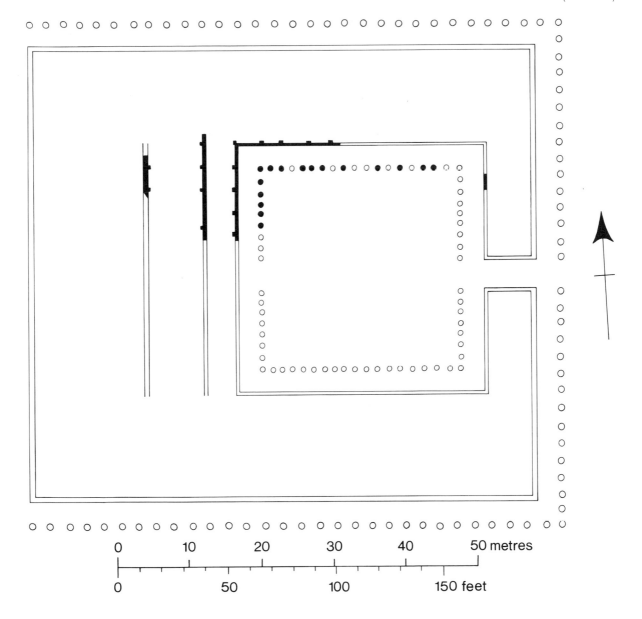

7.6 Reconstructed plan of *principia*.

There are indications of rebuilding during the life of the fortress, and *Legio* II *Adiutrix* might be held responsible for such changes during its short occupation. Apart from the modifications to the defences and to the *principia*, there were alterations at both East Bight and Chapel Lane: only at Westgate School, a poorly-preserved site, were there definitely no signs of modifications to the legionary buildings. This seems to indicate that much of the garrison was in residence, and both its presence and the demand for building materials would have helped maintain the economic basis of the extra-mural settlement.

Colonia foundation

The Flavian advance westwards and northwards spelt the end for the Lincoln fortress. *Legio* II *Adiutrix* was removed no later than AD 78 to settle

7.7 Inscribed dedication stone from Mainz, providing foundation date for *colonia* at Lincoln.

in a new base at Chester. By AD 96, the Lincoln site had become a *colonia*. By analogy, its full name may have been COLONIA (DOMITIANA) LINDENSIUM: the discredited emperor's name was later removed, but it was and is commonly known as LINDUM COLONIA (Richmond 1946, 20; *CIL*, 6679; Wacher 1975, 120). The *terminus ante quem* is provided by a dedication stone to Fortuna set up in Mainz (MOGONTIACUM) by M. Minicius Marcellinus, who describes himself as a citizen of Lincoln: 'VIR LINDO' (fig. 7.7). His voting tribe as given is one of the Flavian period (69–96).

It is generally accepted that the legions were too busy campaigning under the governor Agricola (78–84) for sufficient of them to be discharged into a new veteran colony, and a date after the with-drawal from Scotland and a reorganization of the legionary dispositions is more likely. There is little to support Biro's contention that land remained in possession of the legion until the last soldier serving there had completed his service (Biro 1975). How many ex-soldiers were settled and from which legions they came is difficult to establish: estimates of colonists at the smaller 12ha (30-acre) colony at Timgad in Algeria have varied from a few hundred to about 1000 (Fentress 1979, 128–9). Many at Lincoln will have been discharged from the Ninth *Hispana*, some already having spent several years based there and presumably happy to return.

A caretaker-garrison may have controlled the military land in the interim. The fortress defences were not dismantled throughout this period but were maintained into the early second century. On the other hand, those internal structures examined to date were systematically dismantled, and much legionary equipment discarded, including a dagger scabbard at East Bight (Scott 1985, no 31; Webster 1985).

The *forum*

The *principia* was among the demolished structures, but the evidence for its replacement is not easy to interpret. At one stage a new timber building occupied the site of the cross-hall – perhaps as part of a caretaker garrison. Probably soon after the foundation of the *colonia*, however, the area was developed as a public building or precinct. The main evidence for this came in the form of an extensive area of fine paving, probably covering the whole site of the *principia* (fig. 7.8). On the paving was a huge block likely to have supported an equestrian statue and nearby were two other possible statue bases, such as were common in the piazzas of Roman *fora*. The only wall so far discovered which was contemporary with this precinct was part of a semicircular pier found *c*. 30m (100ft) to the north, beneath the Mint Wall (see below). Finds of building debris from the levels above the paving and probably associated with this period included moulded and painted wall-plaster and quarter-round tiles. Tentatively, one could suggest that an early forum or temple precinct (or both) occupied the site.

While it is difficult to date the extensive colonnade which ran to the east of the complex, along the western side of the main street, it is just conceivable that it too belonged to this period. The colonnade perhaps fits more easily with the subsequent redevelopment of the site, which was probably Hadrianic in date. The style of the column-bases has close links with other major sites to the north and west (although known Corinthian capitals from Lincoln are of the south-eastern type: Blagg 1980).

Part of the east range of the new forum was uncovered in 1979; it consisted of a double range of rooms, with wide porticoes facing both into the courtyard and on to the principal street (figs. 7.8, 7.10). It was built, and its walls dressed, from the level of the earlier paving and this level was more or less retained in the central courtyard. The make-up for the floors in the east range was a metre (3ft 3in) or so thick, and contained no finds dating to later than the Trajanic period: no black burnished ware, associated with the Hadrianic period, was present.

The floor itself was of a thick layer of *opus signinum* with much tile, producing an effect not dissimilar to some modern civic floors. Remains of three small rooms leading from the inner portico were encountered, one of them a semicircular *exedra* (a similar example was found at Silchester). These rooms had painted walls and may all have had an official function. To the east only one larger room *c*. 7m by *c*. 6m (23 × 20ft), with timber subdivisions, was excavated. Finds from its floors suggest commercial activity – these rooms fronted on to the main street. It also contained in its north-west corner an impressive well-house.

This was a rectangular structure, in an excellent state of preservation except for its uppermost courses (its superstructure), which had been rebuilt in the 15th–16th centuries. Four tile-built arches had supported the masonry superstructure, and beneath them the shaft was almost 3m (10ft) in diameter. Its fill was excavated in 1984. This difficult engineering operation produced useful information about the well's capacity and about local geology, but it was disappointing in terms of its contents as the shaft had been recut and cleaned out in the post-medieval period.

The masonry here all clearly belonged to the rebuilt forum, but the well-shaft could have been earlier, possibly legionary in origin. Although wells were not unknown within the rooms of Roman *fora*, a well in the courtyard of the *principia* may be more likely: if so, its location would have had a bearing on the layout of the rooms of the forum's east range. Whatever its origin, the evidence of floor wear and a water tank base indicate that it was also accessible from the room to the west.

The plan as excavated in 1978–9 can easily be linked to the line of the Bailgate colonnade. A substantial portico, *c*. 7m (23ft) wide, is indicated – the grand scale is corroborated by the size of the columns, *c*. 0.75m (2ft 6in) in diameter. There were in all 19 columns, some inosculating: the one triple and five double setts indicated either the corner of the structure or major entrances. Worn stones at the entrance facing the main east gate were noted last century. In all *c*. 84m (92yds) long, the colonnade was formerly interpreted as representing the frontages of three discrete public buildings, but their identification as part of the forum-basilica complex has been securely established by the recent excavations.

The double inosculating columns at the northern end of the colonnade are in line with the remains of

7.9 Mint Wall from north.

the 'Mint Wall', a huge fragment of Roman masonry whose interpretation has been a puzzle (fig. 7.9). It still stands *c*. 7m (23ft) high for a length of over 20m (66ft), and is provided with regular bonding courses of tile. Evidence of three return walls running south from it was noted by early antiquarians, but the main problem has been its complete absence of windows.

Small trenches dug to the south of the wall in 1979 revealed a floor of similar construction to that found in the east range of the forum, but at a higher level. Beyond a wall 14m south of the Mint Wall, the floor level dropped to that of the forum. This all appears to indicate a single aisled hall, the aisle serving also as a portico. Further work in 1980 on the north side of the Mint Wall revealed its foundation at more than 2m (6ft 6in) below the modern ground surface – giving a total height of at least 9.50m (31ft 2in) – and a street contemporary

7.8 Trajanic? paved area over former *principia*, and walls of Hadrianic? forum, east range.

with its construction. The dating evidence suggested that these structures, which overlay the earlier pier base (mentioned above), dated to the Hadrianic or Antonine period.

Obviously, more extensive investigations of this remarkable building are desirable. The most reasonable interpretation of the existing evidence is that the Mint Wall formed the north wall of the basilica, on the north side of the forum. The layout of the postulated complex is of considerable interest in that it did not follow that of the *principia* – as happened at Gloucester – and it hints at more Continental influence than was usual in Britain (figs. 7.10, 7.11). That there would be insufficient space, however, for a temple precinct at Lincoln on the lines of the so-called 'Gallo–Roman' *fora* was proved inadvertently by a small trench dug in 1962–3. As Blagg (1984) and Wacher (1978, 72–3) have suggested for other British towns, the exact plan may have been determined by the local community, using architects who had experience on the Continent. But this whole question is a complex one, and the community's religious needs may also have influenced the design.

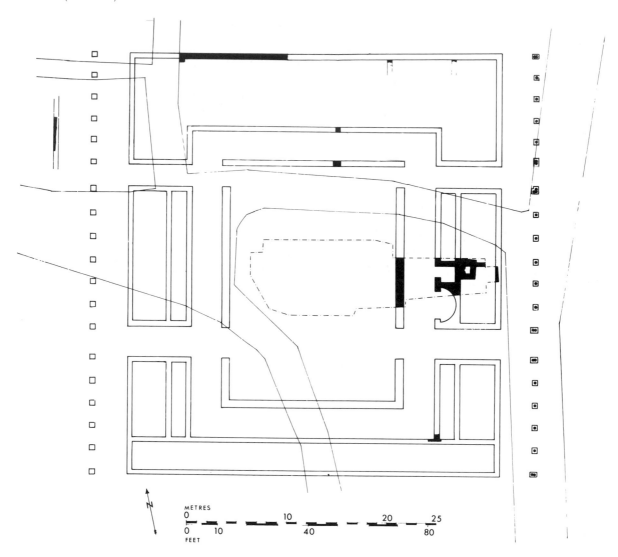

7.10 Suggested plan of forum-basilica.

Other public works

Of the other public buildings of the city, only the baths have been investigated. They were discovered in 1956–8 by Mr D.F. Petch in the north-east part of the town. A full report is now in preparation, and the dating evidence has yet to be studied in detail. The plan (fig. 7.12) suggests that the areas excavated included principally the heated rooms. The building was extended on at least two occasions, not so much to increase its capacity as the level of refinements. In all it may have covered an area *c*. 45m by *c*. 60m (150 × 200ft). The excavated remains are presumed to be a new suite erected for

the *colonia*; legionary period structures and deposits were found beneath, and the legionary bathhouse was probably on another site (cf. Exeter). The baths faced southwards on to an east–west street – a new street for the *colonia* – to the south of which was a row of shops. Beneath the street was found a covered drain, which served the baths outflow. A similar one was excavated in 1981 on East Bight underneath the intervallum road north of the baths. At East Bight, road construction in the early second century had involved the removal of any traces of the legionary street. That the *via sagularis* had lain on the same line was however clear from the building line to north and south.

Presumably there were several such drains which carried off surface and storm water, but

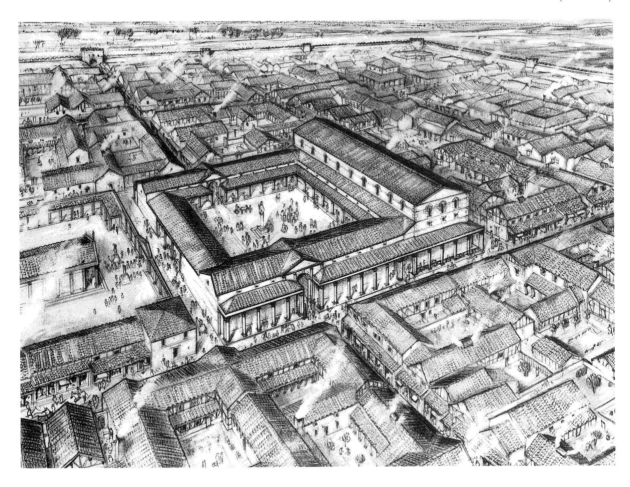

7.11 Reconstruction drawing of forum-basilica.

there is also much evidence for water supply in this part of the town. A tank (*castellum aquae*) was added to the rear of the northern city wall soon after its construction, close to the baths site (fig. 7.13), and one of its functions would have been to serve this building. The source of its water was probably the well-known but imperfectly understood aqueduct, consisting of a ceramic pipe encased in mortar, which tapped a source to the northeast of the city (Lewis 1984). Precise dating for these major public works is not available, but it would appear that the first half of the second century was the critical period for their construction.

Another mainly early development, with some minor changes at a later date, was the *colonia* street pattern (fig. 7.12). We have seen above that the retention of the legionary defences and extension of the gates ensured the continuity of the principal north–south and east–west streets. Excavations

have confirmed that the intervallum road continued on more or less the same line, as we might expect. New streets were necessary to the north and south of the forum-basilica, but that west of the public baths could well have been of military origin (cf. figs. 7.3, 7.12). In several places, the installation of new drains and sewers would have meant considerable ground disturbance. Sewers are known to have been extensive in the southern half of the upper city, presumably lying beneath streets. Their construction provided an opportunity to replan radically certain parts of the town, an operation which may have been facilitated only as long as buildings and property rights had not become firmly established. *Lindum Colonia*, like its model, cannot have been built in a day. Wealthy patrons and the prominent citizens had to pay for its development and its public buildings and the work would have taken perhaps a decade or so. The change to stone building materials and the need for mortar as well as road materials would certainly

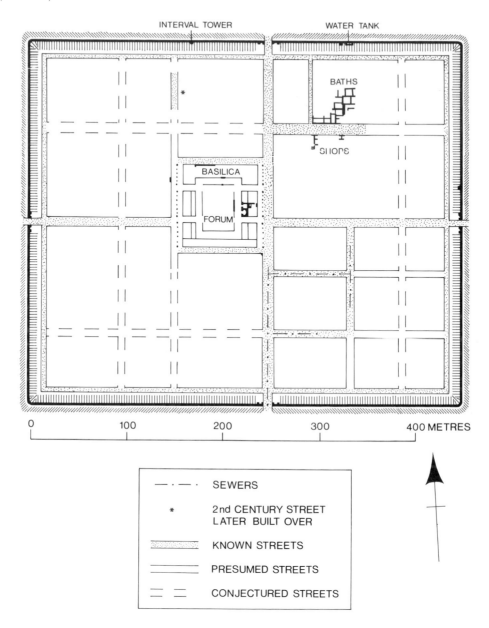

7.12 Plan of upper *colonia* showing known street-grid.

have involved massive undertakings (for the former, see Jones 1980, 37–47). It may have been the city's responsibility to provide the civic centre and the major temples, and possibly some of the cost of the fortifications, the streets and their drains (Duncan-Jones 1985).

Stone defences

The legionary rampart was in due course given a stone front (fig. 7.2). Much of it was subsequently rebuilt, and stretches of the earliest wall can only be identified by a combination of analyses of constructional details, stone and mortar types, and the dating evidence. It was *c.* 1.2m (4ft) wide, and its lowest offset course consisted of larger blocks (figs. 7.13, 7.14). These were not set on foundations, but on the rammed stony fill of the inner ditch. Its rear face was therefore well in advance of

7.13 City wall and foundations of *castellum aquae*, East Bight.

the timber front of the legionary rampart – presuming that the rampart had not been clad in earth. This latter possibility was favoured by some earlier excavators, but is no longer felt to be supported by solid evidence.

There are various possible reasons for the method of constructing the wall: one, so that the new wall-front ran flush with that of the projecting interval towers; more likely, this method allowed the new front to be erected while the old one was still standing, thereby precluding any such disaster as at Boudican Colchester, with the city left unfortified. The rampart was fairly narrow, and it may have been felt that, in order to preserve the line of the intervallum road, the defences had to go outwards. The facing material was in general of inferior quality to that found in the later period, when a much higher proportion of true oolitic limestone was employed. The mortar was derived

from low-lying beds close to the settlement, and the stone could easily be quarried from outcrops on the scarp to the west of the upper walled area.

Dating evidence for the stone front is derived principally from the material infilling the gap between it and the earlier bank. Reliance on one or two investigations can be misleading, although this problem has been thoroughly studied. The general conclusion is that a start may have been made before the end of the first century, but that it was well into Hadrian's reign before it was completed. The regular series of interval towers may have been added shortly after (Darling 1984).

Further development

The provisional placing of some of these major public works in Hadrian's reign is of wider interest, in consideration of the Emperor's known efforts to stimulate urbanization in the frontier provinces (cf. Webster 1980b re Wroxeter), and for which the

7.14 City wall and added interval tower at East Bight.

Emperor is known to have organized a corps of architects. In contrast, what little is known of private houses in the upper and lower cities tends to corroborate the national trend (Walthew 1975, 1983) that they tended to be on a modest scale until the second part of the second century. For example, at East Bight, a narrow building to the south of the intervallum road was only rebuilt on a grander scale at this date. Refurbishment of barracks is not a wholly surprising phenomenon, considering the amount of capital ploughed into public works in the first half of the century.

Most of the public buildings may have occupied the more level ground on top of the hill, with the forum-basilica at the highest point. Perhaps the hillslope could have been utilized for a theatre or conceivably as a *circus*. Certainly, on the basis of finds of mosaics and more recent excavations in the lower city, the south-facing hillside proved an attractive location for domestic buildings.

These residences replaced, to some extent, the timber structures associated with the military occupation. But presumably the main street frontages were still occupied by shopping and public facilities: baths, a temple, and a public fountain are known on the east side of Ermine Street. The street itself was engineered directly up the steep hillside by a series of flights of steps, a feature not otherwise known in Britain. While pedestrians used the steps, wheeled vehicles followed a diagonal or zigzag course. There appears to have been at least one private residence of some quality, built before the end of the first century, perhaps belonging to a wealthy Gallic or Italian merchant (Coppack 1973; see also Esmonde Cleary 1987).

Originally under military control, the hillside was retained in official ownership and in due course designated as part of the *colonia*. The planners' hopes that the presence of prosperous veterans would maintain the settlement and attract new services were realized. Areas available for burial were defined outside the boundary (*pomerium*) of the town, as is confirmed by the presence of cremation cemeteries to east and west of the area later defended (fig 7.15).

Investigations continue into the origin and development of the street pattern on the hillside. At present it appears that the areas east and west of Ermine Street may have been planned as separate exercises, for excavations have failed to find a continuous east–west street linking the gates of the lower town. We might have expected that the steeper hillside, where terracing was obviously necessary, would have proved too daunting for a grid system, and the diagonal street found at the

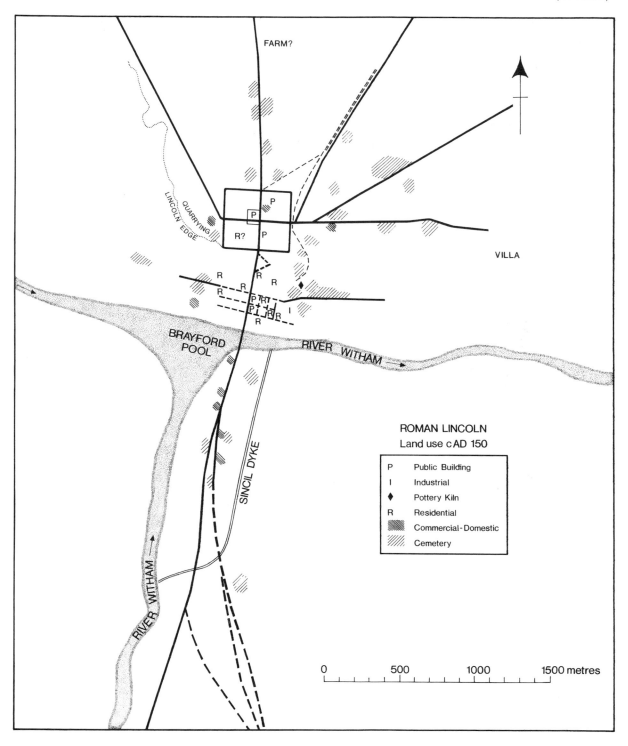

7.15 Map of the *colonia* and its environs in the second century.

bottom of Steep Hill in 1987 confirms this to some extent. The north–south street found south of Silver Street in 1973 (Wacher 1979) was probably laid down in the first half of the second century. A Hadrianic stores building to its east (connected with river-borne supplies?) was soon replaced by a townhouse.

Did this change reflect in any way the commercial development of the town? A major element in the commercial life of the city was the waterfront. To date there have been only slight traces of the wharves and docks which it can be confidently expected were provided, but the location of these discoveries at some distance from the modern river indicates a much larger area of water than today (figs. 7.1, 7.15). The importance of river communication for Lincoln would have been further enhanced by the cutting of the 'Foss Dyke' from the western end of Brayford Pool to the Trent at Torksey, partly by canalizing the course of the River Till. The function of the Car Dyke, linking the Witham east of Lincoln with the lower Nene, now seems to have been primarily for drainage (Simmons 1979). Again, both developments are thought to belong to the first half of the second century, although the Foss Dyke has never been formally dated (see May in Jones and Darling, forthcoming).

At about the same time, the wet ground south of the city along Ermine Street was being reclaimed by drainage programmes followed by extensive dumping to allow for the construction of a row of traders' houses, their shopfronts facing on to the street. New industry was being attracted, as today, to the urban fringes. Whether this can be seen as a single development is uncertain; certainly the city continued to grow in most directions for another century or so (fig. 7.15). But by c. AD 150 the city had assumed its characteristic form, except perhaps for the embellishment of the gates and the lower fortifications. The economic prosperity reflected by the physical growth had its roots in a number of earlier decisions, however, and endorsed the choice of site for fortress and *colonia*. Unlike Gloucester, it did not have an economic rival in close proximity. The hiatus between the departure of the legion and the veteran settlement may have been difficult economically for those civilians who remained, but the foundation of the *colonia* secured their prosperity.

The burial grounds of soldiers and civilians cannot easily be distinguished (as at York: Jones 1984) except by the finds normally associated with women. Some of these were made at Monson Street, an area which also served as a cemetery for soldiers (see above). It continued in use into the *colonia* period, but from the end of the first century areas east of the town appear to have become more important (fig. 7.15).

Beyond the 'town zone' (Rodwell 1975) local resources were exploited for building stone, gravel, and mortar, and for pottery clay. The known sources close to the city would have lain within the *territorium*. The extent of the land in the 'territory' under the direct control of the *colonia*, and thereby outside that of the *civitas*, is a problem still being explored by fieldworkers. It has been suggested that it ran as far as the next forts (or maybe native settlements?) to north and south (probably at Owmby and Navenby; Whitwell 1982, 52–8), but a larger and different area is conceivable (Richmond, 1946, 65–6 expected an area of at least 100 square miles). The initial veteran settlement could have run into thousands, but not necessarily all of these received land. Certainly, there is no evidence as yet for centuriation of the agricultural land close to the city, although such a pattern was apparently normal and might be expected in Britain (Keppie 1984 and forthcoming). Could its apparent absence stem from the fact that field systems already existed in the late Iron Age? (Taylor 1975, 57–8; cf. Hurst this volume). The use of newly drained land would be less unpopular with the native population.

Within this territory one might also identify the farming establishments of the new citizens whose grant was invested in the land. Some may have administered their estates from town residences, however, and in the half-century or so after the colonia's foundation a substantial amount of private wealth would have been expended on urban amenities such as those mentioned above.

There is little evidence about the detailed composition of the settlers. The men of the Ninth Legion were largely Italians but included also men from Spain and Macedonia (Birley 1979, 1983). They presumably made up part of the veterans discharged under Domitian, but probably shared the new town with soldiers retired from other British legions. The upper city could probably have housed no more than a thousand or so in any comfort, but detailed investigation of these early houses is lacking.

A realistic population figure for the growing city in the early second century may be nearer 5000. Finds of inscribed tombstones, few of them dated, include a councillor, a Greek, and a nonagenarian woman (*RIB* 254–7). There were cults of Mercury and Apollo, a burial club, and a youth organization. But extensive excavation and detailed study of a large cemetery is necessary if any advance of knowledge is to be made beyond this tantalizing and unrepresentative sample. Like the town itself, the people are hardly known. Forty years ago Sir Ian Richmond wrote that Roman Lincoln 'offers a glimpse of flourishing Roman urban culture in imported purity, such as has not yet emerged anywhere else on British soil' (Richmond 1946, 68). In spite of some notable recent advances, it remains little more than a glimpse or two.

Acknowledgements

I am grateful to Professor J.S. Wacher and Dr Graham Webster for their comments on an earlier draft of this paper, and to Mr. D.F. Petch for letting me see his draft report on the Cottesford Place site. The plans specially prepared for this article were drawn by Jayne Peacock.

Bibliography

Baynard, D. and Massey, J.L. 1983   *Amiens Romain: samarobriva ambainorum*

Birley, A.R. 1979   *The people of Roman Britain*

Biro, M. 1975   'The inscriptions of Roman Britain', *Acta Archaeologica Academia Scientiae Hungaricae* 27, 13ff

Bishop, M.C. (ed) 1985   *The production and distribution of Roman military equipment, BAR* Internat. Series 275

Blagg, T.F.C. 1980   'Roman civil and military patronage in the province of Britain', *World Archaeology* 13, 27–42

—— 1984   'An examination of the connections between military and civilian architecture' in Blagg, T.F.C. and King, A.C. (eds) *Military and Civilian in Roman Britain, BAR* 136, 249–64

Chantraine, H. *et al*, 1984   *Das römische Neuss*, Stuttgart

Cleary, S. Esmond 1987   *The extra-mural areas of Romano–British towns, BAR* British Series 69

Coppack, G.C. 1973   'The excavation of a Roman and medieval site at Flaxengate, Lincoln', *Lincolnshire History and Archaeology* 9

Crummy, P. 1982   'The origins of some major Romano–British towns', *Britannia* 8, 125–34

—— 1985   'Colchester: the mechanics of laying out a town' in Grew and Hobley, 78–85

Dannell, G.B. and Wild, J.P. 1987   *Longthorpe II: The Military Works Depot (Britannia* monograph series 8)

Darling, M.J. 1981   'Early red-slipped ware from Lincoln', in Anderson, A.C. and Anderson, A.S. (eds), *Roman pottery research in Britain and North-West Europe* (Festschrift for G. Webster), *BAR* International Series 123, 397–415

—— 1984   'Roman pottery from the upper defences', *The archaeology of Lincoln* 16.2, 43–100

Duncan-Jones, R.P. 1985   'Who paid for public buildings in Roman cities?' in Grew and Hobley, 28–33

Drinkwater, J.F. 1975   'Lugdunum, "Natural capital of Gaul?",' *Britannia* 6, 133–40

Fentress, E.W.B. 1979   *Numidia and the Roman army, BAR* Internat. Series 53

Frere, S.S. 1978   *Britannia: a history of Roman Britain* (revised edition)

Frere, S.S. and St Joseph, J.K. 1974   'The Roman fortress at Longthorpe', *Britannia* 6, 1–129

Grew, F. and Hobley, B. (eds) 1985   *Roman urban topography in Britain and the Western Empire*, Council for British Archaeology Research Report 59

Hartley, B.R. 1981   'The early Roman military occupation of Lincoln and Chester' in Anderson, A.C. and Anderson, A.S. (eds), *Roman pottery research in Britain and North-West Europe* (Festschrift for G. Webster), *BAR* International Series 123, 239–47

Hassall, M.W.C. 1983   'The origins and character of Roman urban defences in the West', in Maloney, J. and Hobley, B. (eds) *Roman urban defences in the West*, Council for British Archaeology Research Report 51

Hurst, H.R. 1985   *Kingsholm*, Gloucester Archaeological Reports I

Jones, G.D.B. 1984   '"Becoming different without knowing it": the role and development of *vici*' in Blagg and King, 75–92

Lincoln (*Lindum*)

Jones, M.J. 1980	'The defences of the upper Roman enclosure', *The archaeology of Lincoln*, 7.1, 1–62
Jones, M.J. and Gilmour, B. 1980	'Lincoln, *principia* and forum: a preliminary report', *Britannia* 11, 61–72
Jones, M.J. (ed), 1981	'Excavations in Lincoln: Third interim report', *Antiquaries' Journal* 61, 83–114
Jones, M.J. 1985	'New streets for old: the topography of Roman Lincoln' in Grew and Hobley, 86–93
Jones, M.J. and Darling, M.J. 1988	'Early settlement at Lincoln', *Britannia* 19
Jones, R F.J. 1984	'Death and distinction' in Blagg and King, 219–26
Keppie, L.J.F. 1984	'Colonisation and veteran settlement in Italy in the 1st century AD', *Papers of the British School at Rome* 52, 77 -114
—— forthcoming	'From legionary fortress to military colony' in Breeze, D.J. (ed), *The frontiers of the Roman Empire*
Lewis, M.J.T. 1984	'Our debt to Roman engineering – the water supply of Lincoln to the present day', *Industrial Archaeology Review*, 7.1, 57–73
May, J. 1976	*Prehistoric Lincolnshire*, Lincoln
—— 1984	'Major settlements of the later Iron Age in Lincolnshire' in White, A. and Field, N. (eds), *A Prospect of Lincolnshire* 18–22
Millet, M. 1982	'Distinguishing between the *Pes Monetalis* and the *Pes Drusianus*: some problems', *Britannia* 13, 315–20
Petch, D.F. 1960	'Excavations at Lincoln 1955–8', *Archaeological Journal* 117, 40–70
Reece, R. and Mann, J.E. 1983	'Roman coins from Lincoln 1970–79', *The Archaeology of Lincoln*, 6.2
Richmond, I.A. 1946	'The Roman city of Lincoln', and 'The four *coloniae* of Roman Britain', *Archaeological Journal* 103, 26–84
Riley, D.N. 1977	'Roman defended sites at Kirmington, S. Humberside . . .' *Britannia* 8, 189–92
Rivet, A.L.F. and Smith C. 1979	*The place names of Roman Britain*, London
Rodwell, W.J. 1975	'Milestones, civic territories and the Antonine itinerary', *Britannia* 6, 76–101
Schnurbein, S. von 1974	*Die römischen Militäranlagen bei Haltern*
Scott, I.R. 1985	'First-century military daggers and the supply of weapons for the Roman army', in Bishop (ed) 160–213
Simmons, B.B. 1979	'The Lincolnshire Car Dyke: navigation or drainage?', *Britannia* 10, 183–96
Taylor, C.C. 1975	*Fields in the English landscape*
Thompson, F.H. and Whitwell, J.B. 1973	'The Gates of Roman Lincoln', *Archaeologia* 104, 129–207
Tomlin, R.S.O. 1983	*'Non Coritani sed Corieltauvi'*, *Antiquaries' Journal* 63, 353–5
Wacher, J.S. 1975	*The Towns of Roman Britain*
—— 1978	*Roman Britain*
—— 1979	'Silver Street' in Colyer, C. and Jones, M.J. (eds), 'Excavations at Lincoln, second Interim Report', *Antiquaries' Journal* 59, 50–91
Walthew, C.V. 1975	'The Town House and the Villa House in Roman Britain', *Britannia* 6, 189–205
—— 1983	'Houses, defences and status: the towns of Roman Britain in the second half of the second century AD', *Oxford Journal of Archaeology* 2.2, 213–24
Webster, G. 1949	'The legionary fortress at Lincoln', *Journal of Roman Studies* 39, 57–78
—— 1980a	*The Roman Invasion of Britain*
—— 1980b	'A note . . .' in *Roman Frontier Studies 1979*, Hanson W.S. and Keppie, L.J.K. (eds), *BAR* International Series 111, 291–6
—— 1981	*Rome against Caratacus*, London
—— 1985	'Decorated dagger scabbards found in Britain', in Bishop (ed) 214–19
Whitwell, J.B. 1970	*Roman Lincolnshire*, Lincoln
—— 1982	*The Coritani: Some aspects of the Iron Age tribe and the Roman Civitas*, *BAR* 99

General Bibliography

Short list of books for background reading

Sheppard Frere *Britannia*, latest edition 1987, Routledge and Kegan Paul
Malcolm Todd *Roman Britain 55 BC–AD 400*, Fontana 1981
Peter Salway *Roman Britain*, Oxford History of England 1981

The Conquest Period
Graham Webster *The Roman Invasion of Britain*, Batsford 1980
—— *Rome against Caratacus*, Batsford 1981
—— *Boudica*, Batsford 1978
(Discoveries and excavations over the last ten years have made these three books somewhat out of date.)

Short list of books on the Roman Army

Graham Webster *The Roman Imperial Army* 3rd ed, A. and C. Black 1985
G.R. Watson *The Roman Soldier*, Thames and Hudson 1969
P.A. Holder *The Roman Army in Britain*, Batsford 1982
Lawrence Keppie *The Making of the Roman Army: From Republic to Empire*, Batsford 1984

Classical authors quoted

Augustus *Res Gestae*
Caesar *De Bello Gallico*
Cassius Dio *Roman History*
Historia Augusta
Ptolemy *Geography*

Strabo *Geography*
Suetonius *Lives of the Caesars*
Tacitus *Annals* and *Agricola*
Vitruvius *De Architectura*

Reports on legionary fortresses in Britain in the first century

Colchester Philip Crummy, *Excavations at Lion Walk, Balkerne Lane and Middleborough, Colchester, Essex*, Colchester Archaeol. Rep. No. 3, 1984
Exeter Paul T. Bidwell, *Roman Exeter: Fortress and Town*, Exeter Museum Service 1980
Paul T. Bidwell, *The Legionary Bath House and Basilica and Forum at Exeter*, Exeter Archaeol. Rep. No. 1, 1979
Gloucester H.R. Hurst, *Kingsholm*, Gloucester Archaeol. Rep. No. 1, 1985
Gloucester Roman and Later Defences, Gloucester Archaeol. Rep. No. 2, 1986
Inchtuthil Lynn F. Pitts and J.K. St Joseph, *Inchtuthil: The Roman Legionary Fortress*, Brit. Monograph Ser. No. 6, 1985
Lincoln Graham Webster, 'The Legionary Fortress at Lincoln', *JRS* 39 (1949), 57–78
D.F. Petch, 'Excavations at Lincoln 1955–58', *Archaeol. J.* 117 (1962), 40–70
F.H. Thompson and J.B. Whitwell, 'The Gates of Roman Lincoln', *Arch.* 104 (1973), 129–207
Longthorpe S.S. Frere and J.K. St Joseph, 'The Roman Fortress at Longthorpe', *Brit.* 5 (1974), 1–129
G.B. Dannell and J.P. Wild, *Longthorpe II: The Military Works Depot: An Episode in Landscape History*, Brit. Monograph Ser. No. 8, 1987
Usk W.H. Manning, *The Fortress Excavations 1968–1971*, Univ. of Wales Press 1981

Index

Index